Juvenile Crime and Dissent in Nazi Vienna, 1938–1945

Juvenile Crime and Dissent in Nazi Vienna, 1938–1945

Evan Burr Bukey

BLOOMSBURY ACADEMIC
LONDON • NEW YORK • OXFORD • NEW DELHI • SYDNEY

For my grandchildren Sebastian, Josephine, Lauren, Kathryn, and Gretchen

BLOOMSBURY ACADEMIC
Bloomsbury Publishing Plc
50 Bedford Square, London, WC1B 3DP, UK
1385 Broadway, New York, NY 10018, USA
29 Earlsfort Terrace, DUblin 2, Ireland

BLOOMSBURY, BLOOMSBURY ACADEMIC and the Diana logo are trademarks of
Bloomsbury Publishing Plc

First published in Great Britain 2020
Paperback edition published 2021

Copyright © Evan Burr Bukey, 2020

Evan Burr Bukey has asserted his right under the Copyright, Designs and Patents Act, 1988, to be identified as Author of this work.

For legal purposes the Acknowledgements on p. viii constitute
an extension of this copyright page.

Cover image: Austria, Vienna, 1948. A prison for juvenile delinquents.
(© David Seymour/Magnum Photos)

All rights reserved. No part of this publication may be reproduced or transmitted in any form or by any means, electronic or mechanical, including photocopying, recording, or any information storage or retrieval system, without prior permission in writing from the publishers.

Bloomsbury Publishing Plc does not have any control over, or responsibility for, any third-party websites referred to or in this book. All internet addresses given in this book were correct at the time of going to press. The editor and publisher regret any inconvenience caused if addresses have changed or sites have ceased to exist, but can accept no responsibility for any such changes.

A catalogue record for this book is available from the British Library.

A catalog record for this book is available from the Library of Congress.

ISBN: HB: 978-1-3501-3260-3
PB: 978-1-3502-4671-3
ePDF: 978-1-3501-3261-0
eBook: 978-1-3501-3262-7

Typeset by Newgen KnowledgeWorks Pvt. Ltd., Chennai, India

To find out more about our authors and books visit www.bloomsbury.com
and sign up for our newsletters.

Contents

List of Figures	vii
Acknowledgments	viii
List of Abbreviations	x
Introduction	1
1. Anschluß and Consolidation, 1938–1939	9
Origins and Evolution of Juvenile Justice in Austria	11
Impact of the Depression	17
After the Anschluß, 1938–1939	18
Post-Anschluß Deviance, 1938–1939	25
1. Traditional Offences	25
2. Political Crimes	32
Conclusions	38
2. Nazification: The Impact of Wartime Ordinances on the Austrian Juvenile Penal Code, 1940–1944	41
Wartime Ordinances, 1939–1940	43
Juvenile Court Decisions, 1940–1944	48
1. Juvenile Gangs	50
2. Small Rings and Individuals	56
3. Noncompliant Behavior, Indiscipline, Work Stoppages, Absenteeism	64
4. Violent Crimes	66
5. Moral Offences and Homosexuality	67
6. Subversive Behavior	70
Conclusions	71
3. Juveniles Tried by Hitler's Special Courts, 1940–1945	75
Magistrates of the Special Courts	77
Felonies Committed against Property	80
1. Austrian Juveniles	80
2. Foreign Juveniles	86
Political Offences	87
Sexual Offences	91

	Violence and Assault Felonies	92
	Conclusions	94
4.	Juvenile Political Crimes, 1940–1944	97
	Conclusions	116
5.	Impact of the Juvenile Court Act, 1944–1945	119
	Judicial Reports	123
	Gestapo Reports	125
	Court Records	126
	Break-Ins and Theft	130
	1. Break-Ins	130
	2. Hold-Ups and Robberies	134
	3. Absenteeism, Indiscipline, and Breach of Contract	135
	4. Assault and Sexual Immorality	140
	5. Petty Thefts, Misbehaviors, and Adolescent Shenanigans	141
	Conclusions	143
6.	Postwar and Beyond	145
	Postwar Offences, 1945–1946	153
	Conclusions	156
Final Thoughts		157
Notes		163
Bibliography		185
Index		191

Figures

1.1	Total misdemeanors, gross misdemeanors, and felonies in Vienna, 1930–1950	21
1.1a	Juvenile misdemeanors, gross misdemeanors, and felonies in Vienna, 1930–1950, by case	21
1.1b	Juvenile misdemeanors, gross misdemeanors, and felonies in Vienna, 1930–1950, by percentage	21
1.2	Total felonies in Vienna, 1930–1950	22
1.2a	Juvenile felonies in Vienna, 1930–1950, by case	22
1.2b	Juvenile felonies in Vienna, 1930–1950, by percentage	22
1.3	Total misdemeanors in Vienna, 1930–1950	23
1.3a	Juvenile misdemeanors in Vienna, 1930–1950	23
1.3b	Juvenile misdemeanors in Vienna, 1930–1950, by percentage	23
1.4	Major juvenile felonies in Vienna, 1930–1950, break-ins and theft by percentages	24
1.4a	Major juvenile felonies in Vienna, 1930–1950, robbery by percentages	24
1.4b	Major juvenile felonies in Vienna, 1930–1950, accessory to theft by percentages	24
1.4c	Major juvenile felonies in Vienna, 1930–1950, sex crimes by percentages	25
2.1	Increase in juvenile criminal offenses in Greater Germany, 1933–1944, by percentage	47
2.2	Juvenile indictments in Berlin, 1937–1944	47
2.3	Number of juveniles charged with theft in the French courts, 1937–1947	47

Acknowledgments

This book originated in numerous conversations with Winfried Garscha, who suggested exploring an overlooked but significant topic. Over the years, he provided me with original documents, arranged interviews with Austrian officials, helped me find answers to puzzling questions, and commented on several versions of my completed manuscript. My wife and I are particularly grateful to him and his wife Ulli for their gracious hospitality during lengthy research sojourns in Vienna. Among his colleagues at the Documentation Archives of the Austrian Resistance, I wish to thank Ursula Schwarz, Claudia Kuretsides-Haider, and Wolfgang Neugebauer. In addition, Christian Gerbel, an authority on juvenile dissidence under Nazi rule, deserves my gratitude for a lengthy afternoon interview and subsequent discussion. I also wish to thank the exceptionally cordial staff of the Viennese Municipal and State Archives in the Gasometer and the photographic personnel of the Austrian State Archives. Among Austrian colleagues and friends, I am indebted to Lorenz and Juliane Mikoletzky, Ernst Hanisch, Thomas Grischany, and particularly my "brother" Hans Joachim Weber.

In the United States, I am beholden to Gary B. Cohen for initial advice as well as to Laurence Hare and my brother David Bukey for offering comments on several chapters. For a critical appraisal of the entire manuscript, I wish to thank Peter Steiner, Winfried Garscha, and Kurt Tweraser, each of whom detected errors and provided useful suggestions for revisions. Above all, I am indebted to Matthew P. Berg who devoted countless hours to reading numerous drafts, provided shrewd insights, and helped reconceptualize my approach to the relationship of child-rearing and official views of juvenile delinquency. For technical support, I wish to thank David Kirsch, who configured my statistical tables and Michel Guerreiro, who formatted the manuscript for publication.

My special thanks go to Trish Starks and Robert Knight for suggesting Bloomsbury as a publisher. I am exceptionally grateful to Rhodri Mogford for his encouraging response and subsequent acceptance of the useful advice of two anonymous readers. I also wish to express my gratitude to Laura Reeves and Sophie Campbell for their timely and useful assistance in the production process.

Last but not least, I wish to thank my wife, Anita, who, as in the past, has spent numberless hours probing questionable conclusions, correcting arithmetical errors, and detecting typographical mistakes. Without her love and devotion as well as those of our children, Ellen and David, this study could not have been completed.

Abbreviations

AdR	Archiv der Republik (Archive of the Republic)
AVA	Allgemeines Verwaltungsarchiv (Central Administrative Archive)
BDM	Bund Deutscher Mädchen (League of German Girls)
BJM	Bundesjustizministerium (Federal Ministry of Justice)
DöW	Dokumentationsarchiv des österreichischen Widerstandes (Documentation Archives of the Austrian Resistance)
HJ	Hitler-Jugend (Hitler Youth)
JSLA	Jugendgerichtshilfe (Juvenile Legal Support Agency)
KJV	Kommunistischer Jugendverband (Communist Youth League)
KPÖ	Kommunistische Partei Österreichs (Communist Party of Austria)
NSV	Nationalsozialistische Volkswohlfahrt (National Socialist People's Welfare Association)
ÖJV	Österreichisches Jungvolk (Fatherland Front Youth Organization)
OLG	*Oberlandesgericht* (Higher Regional Court)
ÖStA	Österreichisches Staatsarchiv (Austrian State Archives)
RGBl	*Reichsgesetzblatt* (Reich Law Gazette)
RM	Reichsmark
RSHA	Reichssicherheitshaupt (Reich Main Security Office)
SG	*Sondergericht* (Special Court)
TR	Tagesrapporte Gestapo (Daily Reports of the Viennese Gestapo)
VGH	*Volksgerichtshof* (People's Court)
WSLA	Wiener Stadt- und Landesarchiv (Vienna Municipal and Provincial Archives)
WVN	*Widerstand und Verfolgung in Niederösterreich* (Resistance and Persecution in Lower Austria)
WVW	*Wiederstand und Verfolgung in Wien* (Resistance and Persecution in Vienna)

Introduction

Recent decades have yielded a cornucopia of academic studies, autobiographies, novels, and even films that explore the experience of German and Austrian youth in the Third Reich. These range from bittersweet memories of boys and girls who had belonged to the Hitler Youth (HJ; Hitler-Jugend) to accounts of adolescent disenchantment, nonconformity, dissent, and conscious opposition. Oddly, historians have paid scant attention to the development of the Juvenile Criminal Code under Hitler, let alone to its impact on those youngsters brought before the bench for transgressions and deviant behavior.

This book attempts to address this lacuna by exploring the cases of juvenile delinquents tried in Vienna between 1938 and 1945. There are several reasons to focus on the Danubian metropolis. In the first place, Vienna was the second largest city of the Greater German Reich. Aside from a brief republican interlude, it was also a municipality that experienced three authoritarian regimes between 1918 and 1945. Under Nazi rule, moreover, it did not see the emergence of aggressive teenage gangs such as those that terrorized the bombed-out cityscapes of Cologne, Essen, and the industrial Ruhr. The reasons for this phenomenon are complex, but the most likely explanation is that until September 1944 Vienna remained immune to Allied air attacks. Under such relatively safe conditions it is thus worth exploring what sorts of traditional crimes, misdemeanors, and even acts of opposition were committed by juveniles prior to the last six months of the Second World War. Most importantly, even though Hitler's homeland was incorporated into the Third Reich on March 15, 1938, the Austrian civil and penal codes remained in place throughout the Anschluß era. It is true that Nazi ordinances were introduced between 1939 and 1942, but this study demonstrates that most juvenile malefactors were convicted under autochthonous law. This in turn raises the question of to what extent the Anschluß years represented the "Nazification" of the Austrian legal system. This book contends that while National Socialist institutions pervaded Austrian society between 1938 and

1945 the survival of indigenous others, notably the legal order, preserved a sense of regional identity and judicial continuity that has been overlooked and helps to explain the success of the Second Austrian Republic following the collapse of the Third Reich.

In judging juvenile miscreants, to what extent did the Viennese judiciary under Nazi rule take into account prevailing social and legal norms? What, in other words, did Austrian society consider traditional family values and the proper upbringing of children and young people? In this respect, there was another striking continuity between the Habsburg monarchy and the Second Austrian Republic. Generally speaking, attitudes toward proper child-rearing were based on the traditional Catholic doctrine, modified by Joseph II in the eighteenth century and by bourgeois elites after the Napoleonic wars. Both were patriarchal and authoritarian. By the mid-nineteenth century, the structure of middle-class families had come to be accepted as paradigmatic, both under the law and by respectable society. As heads of households, fathers were expected to provide income and housing for their families. Mothers were charged with hygiene, household chores, and the education of children. Discipline, however, was to be administered by fathers. That this model was not always followed by the vast majority of impoverished Viennese families goes without saying. As for children born out of wedlock, they were consigned to foundling homes, work houses, or sent to the countryside to be reared as unpaid farmworkers.[1]

Rapid industrialization after 1867 saw the influx of hundreds of thousands of workers, who were forced to toil in "dark satanic mills" and workshops and to live in unsafe, overcrowded tenement buildings. Under these conditions, there was a massive surge in illegitimate births. In 1887, for example, 36,364 such babies came into the world out of a municipal population of 2.4 million.[2] As a consequence, imperial officials and social workers felt compelled to reconsider the plight of unwed mothers and their offspring. Their efforts led to the founding of nurseries, orphanages, charitable organizations, the Guardianship Authority (Berufvormundschaft), and the Juvenile Legal Support Agency (JSLA; Jugendgerichtshilfe). While a growing number of certified social workers took expanding interest in impoverished children and adolescents, including arranging for home visits and medical check-ups, their major goal was not the well-being of their charges, but the protection of Viennese society from wayward and delinquent youngsters[3].

In 1911 Dr. Erwin Lazar, a 34-year-old pediatrician at the University of Vienna Children's Hospital, spoke out against existing child welfare measures, particularly those followed by social workers and juvenile court judges. Lazar contended that their reports and decisions on problem children tended to be arbitrary and capricious rather than based on scientific evidence. As Edith Sheffer has explained in illuminating detail, Lazar proposed an entirely new approach to child development combining medicine, psychology, and pedagogy, a system he called "curative education." Supported by a renowned immunologist, Clemens von Pirquet, Lazar and his associates established Curative Education Wards to instruct teachers, social workers, and medical doctors on a holistic understanding of delinquent children. Lazar's major goal was the remediation of as many problem children as possible; however, even he recognized that society had to be protected from negligent and delinquent youth. Further, he became obsessed with the eugenic notion of "dissocial" youngsters, whom he called "morally degenerate" or "waste." In this respect, Lazar's assertions did not differ significantly from prevailing views that would extend from the monarchy to the Second Republic.[4]

During the Great War, as will be discussed below, gangs of fatherless and wayward youngsters roamed the streets of Vienna, contributing to a breakdown of law and order. The searing memory of youthful lawlessness reinforced traditional views of childhood socialization by the founders and elites of the First Republic. Given the deep political, ideological, and religious divisions in Red Vienna, it is astonishing that such authoritarian views prevailed. It is true that there was much talk of reform and some significant achievements, for example, in social welfare, education, and public housing. The renowned physician and city councilor Julius Tandler, to cite one instance, established a public welfare office to assist working-class families. Under its auspices, female social workers were tasked with inspecting living conditions in impoverished homes and, if necessary, removing endangered children from their parents to ensure that they enjoyed a proper upbringing. In practice, however, Tandler's office put much of the population under surveillance. In another case, the Municipal School Superintendent Otto Glöckel introduced school reforms that abolished corporal punishment and extended the leaving age to 14. Perhaps most remarkable was the construction of 25,000 apartments for working-class families.[5]

And yet, Social Democratic elites had little knowledge or understanding of the people they claimed to be representing. This is not to suggest that they were unaware of the plight of impoverished working-class children and youngsters. Believing in the mutability of human nature, they sought to cultivate "neue Menschen" ("new human beings") through a kind of war on poverty. But they also thought it necessary to protect society from juvenile vagrancy, delinquency, and waywardness. Instead of paying attention to the living conditions of working-class families dwelling in single rooms without running water or toilet facilities, many Social Democrats feared that teenage street urchins (*Gassenkinder*) were destined to lead a life of crime. To avoid such a fate, the leaders of Red Vienna instituted a wide variety of educational and welfare programs that ranged from new public schools, to foster housing, a correctional facility that provided vocational training, the construction of public swimming pools, and various leisure organizations such as the Red Falcons. Only such a paternalistic upbringing, it was argued, could prevent mass juvenile delinquency and waywardness.[6]

This is not to deny that enlightened social reformers such as Kathe Leichter, Charlotte Bühler, Alfred Adler, Anna Freud, and August Aichorn undertook psychological studies of impoverished families, but even they made distinctions between "normal" and "abnormal" offspring, noting the need for the latter to be separated from society. Worse, Julius Tandler seems to have embraced Cesare Lobroso's notion that both inherited and environmental factors produced deviance, even calling for the sterilization of those with hereditary maladies or in extreme cases the liquidation of "life unworthy of life."[7] However eudemonistic their intentions, the leaders of Red Vienna established the right of the state to intervene in family life and to assume responsibility for the education and proper upbringing of children.[8] Even Sigmund Freud argued that "psycho-analytic concern with children will benefit the work of education, whose aim is to guide and assist children on their forward path and to shield them from going astray."[9]

The advent of the Great Depression in 1929 led to mass unemployment throughout Austria, particularly in Vienna where over 200,000 persons were thrown out of work. Inevitably, there were drastic cuts in social services, including the closing of childcare centers, orphanages, and reformatories. The establishment of the "Austro-Fascist" regime in 1933 cut municipal welfare payments in half, entrusted mothers with the care of children, and mandated religious instruction in primary and secondary schools. As for the proper upbringing of youngsters, families were required under church supervision to stress the importance of obedience, reverence, and patriotism. But an official journal also wrote that "when possible, socially-abnormal personalities should be kept from society." Further, the question should be addressed as to whether present measures for such persons "are not being wasted."[10]

When the Anschluß occurred, it unleashed a torrent of popular euphoria that may never be adequately explained, not least among the young. Within a year unemployment dropped from 21.7 percent to 3.3 percent, with jobs and opportunities being offered to countless working-class families. Youngsters of all classes felt a sense of liberation from the stifling dictates of parents, church, and school. And in the Hitler Youth and League of German Girls (BDM; Bund Deutscher Mädchen) many perceived opportunities "to be respected and responsible."[11] Further, existing welfare schools and institutions were consolidated and streamlined under the auspices of the National Socialist Welfare Association (NSV; Nationalsozialistische Volkswohlfahrt), most notably a maternal outreach clinic that registered 700,000 Viennese in need of medical or public assistance. With the cooperation of the police, Gestapo, and the Juvenile Welfare Office, Nazi ideologues believed that in Hitler's National Community juvenile delinquency and waywardness would cease to exist. That this utopian fantasy was not fulfilled goes without saying, but it helps to explain that long before the Anschluß Austrian jurists had considered a proper upbringing in trying juvenile cases, even if it meant state intervention in family life and consideration of biological factors in their deliberations.[12]

When considering juvenile crime in Hitler's Greater German Reich, historians have focused their attention primarily on dissident teenage groups active in major cities such as Danzig, the setting of Günter Grass's classic novel Die Blechtrommel.[13] According to the prominent scholar Michael Kater, rebellious youngsters tended to have constituted or belonged to three amorphous cohorts: Hitler Youth members who detested the organization's harsh discipline or in rare cases perceived the evils of National Socialism; nonconformists of all stripes, ranging from wealthy Hamburg Swing Kids to more numerous cliques, bands, and gangs of lower middle-class apprentices or manual workers; and "paracriminal" youngsters found guilty of misdemeanors or felonies as well as those judged guilty of a "criminal disposition" by the regime.[14] While there is undeniable merit in this assessment, it tends to overlook instances of traditional crimes ranging from numerous break-ins and thefts to arson, assault, rape, and even murder.

Unlike other studies, this work is based in large part on court records preserved in the Viennese Municipal and Provincial Archives (WSLA; Wiener Stadt- und Landesarchiv) and to a lesser extent in the Documentation Archives of the Austrian Resistance (DöW; Dokumentationsarchiv des österreichischen Widerstandes). Readers should know, however, that the database is imperfect as a great many records were pruned or unwittingly shredded in 1999. In absolute numbers, 437 judicial records have survived, although in a patchwork universe. There are no records for 1938, 54 for 1939, 171 for the years 1940 through 1943, only 41 for 1944, but a surprising total of 171 for 1945. In addition, Gestapo arrest lists for the entire period of Nazi rule provide information only on 43 individuals. While the records are incomplete, they are not so fragmentary as to preclude researchers from uncovering useful information. When combined with official statistics, the documents can be viewed in percentages so as to provide a sense of the trajectory of juvenile crime and deviance during the Nazi era. These, moreover, can be compared with available percentages from other German cities as well as Vichy France to discern similarities in the juvenile crime wave that swept wartime Europe. Finally, by examining individual cases it is possible to explore family backgrounds as well as to contextualize tensions between adolescent deviancy and normality under Nazi rule. Such an approach will take into account social, gendered, religious, and racial attitudes, not to mention the impact of National Socialist values on childhood socialization.

Exploring the terrain of juvenile delinquency under National Socialism requires knowledge of Hitler's legal system and how it actually functioned. Until recently, historians, jurists, and scholars have tended to dismiss the law of Greater Germany as an oxymoronic contradiction designed to mask a lawless tyranny. However, as early as 1938 the Berlin legal scholar Ernst Fraenkel characterized Hitler's regime as a "dual state" combining "normative" and "prerogative" measures. Precisely because the Nazi system rested on popular consent, Fraenkel contended, the Führer and his henchmen opted to retain most of the judicial order in place, if for no other reason than to proceed legally against their opponents. That the German civil and penal code remained untouched, in other words, was hardly a coincidence.[15]

Following the collapse of the Third Reich in 1945, Fraenkel's explanatory model seemed outmoded or no longer apposite. In the horrified view of Allied occupation authorities and contemporary observers, Hitler's regime had evolved into a prerogative tyranny dominated by the party, the Gestapo, and SS. It was a system in which laws were either ignored, for example, in concentration camps, or in which legal decisions were handed down by highly politicized courts, such as the Special Courts (SG; *Sondergerichte*) or the notorious People's Court (VGH; *Volksgerichtshof*).[16] Even at the local or regional level, judges seemed to have ruled according to the principle *quod principi placuit legis vigorem habet*: what pleases the prince has the force of law. Among the few individuals to question this monolithic view were the writer Abby Mann and the Hollywood director Stanley Kramer. In their 1961 film, *Judgment at Nuremberg*, they provided a glimpse, albeit fictional, of how German courts meted out justice between 1933 and 1945.

Contemporary scholars, as suggested above, have recently taken another look at the complexities of Nazi jurisprudence. They have stressed that because

Hitler came to power constitutionally, it was in his interest, albeit against his will, to maintain the facade of legality as long as possible. They have also pointed out that while radical legislation such as the Nuremberg Laws altered the legal landscape and paved the way for "extralegal terror," judicial decisions tended to be based more on Nazi ideology than on existing statutes. Even after the passage of drastic wartime decrees in 1939, state prosecutors and judges would examine the "inner motivation" of defendants to determine whether they were criminal types that should be excluded from the National Community. Intent and personal characteristics, in other words, became more important than the crime itself. The rule of law was also undercut by a statute altering the legal principle *nulla poena sine lege* (no punishment without the law) to the precept *nullum crimen sine poena* (no crime without punishment). As a consequence, jurists became inclined to reach decisions on the specious principle of fulfilling the Führer's will.[17] And yet, as Alan Steinweis and Robert Rachlin have noted, even individuals accused of racial and political transgressions continued to be "indicted by state prosecutors and tried in established courts."[18] Recalling that the civil and penal codes remained largely in place, Germans brought before the bench found themselves caught in what one authority has called a "parallel judicial universe."[19] This was even more the case in incorporated Austria following the Anschluß, as the next chapter will make clear.

1

Anschluß and Consolidation, 1938–1939

German and Austrian jurists in the euphoria following the Anschluß believed that the opportunity to combine the legal systems of both countries into a single Germanic law was at hand, even though Hitler himself recognized the difficulties of coordinating such an effort. Thus although a flood of German laws, ordinances, and regulations were extended throughout the "Ostmark" between 1938 and 1945, legal uniformity was not achieved. There were multiple reasons for this failure, as this chapter explains in detail. Yet, as it will also demonstrate, in many ways the Austrian judicial thinking and procedures had already been aligned with those in the Third Reich before March 1938. First, although the Minister of Justice Franz Gürtner lobbied incessantly for the passage of an all-embracing National Socialist law (*Verreichlichung*), he was stymied by the resistance of economic and administrative officials as well as by a shortage of trained personnel. The shortages were exacerbated by the dismissal or forced retirement of 207 Austrian state prosecutors and judges, including 130 in Vienna, as well as the call up of other jurists to the armed forces. Second, Gürtner faced the opposition of Rudolf Hess, who sought party supremacy and the Minister of the Interior Hans Frick, who argued persuasively that hard-pressed Austrian jurists were in no position to master the intricacies of the German Civil Code (*Bürgerliches Gesetzbuch*) in an atmosphere of international crisis that might well lead to military conflict. In the accelerated run-up to the war, Hitler conceded the point, leaving the Austrian Civil Code of 1811 and the Penal Code of 1852 in place.[1]

There were, however, some exceptions; a number of decrees and ordinances were extended to Austria shortly after the Anschluß. These included the Law Against the Formation of New Parties, the Reich Flag Law, the Four Year Plan Law, the Wehrmacht Law, and the Law for the Protection of German Blood and Honor, that is, the Nuremberg Laws. On June 20, 1938, the Nazi regime replaced the Austrian laws on treason, which according to Articles 58–62 had been defined as betrayal of the country or the federal president. During the First Republic, the maximum penalty had been life imprisonment, though in 1934 the Dollfuss regime restored the death penalty. The new post-Anschluß law on treason was based on Prussian jurisprudence. It distinguished between two types of treason: high treason (*Hochverrat*), which meant acts against the government and its institutions, and state treason (*Landesverrat*), which corresponded roughly to espionage. In coming years, those charged with treason would be tried by the People's Court, whose judges would abuse, humiliate, and sentence those found guilty to death or to lengthy prison terms. Others indicted on lesser charges of sedition or espionage would suffer similar abuse in the chambers of the Higher Regional Court (OLG; *Oberlandesgericht*). Technically speaking, these measures constituted the "Nazification" of the Austrian legal system. Even so, the Austrian criminal code remained in place until the collapse of the Third Reich. This meant that in addition to legislation introduced or passed in Berlin after the Anschluß two parallel or arguably three legal systems existed in the "Ostmark."[2]

There was another reason that the Austrian criminal code remained largely untouched. It lay in the conviction of Nazi jurists that in time the Austrian code's more authoritarian legal precepts would add strength and vitality to the sort of "German Common Law" envisioned in the NSDAP's (National Socialist Workers Party) platform.[3] These included laws based on the "personality principle" excluding noncitizens from established judicial rights and "material law" permitting judges to discard evidence at their own discretion. In addition, there were several severe laws punishing vagabonds, sex offenders, dangerous habitual criminals, and individuals considered harmful to society.[4] A number of these had been tightened by the Dollfuss-Schuschnigg dictatorship, for example, through decrees curtailing trial by jury, restricting judicial tenure rights, eliminating the procedural defense of double jeopardy, and establishing Special Courts. In September 1934, moreover, the government had assumed extralegal power to incarcerate political opponents in detention centers.[5] Also significant and particularly attractive to Reich German judicial officials was a statute condemning juvenile delinquents to "indefinite imprisonment" (*unbestimmte Verurteilung*), a measure designed both to penalize and to monitor youthful offenders; this will be explained in greater detail below.[6] Between 1938 and 1945, a number of Austrian precepts would be woven into the legal system of Greater Germany, including territories annexed after the Munich settlement and during the Second World War. Even so, the criminal code in Hitler's homeland remained fundamentally intact. What altered it and the German code, as numerous scholars have pointed out, was not so much the introduction of new laws and decrees as the interpretation of existing laws through *völkisch* norms.[7] Operationally, judges were expected to reach decisions protecting both the race and the National Community (*Volksgemeinschaft*), identifying criminal types, and even anticipating the will of the Führer. According to one legal authority, "the purpose of a trial now became not so much to determine whether the accused had broken a law but rather 'whether the wrongdoer still belongs to the community.'"[8]

Origins and Evolution of Juvenile Justice in Austria

Austrian criminal law originated in the provinces of the Habsburg Hereditary Lands, most notably in 1499 when Emperor Maximilian I proclaimed a penal code in Tyrol. Two and half centuries later Maria Theresia promulgated a uniform system of criminal justice for her entire realm. Based on inquisitional procedures, it was exceptionally harsh, permitting the use of torture and imposing penalties for theocratic offences such as blasphemy, sorcery, and witchcraft. In 1787, Joseph II abolished capital punishment and introduced the principle *nullum crimen sine lege*. The emperor's "enlightened" reforms were accompanied, however, by severe criminal penalties intended to terrify his subjects, for example, through branding, imprisonment in irons, and lethal barge hauling on the Danube.[9] Following the French Revolution, a more humane penal code came into force in 1803. It adopted the Napoleonic model of dividing offences into misdemeanors, gross misdemeanors, and felonies. Sanctions remained severe, but the new code also stipulated that both the nature of the crime and the personality of the defendant had to be considered in judicial procedures. These and other elements were woven into the General Civil Code (*Allgemeines Bürgerliches Gesetzbuch*) of 1811, based largely on Roman law but also heavily influenced by eighteenth-century Enlightenment precepts. It thus distinguished between private and civil law and recognized individuals as citizens rather than subjects liable to servitude.[10] The General Civil Code constituted what one authority calls "a major endorsement of notions of civil liberty within the framework of the bureaucratic-absolutist state."[11]

On May 27, 1852, Emperor Francis Joseph enacted a revised penal code. Although amended in 1867, 1873, and after the world wars, it remained in force until 1974. Authoritarian and patriarchal, the code recognized matrimony, family, and private property as the foundations of society.[12] During the course of the next two decades, however, the code was modified to guarantee civil liberties, regulate police regulations, and abolish corporal punishment. In 1918, convicted individuals were permitted to petition for the effacement of criminal records after serving their sentences. The following year capital punishment was abolished, and in 1920 a law was passed authorizing judges to reduce the time served for certain criminals by imposing punishment of "indefinite imprisonment" (*unbestimmte Verurteilung*). The legislation called for the early release of prisoners deemed capable of rehabilitation by placing them under supervised parole for a period of one to three years. Most important for our study was the enactment in 1928 of the Juvenile Court Law, a measure designed to protect society by seeking to rehabilitate certain youthful offenders through education. The new statute distanced itself in some ways from the Penal Code of 1852, but even during the Anschluß years it required courts and judicial officials in Nazi Austria to consider mitigating circumstances in reaching decisions.

As early as 1811, the General Civil Code attempted to address the problem of juvenile negligence and deviance in Austria by permitting judges to appoint guardians to care for orphans or illegitimate children. Later rulings included children who were either neglected or abused by their parents. Throughout the nineteenth century, various charitable associations, comprised largely of women, sought to offer advice and counsel to juvenile court officials in assessing the behavior of wayward adolescents. Their efforts led to the founding in 1911 of an umbrella organization by Countess Luise Fünfkirchen-Lichtenstein designed to assist juvenile authorities in investigating family backgrounds, living conditions, and other factors contributing to the criminal activities of youthful offenders. Seven years later her JSLA Juvenile Legal Support Agency (Jugendgerichtshilfe) would become an integral component of the Austrian law.[13] As for illegitimate youngsters, the Guardianship Authority was established to place wayward youngsters in foster homes, though most appear to have been accepted only with great reluctance.[14]

In contrast to France, and to a lesser extent Britain, the Austrian legal system prior to 1918 paid little attention to the nature or causes of juvenile crime. This meant that the judicial order of a Catholic monarchy regarded adolescent malefactors as "child criminals," disposed to original sin and thus deserving punishment. Little thought was given to notions of personal responsibility, let alone to Rousseau's ideas of childhood innocence or more modern concepts of rehabilitation. As a consequence, juvenile offenders ranging from 10 to 20 years of age might find themselves imprisoned with hardened criminals or later consigned to special sections of a penitentiary. On the other hand, the number of incarcerated youth seems to have been relatively small prior to the 1870s, even though the absence of statistics makes it impossible to say for sure.[15]

In the decades following the collapse of the Viennese Stock Exchange in 1873, elites and the general public expressed alarm at what they perceived as a dramatic increase in adolescent crime within the Austrian half of the Habsburg monarchy. Officials, politicians, criminologists, and opinion makers gathered statistics that would justify harsh measures aimed at stemming juvenile delinquency and waywardness. The most significant of these was the Vagrancy Act of 1885, according to which judges could order the confinement of minors who were 10 to 18 years of age in reformatories or workhouses for aversion to work, begging, vagabondage, prostitution, and other offences. There was general agreement that the major causes for the youthful "crime wave" lay in the transition from artisanal manufacturing to factory labor, a process that severed the supervision of masters over apprentices so as to allow minors to gather in precocious gangs and fall prey to alcoholism, gambling, and prostitution. Other putative causes lay in the breakdown of the family, secularization, and moral degeneracy. The general fear of the rise of a "dangerous class," as in France, was reinforced by a study contending that between 1882 and 1892 juvenile crime had risen 51 percent. In actual fact, as recent research has revealed, indictable offences for misdemeanors such as petty theft, begging, or trespassing had not risen substantially. Rather, formal legislation criminalized what had previously been considered minor police infractions. This meant that, despite various reform measures, the prevailing view of "dangerous youth" as opposed to that of "endangered youth" would persist in Austria through both world wars and even into the 1960s.[16]

Meanwhile, the disastrous failures of the Habsburg army during the First World War combined with the loss of Hungarian grain, the Allied blockade, and an inadequate food distribution system led to a "starvation crisis," particularly in Vienna. The impact of malnutrition on the health of children and adolescents was disastrous. By 1916, mass deprivation had stunted growth, taken the lives of thousands, and precipitated radical changes in youthful behavior. With roughly 70 percent of Viennese married men serving in the armed forces, many of them never to return, municipal officials confronted a "fatherless society," one in which adolescent crime began to skyrocket. The exact causes of juvenile neglect and delinquency (*Jugendverwahrlosung*) then became the subject of heated debate. At first, movie theaters were held to blame for showing violent detective films and encouraging the spread of raunchy magazines, pamphlets, and novels. Given the absence of statistics, journalists, teachers, and clergymen disagreed on root causes. Nevertheless, wide publicity was given to cases of theft, loitering, smoking, aggravated assault, and sexual promiscuity. Objections were also raised to youngsters hanging out in cafes, organizing street gangs, and playing cards or billiards in public places. Eventually, a rough-hewn consensus emerged that "absent fathers and weak mothers" along with the "Jews and their press" were primarily responsible for the upsurge of teenage crime.[17]

In 1918, military defeat and the disintegration of the Habsburg monarchy had a disastrous impact in Vienna. An imperial capital that had dominated Central and Eastern Europe for centuries, Vienna was suddenly reduced to the seat of government of a small republic, a "state that nobody wanted." Accompanying the social and political turmoil was an influenza epidemic that took the lives of 3,927 Viennese, many of whom were children.[18] Cut off from foodstuffs and coal in neighboring Hungary and Czechoslovakia, the Austrian provisional government appealed to the Inter Allied Relief Commission for aid. British, American, and Quaker relief workers responded by providing schoolchildren with rations of cocoa, sugar, milk, fat, flour, and soap as well as warm clothing. Even so, in 1920, 96 percent of Viennese minors under the age of 15 remained severely malnourished. Not until another three years had passed, during which 200,000 Austrian children had been sent to Switzerland, Britain and Scandinavia to recuperate, did the Society of Friends conclude that the hunger crisis had passed.[19]

The severe suffering of children and adolescents during the Great War resulted in measures designed to address problems of "juvenile negligence and delinquency." Reforms passed in 1914, 1916, and 1919 sought to protect foster and illegitimate children by establishing public boards to provide legal, familial, and educational assistance through the Guardianship Authority. In Vienna, the Juvenile Welfare Board (*Jugendamt*) was made up of professional social workers assisted by volunteers from charitable associations. On January 25, 1919, the provisional assembly passed legislation to establish a juvenile court system that began proceedings 19 months later. But as mentioned above, it was the Juvenile Court Law, enacted in July 1928, that sought to reexamine the causes of juvenile deviance, limit punishment, and institute alternatives to incarceration. The new law stipulated that adolescents under the age of 14 could no longer be arrested, indicted, or tried as adults. Instead, youthful offenders between 14 and 18 were to be judged only after careful scrutiny of the nature of their crime and consideration of their personality development.

The underlying assumption of the Juvenile Court Law was that delinquents under 18 years of age lacked "education," an elastic belief shared by many criminologists, sociologists, jurists, and psychologists in Western Europe. And because most youthful malefactors came from impoverished or dysfunctional families this was hardly an unreasonable notion. Social workers thus prepared dossiers identifying problems such as neglect, abuse, poverty, malnutrition, low intelligence, peer group pressure, or even an inability to distinguish right from wrong. As a large number of the personnel were unmarried women, most notably in France and Austria, many took a keen maternal interest in the children of troubled or dysfunctional families. Prior to the Anschluß the Viennese investigative reports tended to focus on the moral behavior and conduct of delinquent offenders as inseparable from their social milieu or living conditions.[20] Their inquests provided a "social diagnosis" that refrained from assessing the personal character of the accused. However, during the Dollfuss-Schuschnigg dictatorship some officials of the JSLA added information on medical abnormalities suggesting "antisocial" biological disorders. Between 1928 and 1938, judges were required to decide the "problematic maturity" of the defendant at the moment the crime had been committed.[21] In this respect the juvenile justice system in Austria bore a striking resemblance to that in France. Here courts exercised the power of *discernement*, that is, an obligation to discern if minors understood the consequences of transgressions of which they had been convicted. Upon reaching such a conclusion French judges could impose adult sentences on defendants between the ages of 13 and 18.[22]

Although Viennese courts continued to mete out stiff sentences to youthful malefactors, particularly those convicted of felonies, the magistrates could impose imprisonment only for a maximum period of ten years to be served in jail rather than in prison. Those convicted of lesser crimes or misdemeanors might receive "indefinite imprisonment" as a kind of preventive punishment designed, as we have seen, both to penalize and monitor youthful delinquents. The major goal of the Juvenile Court Act, however, was care and rehabilitation rather than punishment. Even in cases of incarceration, the objective was "to change the character and to overcome the harmful inclinations of the juvenile."[23]

By far the most ambitious attempt to combat "juvenile waywardness and delinquency" was the establishment of a reform school for convicted minors from negligent families or deemed educationally disadvantaged. Located at Kaiser-Ebersdorf, near Simmering, the Federal Institution for the Educational Needy (Bundesanstalt für Erziehungsbedürftige) provided room, board, and clothing for delinquent boys. The director, Richard Seyss Inquart, was a former priest who had provided pastoral care for Empress Zita and her children during the Great War. Thereafter, he left the priesthood, got married, and became a prison counselor. As director, Seyss hired teams of vocational instructors, social workers, and psychotherapists to assess each boy's aptitude, sense of morality, and potential for social integration as adults. According to one associate, Viktor Matejka, Seyss was initially impressed by the Soviet approach to correctional education. Whether this was actually the case is unclear. What is indisputable is that Seyss threw himself into his work with pedagogical zeal, constructing fourteen manual-training workshops, establishing an apprentice training center, and even renting a large estate to train agricultural workers. He also made sure that each pupil, as he called his charges, received personal vocational and psychological counseling designed to preempt them from leading a life of crime. By 1938, Seyss had become an ardent National Socialist, convinced that the Anschluß orchestrated by his brother, Artur Seyss Inquart, would enable him to expand his vocational and psychotherapeutic programs. In this he was sorely disappointed. Shortly before his death in June 1941, Richard Seyss Inquart published a bitter article in a psychoanalytic journal regretting that Kaiser-Ebersdorf had been transformed into a penal institution for youthful deadbeats and convicts[24].

By 1944, those incarcerated in Kaiser-Ebersdorf were being treated more as hardened criminals than as wayward youth. According to a report filed by the Viennese NSDAP, the reformatory housed 388 delinquents serving terms ranging from seventy-three weeks of detention to nineteen months in jail. An unspecified number had been convicted of subversive activities such as listening to foreign radio broadcasts, fifty-four for breach of labor contract or absenteeism, and the rest for conventional offences such as theft, vandalism, and loitering. Nearly all were forced to work in filthy, often dangerous enterprises for the party or the Wehrmacht. These included interweaving metal strands for artillery shells and fabricating crates for military vehicles; washing, cleaning, and repairing Storm Troopers (SA) clothing; and refurbishing "shoes taken as booty."[25] One survivor later recalled that Kaiser-Ebersdorf was "really, one could almost say, a concentration camp."[26]

Who were these youthful miscreants? Had most been found guilty of serious misdemeanors or felonies? Had they belonged to street gangs? Had a number simply joined together in nonconformist groups or engaged in youthful high jinks? How many had been arrested for political crimes? If so, had they actually opposed the Nazi regime or had they been taken into custody for violating wartime ordinances that included loitering after dark, forging ration coupons, or engaging in black marketeering. How many had been victims of Himmler's crackdown on homosexuality? To what extent did the youthful crime rate in Vienna compare to that in other major cities of Hitler's Greater German Reich? These and other problems related to juvenile delinquency in Nazi Vienna are the major issues this study seeks to address.

Impact of the Depression

Interestingly, the advent of the Great Depression had not unleashed a youthful crime wave in Vienna. As in the great cities of the German Reich, the numbers of juvenile misdemeanors, gross misdemeanors, and felonies actually declined; the percentage of misdemeanors fell from 5.2 in 1930 to 3.2 in 1935 and that of felonies from 4.2 in 1930 to 2.8 in 1935. During the next two years, the rate of misdemeanors remained steady, but those of felonies rose in 1936 to 4.8 percent and in 1937 nearly doubled to 5.7 percent.[27] Elsewhere in Austria, the rate of juvenile convictions appears to have paralleled that in the capital city. One set of statistics indicates, however, that underage felonies in Graz, a much smaller jurisdiction, rose dramatically in 1936 to 7.1 percent.[28] Given the upsurge of Nazi violence the following year, instances of juvenile crime in the provincial capital most likely continued to accelerate.

Austria, unlike Germany, remained impoverished throughout the 1930s. Nevertheless, the types of juvenile misdemeanors and felonies committed in Vienna between 1930 and 1937 paralleled those undertaken by urban teenagers in the Third Reich. Two-thirds of the offences involved petty theft, minor assaults, break-ins, robbery, forgery, and larceny.[29] A court record from January 1938 suggests that extreme poverty may have driven many youngsters to break the law. On September 25, 1937, 14-year-old Friedrich J. had been apprehended for damaging a garden fence and stealing plums, an amount assessed by the court to be worth ten schillings. Found guilty on January 15, 1938, he was sentenced to three years of closely supervised probation.[30] Another distinguishing feature of juvenile deviance in Vienna was the conviction of a fair number of minors for sex crimes and moral offenses. The statistics do not reveal whether the teenagers were prosecuted for prostitution, indecent exposure, sexual assault, or sodomy, but they do indicate the percentages of convictions rose from 7.1 percent in 1930 to 9.5 percent in 1935 while tapering off to 5.2 in 1937. During the same period in the German Reich, cases of teenage moral offences, particularly homosexuality, climbed slowly from 3.2 percent in 1931 to 4.5 percent in 1936. Thereafter, they rose sharply, as we have already seen.[31] According to official statistics, the percentage of juvenile misdemeanors, gross misdemeanors, and felonies skyrocketed from 4.5 percent in 1937 to 12.8 percent in 1939. However, the actual numbers rose only slightly from 2,818 convictions in 1937 to 2,939 in 1939.[32] The relatively unchanged low level of teenage crime in Vienna may be attributed to a federal law passed in 1922, a stern measure designed to prevent the sort of youthful misbehavior that had plagued the city during the Great

War. The law banned minors under 16 from attending cinemas, distributing lascivious or pornographic pictures, and consuming alcoholic beverages. For the same age group it mandated a curfew, prohibited smoking and card playing in public places, and laid down strict rules for dancing. Finally, the penal code prohibited youngsters under 16 from visiting prostitutes and imposed severe penalties for homosexual behavior for teenagers of both sexes.[33]

After the Anschluß, 1938–1939

On March 13, 1938, in Linz, Adolf Hitler sat down to dinner at the Hotel Weinzinger. Supping on pea soup and rice he signed a legislation that proclaimed the Reunification of Austria with the German Reich. The new law incorporated Austria into Germany and called for a plebiscite to be held on April 10; it also stipulated that until further notice existing Austrian law remained on the books. Two days later a Führer decree ordered the dismissal of all Jewish civil servants, military personnel, judges, notaries, and patent attorneys. It was followed by an amendment charging Heinrich Himmler with the maintenance of law and order. Subsequent weeks saw the introduction of the Four Year Plan, a decree requiring the registration of Jewish assets above 5,000 marks, the extension of the Nuremberg Laws, and the division of incorporated Austria into seven semiautonomous Reichsgaue. Berlin, however, retained central control of the railroads, postal service, finance, and, most significantly, the judiciary.[34]

Reich Minister of Justice Franz Gürtner now sought to take advantage of his enhanced position to pass an all-encompassing Germanic Law according to Point 19 of the Nazi Party program. However, as we have already seen, he not only confronted a shortage of trained legal personnel, but also encountered the resistance of Hess, Frick, and a number of competing bureaucratic agencies. As a consequence, the Austrian penal code remained in place as did nearly all non-Jewish members of the judiciary, most of whom were German nationalists (*deutschnationale*) sympathetic to the Nazi cause. On the other hand, the jurisdiction of the *Volksgerichtshof* was extended to the "Ostmark" on June 20, 1938, and that of Special Courts five months later. There were also a number of technical changes. These included the establishment of a Senate of the Ministry of Justice in Vienna, a branch that both assigned a criminal division to the Higher Regional Court and authorized it to try cases of espionage and treason. In addition, the Juvenile Court was officially dissolved but continued to function under the auspices of the Higher Regional Court located in the Gray House.[35]

Indeed, prior to the outbreak of war the only formal measure affecting juvenile delinquents was the adoption of the German firearms law, criminalizing the ownership and use of firearms by underage Jews, gypsies, sex offenders, and other "enemies of the state."[36]

German jurists, criminologists, social workers, and officials had long wrestled with problems of juvenile waywardness and deviance. As in Austria, they had been alarmed by a massive surge of juvenile crime during the Great War, particularly in Berlin where orphan gangs, armed with knives and revolvers, had roamed the city engaging in street fights, assaulting pedestrians, and committing other crimes. Even though delinquency declined during the Weimar period, a majority of attorneys, judicial officials, and legal scholars such as Carl Schmitt had welcomed Hitler's rise to power, even hailing him as the "Guardian of Justice."[37]

Between 1933 and 1938, Nazi anticrime measures, both legal and illegal, reduced criminality in Germany, particularly among juveniles. Youthful convictions initially dropped in major cities by a third, in medium-sized towns and villages by nearly a half. The major reason for the sharp decline in juvenile delinquency was the dramatic recovery of the German economy, which provided work for youthful apprentices, clerical trainees, and other adolescents under the age of 18. For others, the Hitler Youth and the League of German Girls provided opportunities to escape the misery of poverty or even monitor the activities of wayward youth. And yet the return of economic recovery also provided opportunities for a recrudescence of petty theft, most notably of vending machines and pay telephones as well as shoplifting in department stores. Bicycles, motorcycles, and even automobiles also became targets. On the other hand, other forms of juvenile larceny such as burglary, fraud, and embezzlement did not increase. There was a slight rise in vandalism, as one might expect, though the rates of violent crime such as assault, manslaughter, and murder remained low. In these areas, the Nazi goal of eradicating teenage crime appears to have come close to success.[38]

Given this record of achievement, it was hardly surprising that Berlin officials would introduce small but significant steps to alter courtroom procedures in the Austrian penal code. One of the most important of these was to enhance the power of the state prosecutor at the expense of the judge. The aim was to divest judges of the authority to question pretrial irregularities or set aside decisions that might "dishonor the race" or be at variance with "healthy common sense." Further, the state prosecutor was empowered to refer sensitive or egregious cases to Special Courts, in which defense attorneys had no right to question evidence, those found guilty had no right of appeal, and a panel of three judges could sentence defendants to be executed within hours of handing down a verdict. The implementation of the "expeditious trial" (*kurzer Prozess*), as it came to be known, made it possible both to "eliminate formalism" in legal proceedings and to ensure immediate punishment at minimum cost. In incorporated Austria, the expeditious trial also enabled the courts to proceed without replacing the hundreds of prosecutors and judges purged in 1938.[39] Looking back, the Austrian judicial system appears to have remained largely intact following the Anschluβ, most notably in the eighteen months prior to the outbreak of the Second World War. That said, widespread approval of Nazi ideology among the justices as well as their previous support of the authoritarian Dollfuss-Schuschnigg dictatorship meant that the judiciary would eventually evolve into a "tool of the National Socialist regime."[40]

To what extent these procedures were applied to juveniles brought before the Viennese bench in the months following the Anschluβ is impossible to gauge. There can be little doubt that hundreds of youngsters participated in the waves of violence that swept through the Danubian city in 1938, particularly those directed against Jews and supporters of the Dollfuss-Schuschnigg dictatorship. Many surely belonged to the Hitler Youth, but others may have been hooligans. We shall never know. Statistics on penal offenses committed in 1938 were neither gathered nor published. As previously noted, moreover, many of the juvenile court records for the years 1930 to 1945 were unintentionally shredded by the University of Vienna.[41] That said, what appears to be a complete file of juvenile cases tried between July and December 1939 has survived.[42] Because nearly all these offenses were committed before the issuance of drastic wartime ordinances in October 1939, they provide a glimpse of juvenile deviance during a stable period of Nazi rule. When compared with official statistics published between 1930 and 1937 and in 1939, they reveal an even clearer image. In addition, the daily reports of the Viennese Gestapo prior to the outbreak of Hitler's war reveal that between September 1, 1938, and August 9, 1939, no fewer than seventy-three youngsters were arrested for "political crimes." For the period 1940–1944, a handful of court transcripts preserved in the Documentation Center of the Austrian Resistance provide additional data. Although exiguous, these records along with those of seventy-two youngsters tried by Hitler's Special Courts are also revealing. Combining them with Christian Gerbel's outstanding studies of adolescent dissidence in wartime Vienna makes it possible to understand the complex aspects of juvenile justice under Nazi rule prior to the enactment of a comprehensive Reich Juvenile Court Law on October 6, 1943.[43] Thereafter, the

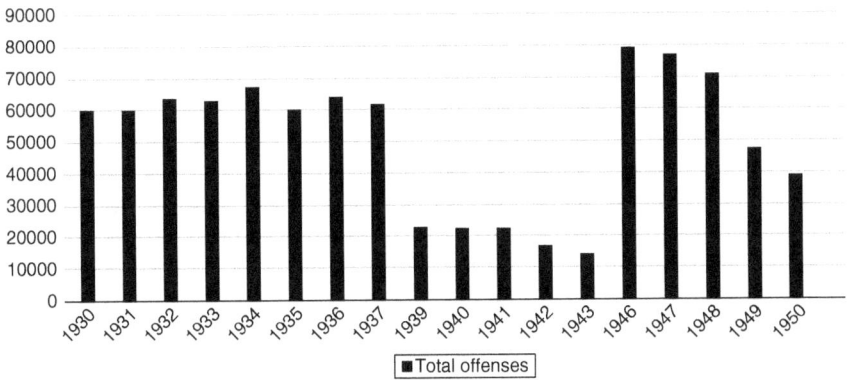

Figure 1.1 Total misdemeanors, gross misdemeanors, and felonies in Vienna, 1930–1950.
Sources: *Statistisches Jahrbuch der Stadt Wien* 3 (1930–1945), 4 (1937), 5 (1938), 6 (1939–1942), 7 (1943–1945), 8 (1946–1947), 9 (1948), 10 (1949), 11 (1950).

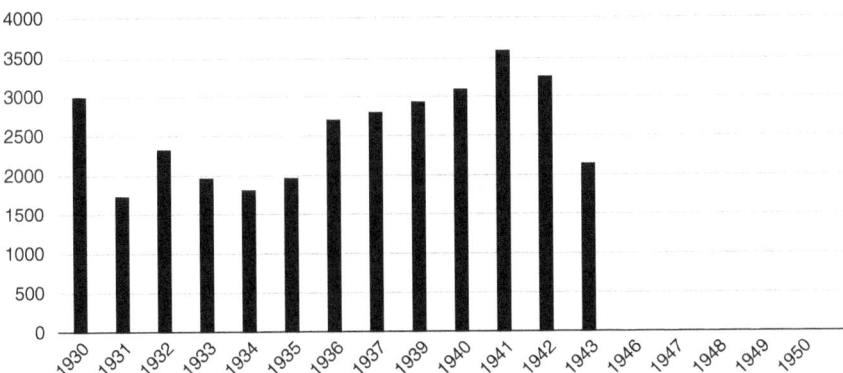

Figure 1.1a Juvenile misdemeanors, gross misdemeanors, and felonies in Vienna, 1930–1950, by case.
Sources: *Statistisches Jahrbuch der Stadt Wien* 3 (1930–1945), 4 (1937), 5 (1938), 6 (1939–1942), 7 (1943–1945), 8 (1946–1947), 9 (1948), 10 (1949), 11 (1950).

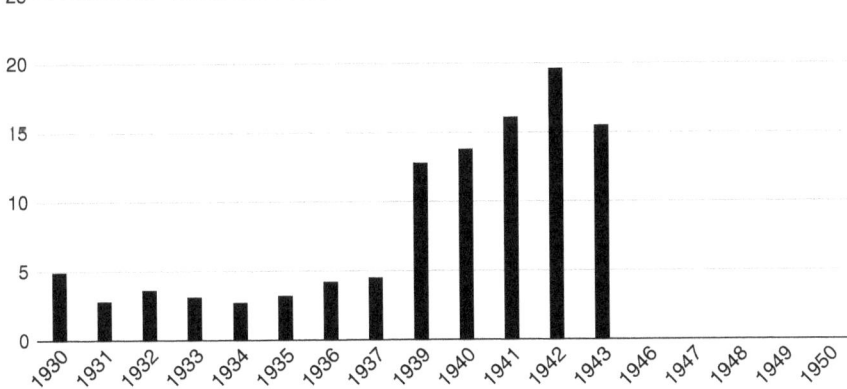

Figure 1.1b Juvenile misdemeanors, gross misdemeanors, and felonies in Vienna, 1930–1950, by percentage.
Sources: *Statistisches Jahrbuch der Stadt Wien* 3 (1930–1945), 4 (1937), 5 (1938), 6 (1939–1942), 7 (1943–1945), 8 (1946–1947), 9 (1948), 10 (1949), 11 (1950).

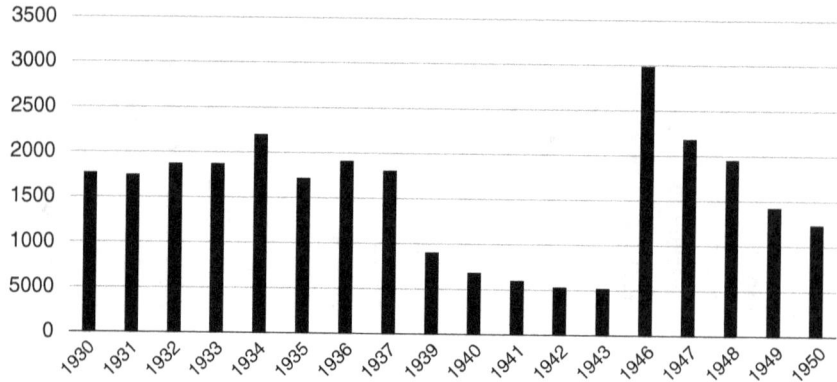

Figure 1.2 Total felonies in Vienna, 1930–1950.
Sources: *Statistisches Jahrbuch der Stadt Wien* 3 (1930–1935), 4 (1937), 5 (1938), 6 (1939–1942), 7 (1943–1945), 8 (1946–1947), 9 (1948), 10 (1949), 11 (1950).

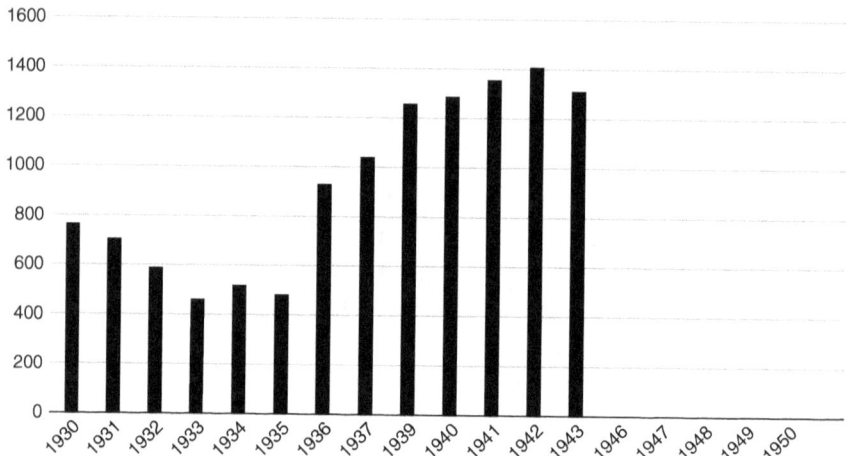

Figure 1.2a Juvenile felonies in Vienna, 1930–1950, by case.
Sources: *Statistisches Jahrbuch der Stadt Wien* 3 (1930–1945), 4 (1937), 5 (1938), 6 (1939–1942), 7 (1943–1945), 8 (1946–1947), 9 (1948), 10 (1949), 11 (1950).

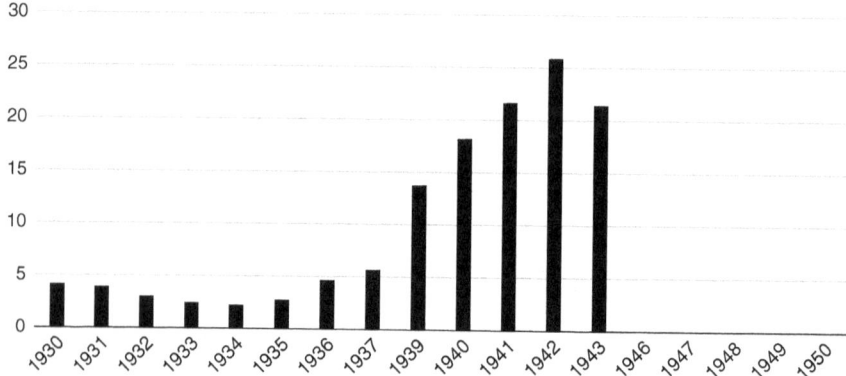

Figure 1.2b Juvenile felonies in Vienna, 1930–1950, by percentage.
Sources: *Statistisches Jahrbuch der Stadt Wien* 3 (1930–1945), 4 (1937), 5 (1938), 6 (1939–1942), 7 (1943–1945), 8 (1946–1947), 9 (1948), 10 (1949), 11 (1950).

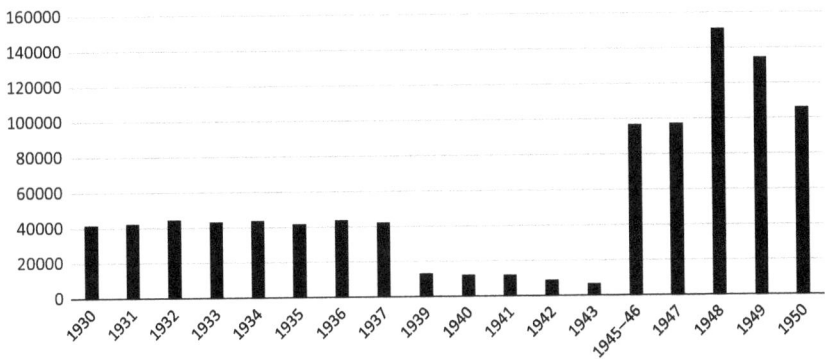

Figure 1.3 Total misdemeanors in Vienna, 1930–1950.
Sources: Statistisches Jahrbuch der Stadt Wien 3 (1930–1945), 4 (1937), 5 (1938), 6 (1939–1942), 7 (1943–1945), 8 (1946–1947), 9 (1948), 10 (1949), 11 (1950).

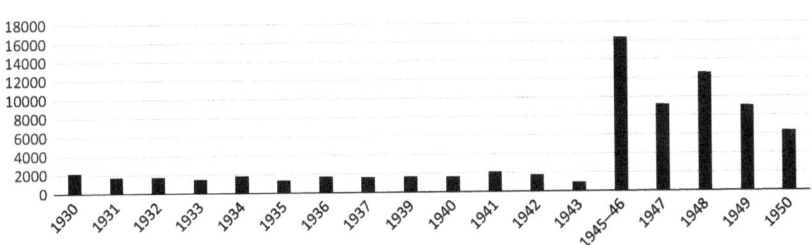

Figure 1.3a Juvenile misdemeanors in Vienna, 1930–1950.
Sources: Statistisches Jahrbuch der Stadt Wien 3 (1930–1945), 4 (1937), 5 (1938), 6 (1939–1942), 7 (1943–1945), 8 (1946–1947), 9 (1948), 10 (1949), 11 (1950).

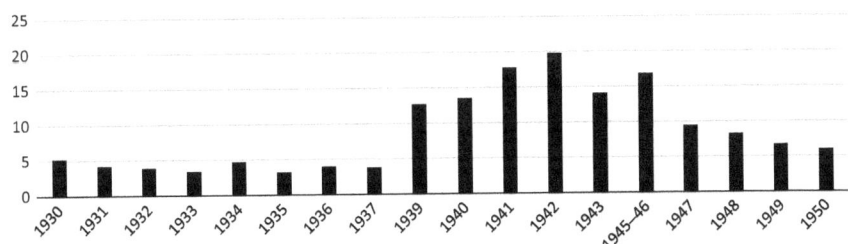

Figure 1.3b Juvenile misdemeanors in Vienna, 1930–1950, by percentage.
Sources: Statistisches Jahrbuch der Stadt Wien 3 (1930–1945), 4 (1937), 5 (1938), 6 (1939–1942), 7 (1943–1945), 8 (1946–1947), 9 (1948), 10 (1949), 11 (1950).

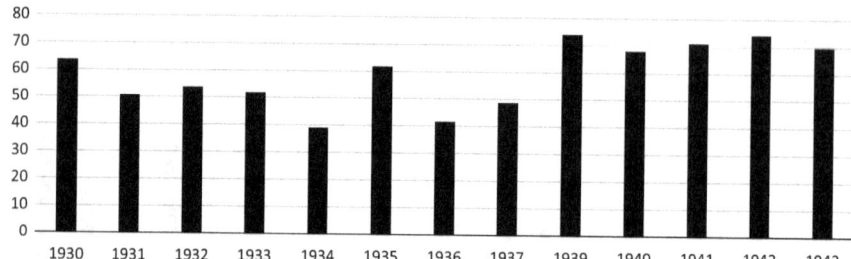

Figure 1.4 Major juvenile felonies in Vienna, 1930–1950, break-ins and theft by percentages.
Sources: *Statistisches Jahrbuch der Stadt Wien* 3 (1930–1945), 4 (1937), 5 (1938), 6 (1939–1942), 7 (1943–1945), 8 (1946–1947), 9 (1948), 10 (1949), 11 (1950).

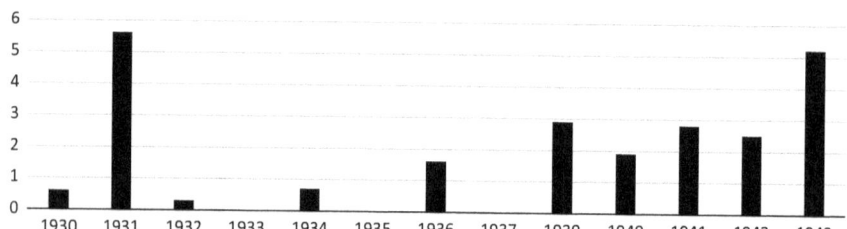

Figure 1.4a Major juvenile felonies in Vienna, 1930–1950, robbery by percentages.
Sources: *Statistisches Jahrbuch der Stadt Wien* 3 (1930–1945), 4 (1937), 5 (1938), 6 (1939–1942), 7 (1943–1945), 8 (1946–1947), 9 (1948), 10 (1949), 11 (1950).

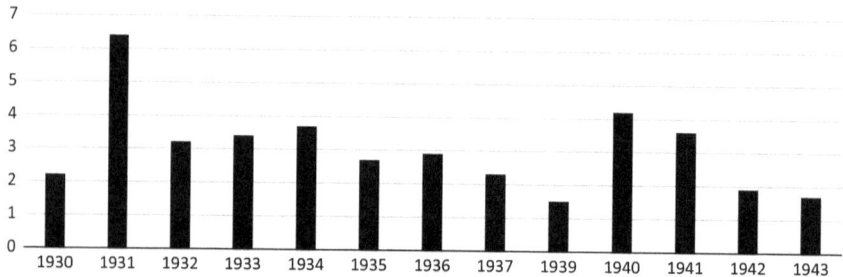

Figure 1.4b Major juvenile felonies in Vienna, 1930–1950, accessory to theft by percentages.
Sources: *Statistisches Jahrbuch der Stadt Wien* 3 (1930–1945), 4 (1937), 5 (1938), 6 (1939–1942), 7 (1943–1945), 8 (1946–1947), 9 (1948), 10 (1949), 11 (1950).

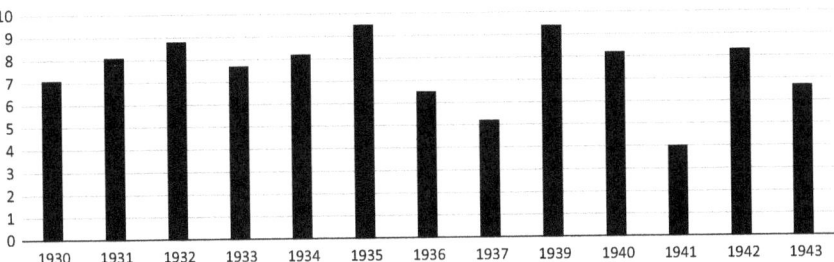

Figure 1.4c Major juvenile felonies in Vienna, 1930–1950, sex crimes by percentages. *Sources: Statistisches Jahrbuch der Stadt Wien* 3 (1930-1945), 4 (1937), 5 (1938), 6 (1939-1942), 7 (1943-1945), 8 (1946-1947), 9 (1948), 10 (1949), 11 (1950).

record is more complete, particularly for the last year of the war. Also significant are the day-to-day reports of the Viennese Gestapo that indicate that during the wartime years 374 juveniles were prosecuted for political crimes. A handful of these were tried as adults, but the vast majority had been engaged in subversive or criminal conduct as minors.

Post-Anschluß Deviance, 1938–1939

Assessing juvenile crime in Vienna between the Nazi takeover in 1938 and the outbreak of the Second World War constitutes a complex and challenging task. Theoretically, those delinquents accused of traditional offenses such as theft, fraud, sexual assault, manslaughter, or murder were to be arrested by the criminal police, while those charged with subversion, espionage, or treason by the Gestapo. Officials of the Security Police (SD) Sicherheitsdienst and state prosecutors would then determine whether those in custody should be remanded to the courts or dispatched to concentration camps. During the eighteen months of peace, there appears to have been some confusion and overlap. The arrest of homosexuals, for example, was to be entrusted to the criminal police, but prior to the war Gestapo agents picked up 120 individuals including half a dozen youngsters for sodomy, pederasty, or other "immoral acts."

1. Traditional Offences

In considering traditional juvenile offences committed in 1939, this study will rely primarily on surviving Viennese court records from July through December. The documentation is somewhat fragmentary, limited here and there to arrest records, police reports, or formal indictments. But when combined with actual trial records one gains a sense of the impact of the Anschluß on nonpolitical delinquency prior to the Second World War. During those six months, fifty-four cases involving eighty-six individuals were brought before the bench. Those indicted consisted of seventy-four boys and twelve girls as a group averaging 17 years of age. The judicial officials recorded that half of the accused were apprentice craftsmen, domestics, or workers; eight vocational school pupils; and four without work. As for the rest, there is no information on occupational background. Of the youngsters tried in the Gray House, forty-five were found guilty, six not-guilty, and the rest either released or held in custody for further investigation. The major charges were for break-ins and theft (73 percent), homosexuality (11 percent), unauthorized border-crossings (9 percent), illegal possession or misuse of firearms (6 percent), and abortion (3 percent).[44]

Both statistics and court records reveal that nearly three-quarters of all juvenile cases to come before the bench involved theft. This was a trend that persisted throughout the entire Nazi period, not only in Vienna but also throughout Greater Germany and later occupied Europe, particularly in Vichy France. Most of the Viennese minors apprehended in 1939 for break-ins and theft acted in teams of two or three or on their own. Some were planned; others appear to have been spontaneous. On March 20, 1939, for example, 15-year-old Erwin S. was arrested for stealing an expensive camera from a photo shop. His accomplice claimed that the two intended to use the proceeds to emigrate to the United States. Erwin denied this by calling the court's attention to his membership in the Hitler Youth. Because the youthful defendant had a lengthy arrest record for stealing and fencing goods from small shops as well as from the Gerngross department store, the judges were unimpressed. Additional testimony revealed evidence of disruptive school behavior that included bullying and throwing inkwells in the classroom. On May 5, 1939, the court sentenced Erwin to four months of hard labor in Kaiser-Ebersdorf reformatory. Upon release, he appears to have continued a life of crime. In 1956, the judiciary refused to expunge his record on the basis of additional arrests and imprisonment.[45]

A similar case involved two 17-year-olds, employed in the Anton Ketele woodworking plant in the 8th District. On July 21, 1939, Johann T. and Kurt Z. made off with RM 600.37 in cash, four fountain pens, 11 kilograms of nails, and two shoulder holsters. As no damage had been done and neither boy previously been in trouble, the court handed down a reduced sentence of two months incarceration with the hope that relatively mild punishment would serve as a salutary lesson.[46] More serious in the view of the juvenile authorities were a rash of thefts from small tobacco shops by Franz S. and Anton T. Because the pilfered items were cheap and worth little money, the two youngsters petitioned for release from protective custody. The court denied the request, primarily because Franz and Anton were frequently absent from work and spent most of their ill-gotten gains playing cards in coffee houses.[47]

Among half a dozen bicycle thieves, the most successful was 13-year-old Kurt M.; in early 1939, he had managed to steal, refurbish, and sell thirty bikes in the 15th District. As he was too young to be prosecuted under the Austrian penal code, court-appointed social workers recommended that he be placed in a foster home. Whether they succeeded is not revealed in his small surviving file.[48] Other apprehended individual robbers included a waiter's assistant indicted for stealing wine and liquor worth RM 10 from his employer, a day laborer for breaking into a vending machine, a 14-year-old seamstress-apprentice for purloining her employer's wallet from a desk, a teacher's assistant for the theft of golden earrings and a watch, and a 15-year-old girl for picking flowers from fields and private gardens, and four 17-year-old youngsters for making off with 3 kilograms of apricots. None of the adolescent reprobates appears to have received anything other than a reprimand.[49] On the other hand, two boys who stole 150 tulips and unstipulated number of lilacs from a private garden were sentenced to three years of supervised probation.[50]

A major exception consisted of a small gang of school boys led by Heinz P., born on April 18, 1924. Between January and July 1939, he and seven older accomplices managed to pull off an astonishing number of robberies in Klosterneuburg. Most of the loot consisted of boating gear and personal belongings stored at the Viennese Kayak and Rowing Club. The police inventory listed a canoe, two paddles, two tents, three sleeping bags, three sets of training clothes, twenty-one phonograph records, a gramophone, five woolen blankets, and other items worth RM 312. On other occasions, the juveniles stole footballs, twelve additional phonograph records, and other athletic equipment. Led by Heinz with a loaded revolver, they also broke into private homes, making off with cash, wood carvings, tableware, and various other valuables assessed at RM 250. Once apprehended in late summer, three of the boys were remanded immediately to the custody of their parents and four others to that of juvenile authorities. Young Heinz was not tried until November 1940 after which he received only a mild sentence. While the Austrian penal code called for severe imprisonment of six months to five years, both the State Prosecutor Dr. Baumann and Judge Anton Nirschl, an ardent National Socialist, concurred that the code also stipulated that a minor under 16 at the time of his arrest could not be prosecuted as an adult. The court thus sentenced the boy to pay the full cost of legal proceedings but allowed him to remain free under three years of delayed probation. The fate of the other youngsters is unknown.[51]

Fragmentary records of three other cases brought before the bench in late 1939 suggest that the judicial authorities were confounded by a rash of thefts from Jewish shops, which were abandoned or seized by Nazi gangs in the wake of Kristallnacht. Shortly after the pogrom, in December 1938, for example, Otto P., born in 1924, broke into a candy store owned by Ester Peistl. In his defense, Otto contended that he had been joined by others including uniformed Brownshirts. Whether this case ever came to trial is not known, though the official indictment reports that a great many "aryanized" shops had been broken into by gangs of youngsters seeking chocolates and other sweets. Two other boys, August H. and Wilhelm P., confessed to smashing the windows of a Jewish owned dry-goods enterprise and stealing a sack of blankets. Admitting his offence, August contended that that he and his accomplice had assumed Jewish goods were simply there for the taking. On July 17, 1939, the state prosecutor drew up a sympathetic indictment, pointing out that although the dry-goods store now belonged to the Property Transfer Agency, the boys sincerely believed they had acted in good faith proceeding against a Jew. Thereafter legal proceedings appear to have been dropped.[52]

In 1939, some 113 Viennese youngsters were convicted of "crimes contrary to nature" or related sexual offenses, amounting to 9.4 percent of all juvenile felonies. These figures did not reflect Hitler's well-known obsession with protecting society from abnormal sexual behavior, as might be believed. Rather they represent a continuity of attitudes and proceedings within Austria itself. Toward the end of the nineteenth century, Viennese physicians, writers, artists, and intellectuals devoted increasing attention to problems of sex and sexual behavior, particularly the tension between traditional moral values and natural instincts.[53] Although the official number of sexually related offences remained low among the general population, an epidemic of venereal disease during the Great War unleashed widespread discussion about sexual education and reform. In the confusion following the collapse of the monarchy, debates raged between those calling for the "liquidation of the bourgeois family," "orgiastic emancipation," and promiscuity on the one hand, and the maintenance of traditional conjugal and family relations on the other. Prelate Ignaz Seipel even called for a "cleansing of the soul." As for the general public, interest in eroticism, sexuality, and changes in gender relations appears to have been considerable; Hugo Bettauer's *He and She: Weekly Journal for Lifestyle and Eroticism*, for example, enjoyed widespread readership before its ban by the Viennese Juvenile Welfare Board in 1924.[54]

Ultimately, as Ernst Hanisch has pointed out, the state prevailed—even in Red Vienna. Restrictions on adolescent behavior imposed in 1922 remained in place, particularly on dating habits. They were tightened by the prudish Dollfuss-Schuschnigg dictatorship, which banned the sale of contraceptives, did away with coeducational schooling, and ordered the placement of fig leaves on nude statues.[55] Further, no attempt was made between 1918 and 1938 to alter Articles 125–33 of the Austrian penal code that mandated harsh punishment for moral felonies ranging from rape, to incest, pandering, and particularly homosexuality. This may explain why the percentage of convictions in Vienna for "crimes contrary to nature" remained high long before the Anschluß. The police, in other words, were accustomed to patrolling bath houses, bars, public toilets, and other homosexual gathering places such as the sylvan glens of the Prater, the huge park in the 2nd District.[56]

In 1939, according to official Viennese statistics, some 293 individuals were convicted of "crimes contrary to nature" or abnormal sexual behavior of whom 113 were minors under 18 years of age.[57] In the course of the same year, the Gestapo arrested 120 persons for "homosexual activities," including two SS officers, though only five minors.[58] Whether those arrested by the Gestapo were included in the official statistics is not clear. The surviving 1939 trial records indicate that thirteen juveniles including three girls were charged with moral offenses. The most dramatic involved four 17-year-olds indicted for homosexual molestation, assault, and blackmail. They belonged to a larger group headed by three adults. Late in the afternoon of October 21, 1938, while strolling through the Prater, a postal official, Johann Meyer, was beaten and robbed near St. Mary's Church. After escaping his assailants, he managed to alert the police, who took the three of the hooligans into custody. According to the arrest report, their ringleader, Ferdinand S., had been making homosexual advances to roughly 200 teenagers since 1936, seducing most of them in a remote wooded area of the enormous park. Immediately thereafter, his accomplices, Alfred K., Rudolf J., and Josef L., would turn up, threatening to report the victims to the police unless paid off with a bribe. After a thorough investigation, two of the adult members of the gang were sentenced to two and half years in prison and the third to twelve years of hard labor. The fate of the minors does not appear in the records, though Rudolf appears to have been placed on parole.[59]

A more bizarre case involved charges of sadomasochistic beatings by a 15-year-old barber trainee. The accused, Karl M., admitted that he had befriended a certain Franz S. and even cut his hair without requiring payment for his services. Careful investigation by the Viennese vice squad revealed that Franz had concocted the charges as a means of extorting blackmail. In October 1939, Karl was found not guilty, and Franz was sentenced to five months in jail.[60] Among other adolescents apprehended for homosexuality were two 17-year-olds who had met at a coffee house. Several days later, they appear to have been spotted in a small cottage house engaged in mutual masturbation. As was frequently the case, one claimed to have been a victim, while the other freely admitted to being attracted to young boys and men. The fate of this couple is undocumented. The records of two boys apprehended for fellatio indicate that youthful homosexuals were regularly sentenced to serve time in Kaiser-Ebersdorf.[61]

Among other moral offences considered by the juvenile authorities in late 1939 were three cases of abortion and one of statutory rape. Theresia M., for example, was a 17-year-old domestic; her mother arranged for an abortion that took place in July 1939. The following March, Theresia was sentenced to four months in jail to be followed by a "salutary lesson" of three years of supervised probation.[62] A most unusual case involved Franziska H., a seamstress trainee who had taken up with Jaraoslav J., a mechanic apprentice in September 1938. After missing her menstrual period the following spring, she consulted a shady midwife and on July 3 underwent an abortion. According to a very thick file, the police took all parties into custody and conducted a thorough investigation. On August 31, the Juvenile Court dismissed all charges. Their decision was based on medical evidence that the defendant had never been pregnant. As for the midwife and putative abortionists, they were most likely sentenced to five years in prison as stipulated by Article 145 of the Austrian penal code.[63]

In the one case of statutory rape to come before the juvenile bench in 1939, the judges exercised leniency. They found the defendant, Franz L., born in 1922, guilty of "deflowering" a 14-year-old high-school girl, reputed to have run in loose company and, much to the consternation of her parents, to have spent nights away from home. The law stipulated imprisonment for three years, but the state prosecutor and judge concurred that because the precocious girl had lied about her age, there seemed no point in imposing a punishment harsher than a three-year probation.[64]

The evidence examined here suggests that neither the kinds of traditional offences committed by Viennese juveniles in 1938–1939 nor the sentences handed down by the courts differed in any significant way from those prior to the Anschluß. Indeed, there was a striking continuity stretching back to the First

Republic. This was not the case with a handful of youngsters apprehended for violating German passport regulations or firearms law.

In the first instance, persons apprehended crossing the German frontier without a visa or valid passport could be fined or imprisoned for a year according to a decree drawn up by Reich President Friedrich Ebert during the Ruhr crisis of 1923.[65] Between July and December 1939, five adolescents were tried and convicted for violating a measure drawn up to preserve the democratic Weimar Republic. On June 26, 1938, two underage gypsy girls were apprehended for smuggling Hungarian vegetables into the Burgenland. The following summer they were convicted by the Viennese juvenile court. The judge saw no point in imposing the mandatory penalty, however, and released them on parole.[66] Also fortunate was 17-year-old Helene H., picked up in Nikelsdorf on July 29, 1939. On September 10, the juvenile judge sentenced her to three weeks incarceration, but allowed her to walk free, ruling that she had already served time in protective custody. More complex and sordid was the case of 16-year-old Viktoria B. On September 13, 1939, she was found guilty of operating on both sides of the Hungarian frontier to solicit customers for a prostitute in Oedenburg. The law stipulated punishment of six months to a year in jail. As with Helene H., the judges took into account her age and willingness to cooperate. They imposed a sentence of four months considered already completed in protective custody. She too was released but compelled to pay full court costs. The final case in the surviving files concerned an 18-year-old Reich German, who had made his way to the Hungarian border from Gera in Thuringia, most likely to find refuge in an authoritarian though more tolerant country. Again, the juvenile court treated the defendant with leniency, handing down a sentence of one-year probation.[67]

In the second instance, Berlin passed legislation on March 18, 1938, relaxing strict gun ownership laws dating from the Weimar Republic. However, juveniles under 18 were still not allowed to possess or use firearms without a license or special permit. There seems to have been some confusion about the details of the new regulations, which may explain why several youngsters ran afoul of the law. Three of those taken into custody were accustomed to using Flobert guns, a nineteenth-century French rifle with a limited range of roughly 32 meters. Popular at shooting galleries and used by individuals to kill garden pests, Floberts were in wide circulation. In early spring 1939, Robert H., a cooking apprentice, became involved in a tragic accident in his grandmother's community garden. With his Flobert he fired at a flock of blackbirds perched in the foliage of a thick hedge. His bullet scattered the birds but also hit and killed a young woman on the other side of the tangled bushes. Although indicted for negligent homicide, he seems not to have been tried. A similar, though harmless case involved youthful high jinks. On June 19, 1939, two teenage apprentices from Gross Enzendorf went target shooting with a Flobert in the Prater. They affixed targets on a tree and fired off thirty-six rounds of ammunition before being apprehended. The police report concluded that although no one had been hurt, it was both illegal and dangerous to discharge a firearm in a public park. As there no record of a formal indictment or trial, it appears the two boys were let off with a reprimand. During the same month, two school boys were picked up for carrying an antique wheel-lock pistol into a classroom. Given the rash of American school shootings in the twenty-first century, such an incident from today's perspective might be considered a harmless prank. Nevertheless, the state prosecutor indicted the teenagers for violating the 1938 weapons act. Before coming to trial, however, they were released on October 2, 1939, according to a Führer amnesty issued the previous month. Finally, there was the case of 18-year-old commercial apprentice, Karl D., who had purchased a Mauser 6.55 revolver in late 1937. According to Article 34 of the Austrian penal code, he was subject to felonious prosecution. But since the defendant had sought to purchase a gun license after the Anschluß, the state prosecutor reduced the charge to a misdemeanor. Whether the case came to trial as scheduled on September 10 is not revealed in the surviving records.[68]

2. Political Crimes

In one important respect, a significant number of juveniles prosecuted for criminal misconduct in Vienna under Nazi rule had committed politically conscious acts of defiance that differed from similar violations elsewhere in Hitler's realm. This is not to deny the courage of German adolescents such as 17-year-old Hellmuth Hübner, who in 1942 was executed for listening to the BBC and distributing anti-Nazi flysheets in Hamburg, or for that matter that of the older members of the famous White Rose Society in Munich.[69] The daily reports of the Viennese Gestapo reveal that between November 1938 and April 1945 some 14,367 individuals, including over 440 minors, were arrested in Vienna and Lower Danube for offences considered a threat to Hitler's regime. Obviously, not everyone taken into custody by the Gestapo for political misconduct were resistance fighters. Neugebauer's meticulous quantitative research reveals that one-third of those arrested had been involved in labor disputes, of whom 15.7 percent were foreign laborers or prisoners of war. Another 16.6 percent were charged with economic offences. There were also a large number of persons (13.4 percent) picked up for listening to foreign radio broadcasts, violating curfew restrictions, or "subversive" outbursts. Most likely, many of these offenders resented Nazi rule or some aspect of it. But others may have been turned in by petty officials, employers, or jealous lovers to settle personal scores. To what extent their offences constituted acts of active resistance thus remains ambiguous. There were also innocents criminalized by the regime including 13.4 percent for "Jewish related offences as well as Jehovah's Witnesses, and homosexuals."[70]

Neugebauer's research identifies three groups whose members engaged in active resistance as Austrian patriots opposed both the Anschluß and National Socialism. The first were Communists, socialists, and labor functionaries (29.2 percent) of whom most belonged to the Communist Party of Austria (KPÖ; Kommunistische Partei Österreichs). The second consisted of Habsburg loyalists, Catholic conservatives, individual clergy, and various other Austrian patriots such as Otto and Fritz Molden. Overall, these groups tended to be more active in traditionally Catholic regions such as the Tyrol, but in Vienna, the Gestapo arrested 1,231 such persons (8.6 percent). What these groups had in common was the rejection of the Anschluß and a keen sense of Austrian identity. The third largest group of resisters consisted of individuals who had spoken out against the regime, distributed anti-Nazi pamphlets, provided assistance to Jews, or engaged in noncompliant behavior. Many of these arrested were tried for subversion, sabotage, and occasionally treason by Special Courts, which tended to dispatch them to concentration camps or hand out long prison terms. Exactly how many consciously opposed Nazi rule, as mentioned earlier, is difficult to ascertain.[71]

My own examination of the Viennese Gestapo arrest records reveals that no fewer than 441 Austrian youngsters were prosecuted for political crimes during the Anschluß years. Of these, sixty-seven were 19- or 20-year-old adults, but they had been engaged in subversive or criminal misconduct as minors. In contrast, another 98 were 16 years old or younger, including a dozen 12-year-olds. The offences tended to parallel those of adult resisters. Of the youthful culprits, 168 (38 percent) were Communists, primarily though not exclusively, belonging to the Communist Youth League (KJV; Kommunistischer Jugendverband) while 58 (13 percent) belonged to Catholic conservative or legitimist groups such as the Austrian Youth League (Österreichisches Jungvolk), the Anti-Fascist Freedom Movement, or smaller organizations. Some 8.4 percent of juveniles were picked up for "Jewish-related" offences, including "non-Aryan boys and girls caught in hiding or attempting to flee abroad."[72]

The other half of those juveniles arrested by the Gestapo in Vienna and Lower Danube had committed a wide variety of transgressions: Five were Jehovah's Witnesses, eight had engaged in homosexual acts, and nineteen teenage girls had slept with foreign workers or prisoners of war. While those convicted of sexual improprieties were severely punished, they had not actively opposed the regime. This was certainly not the case of the five Jehovah's Witnesses or most of the others appearing on the daily Gestapo arrest list. Twenty-two were convicted of insulting Hitler, daubing anti-Nazi graffiti in public places, or composing and distributing anti-regime pamphlets. Fifteen others were indicted for vandalism, which included cutting cables in an armaments plant, throwing a crowbar into a cutting machine, placing explosives in a telephone booth, or, in one remarkable case, disrupting the Viennese trolley system for months by derailing streetcars with cinders or opening brake clutches. Thirty-five other youngsters were punished for assaulting members of the Hitler Youth and League of German Girls, in some cases trashing their meeting halls. In astonishing contrast, the Gestapo uncovered an entire branch of the Hitler Youth in Pulkau whose members had turned against the regime by seeking British and American aid in restoring Austrian independence. Taking into account the large number of youngsters who downed tools, refused to work, or walked off the job during the last year of the war, the evidence suggests that many of those who broke ranks with Nazi rule in Vienna were not simply dissidents or nonconformists, not least because ten teenagers were sentenced to death for treason between 1943 and 1945.[73]

In the months immediately following the Anschluß, the Nazis arrested or detained between 40,000 and 50,000 individuals, disbanded civic and associational organizations, and clamped down on the press. They also unleashed or tolerated waves of violence that took the lives of hundreds, including twenty-two Jews murdered in November 1938 on Kristallnacht. A few days later, 3,000 Viennese Jews were deported to Dachau of whom seventeen died or were tortured to death.[74] With access to member lists compiled by the Austro-Fascist regime, the Gestapo moved rapidly to arrest or detain Revolutionary Socialist or Communist functionaries, if only for a few days. Under these circumstances, it was virtually impossible to organize political resistance, although the first legitimist and labor cells began to emerge in late 1938.[75]

Significantly, the first organized resistance group uncovered by the Gestapo consisted of twenty teenagers under 16 years of age. All were residents of the Fuchsenfeldhof, a huge municipal housing complex constructed between 1921 and 1924 in Meidling, later the scene of bitter fighting during the 1934 civil war. Exactly who organized what may have been the first cell of the KJV in Vienna is not altogether clear, although the activist Bruno Dubber, returning from Prague in mid-September, may have taken the initiative. Another source suggests that an older girl, Erna Wimmer, laid the foundation for a Communist network in Meidling shortly after the Anschluß.[76] What is indisputable is that in the afternoon of October 4 a Gestapo agent stumbled upon an 11-year-old boy scribbling "Hail Moscow" on small scraps of paper in a local toy store. This discovery led to the arrest of twenty other youngsters in the Fuchsenfeldhof. According to court records, the authorities singled out Franz Müller and Franz Cauze, both 16 years old, as ringleaders. The two were held in custody until January 21, 1941, when the Higher Regional Court sentenced them as adults to eight and seven months in jail respectively. Presumably, the younger boys had been released and placed under surveillance.[77]

Between January 1939 and the outbreak of war nine months later, the Viennese Gestapo arrested no fewer than thirty-two underage members of the KJV. They were not the only juveniles actively to oppose the Anschluß regime, but they were the most numerous, best organized, and initially the most difficult for the Gestapo to penetrate. Those familiar with the Communist resistance in incorporated Austria know that in late spring 1938 party functionaries loosened the Stalinist command structure to establish small cells seeking to infiltrate Nazi organizations and spread propaganda particularly in municipal enterprises and public utilities. As for the KJV, its members were to join the Hitler Youth and sporting clubs in order to undermine the regime from within. Vienna itself was then divided into four regions with particular emphasis on agitation within the Inner City, Landstrasse, and Meidling.[78]

Of the thirty-two other Communist youngsters arrested during the last year of peace, there is only scant information on a handful of cases and individuals. In late October 1938, for example, the daily Gestapo arrest list simply noted that three youngsters had been picked up in working-class Favoriten for singing the "International."[79] In contrast, an entry in late February provides details about a group consisting of eleven boys under age 21. Apprehended for distributing pamphlets and in working-class Simmering, these youngsters were convicted the following January for "attempted treason," apparently a relative minor offence warranting relatively short jail sentences.[80] In another case, a constable in Eisenstadt picked up 16-year-old Josef Laskakovitz two months later for distributing thirty handwritten flysheets. Written in red ink on one side were the words "Red Front," and on the other "Hail Moscow." Further investigation led to the arrest of three other boys, including two 13-year-olds, each of whom belonged to a miniscule Communist cell. This information was forwarded to the Viennese Gestapo, but the fate of the youthful resisters is unknown.[81]

In late June, the Security Police picked up fourteen underage members of the KJV. One cell consisted of ten young adults under the age of 21 as well as two boys born in 1922. The leader of the group was a 19-year-old saddler apprentice, Franz Martinak, an activist who had joined the National Socialist Motor Corps (NSKK) Nationalsozialistisches Kraftfahrkorps following the Anschluβ. After careful preparation, his team struck on the evening of June 13. While Martinak provided cover dressed in his Nazi uniform, the young Communists ripped up and destroyed thirteen public telephone booths in Alsergrund. Within days the Gestapo swept up the political vandals and held them in custody for two years. On May 7, 1941, the Higher Regional Court found them guilty of treason, imposing harsh sentences ranging from two to four years in prison.[82]

Little is known about other Viennese juveniles taken into custody after being charged with Communist subversion before the war. The daily Gestapo arrest lists indicate that a number of individuals belonged to the KJV, but provides few details about their cells, activities, or subsequent fates. Two boys appear to have acted as what today would be called "lone wolves." Eighteen-year-old Karl Horwarth, for example, deserted the Reich Labor Service in early May 1939. When he returned home, his enraged father forced him to rejoin the ranks, whereupon Karl saluted his squad leader with the words "Hail Moscow!"[83] Another 18-year-old, Thomas Knauder, was arrested in a hotel room where several Communist pamphlets were found. Unlike Horwarth, Knauder claimed to have been stiffed by workmates who placed the flysheets in his locker.[84] The subsequent fate of both boys remains unknown. In addition to young Communists, the Gestapo arrested several adolescents involved in the diminutive Revolutionary Socialist movement, even though many industrial workers had been initially co-opted by the Nazis or decided to lay low. Nevertheless, the Gestapo arrested two teenagers in October 1938 as underground activists as well as two others for demonstrably wearing red carnations in their lapels.[85]

Of the seventy-three adolescents arrested by the Gestapo for political crimes between September 1938 and the outbreak of war exactly a year later, 71 percent were Communist activists and another 6 percent were underground Socialists. Three-quarters of the young resisters, in other words, sprang from the labor movement, a much higher percentage than the total number of those engaged in resistance during the entire period of Nazi rule. Only one teenager, 17-year-old Philipp Kaplan, was apprehended for belonging to the "Austrian Legion," a small group affiliated with Habsburg loyalists or Catholic conservative circles. On the other hand, it should not be forgotten that on October 7, 1938, some 7,000 to 10,000 youngsters under 30 thronged the St. Stephan's Cathedral to stage what became the largest anti-Nazi demonstration in the history of the Third Reich.[86] The police arrested only a handful of the participants in the Cathedral Square, although one of them, 18-year-old Hermann Lein, was subsequently dispatched to a concentration camp.[87] Even so, it would not be until 1940 that the Gestapo would detect and arrest the more youthful legitimists, Catholic conservatives, individual clergy, or members of the Austrian Freedom movement.

Significantly, the second largest number of juveniles arrested by the Gestapo before the war for political crimes were homosexuals. In fact, prior to the outbreak of war well over a hundred Viennese of all ages were picked by the Gestapo for "crimes contrary to nature." Thereafter, the vice squad of the uniformed police undertook such arrests. That homosexual acts should be considered acts of political defiance or resistance is obviously absurd, although the National Socialists considered aberrant sexual behavior a threat to the National Community. In a sense this was a distinction without a difference in that the Austrian penal code considered homosexuality a societal menace long before the Nazi takeover. Unlike the court records examined previously, however, the Gestapo arrest lists do not provide salacious details, except for one case of a 19-year-old observed performing fellatio on a platform at the Wöllersdorf train station. Those under 18 were remanded to the Juvenile Court.[88]

Turning finally to the problem of individual teenage resistance, it is difficult to discern a pattern. The first minor arrested by the Gestapo as an opponent was a 16-year-old member of the Hitler Youth, a boy charged with vagrancy, hardly a political offence let alone an act of resistance. Shortly thereafter, in late September 1938, at the height of the Munich crisis, two Czech teenagers attempting to flee across the frontier into Czechoslovakia were taken into custody.[89] The first documented instance of individual youngsters actively opposing the Nazi regime appears in the Viennese Gestapo arrest list of March 17, 1939. The authorities assumed the perpetrators were Communists, but provided no evidence. On the evening of the March 13, six members of the Hitler Youth, after leaving a cinema in Atzgeradorf, were attacked by three 17-year-old boys. Following a brief scuffle, one of the assailants pulled out a handgun and fired three shots at the fleeing Hitler Youths. The presence of a uniform patrolman led to the arrest of Otto H., Hugo W., and Johann H., followed by a house search that uncovered a gold-plated revolver. While proclaiming their innocence, it is unlikely the three perpetrators escaped punishment.[90]

More clear-cut were the cases of Adolf K. arrested in October 1938 for sabotage in a Viennese roofing plant as well as those of Rudolf K. and Josef L., who were picked up at the same time for insulting the Führer. To this very short list should be added the names of 19-year-old Josef K., arrested for smuggling Jews over the frontier, 16-year-old Rosa R., for preserving letters and belongings of Jewish refugees in Palestine, and the 15-year-old carpenter's apprentice Edmund K., who on August 9, 1939, shouted out in public, "The Führer guzzles on and on about a thousand year history. Austria, however, has not rejoined the Reich but been stolen by Hitler."[91]

Conclusions

This survey of eighty-six youngsters arrested or tried in Vienna between July and December 1939 for traditional offences cannot be viewed as a comprehensive portrait of the impact of the Anschluß on juvenile deviance in the metropolis. The loss of previous court records and the relatively small number of individuals involved makes that impossible. Even so, examination and analysis of the surviving evidence does provide a glimpse corresponding to statistical data and behavior patterns detected by criminologists and Nazi officials. First, nearly three-quarters of those brought before the bench were charged with crimes against property, most commonly break-ins and theft, particularly of bicycles. The percentages approximate the overall rate in Vienna (74 percent) as well as that in other cities of Greater Germany, most notably Munich, Hamburg, and Berlin. As in those municipalities, the sentences handed down tended to be relatively mild, not least for those under 16 years of age. Most were placed on parole or released from protective custody on the basis of jail time already served. Those apprehended for making off with sweets or blankets from "aryanized" Jewish stores seem to have been treated with kid gloves. On the other hand, at least half a dozen, or possibly more, teenagers found guilty of stealing expensive goods such as cameras or hundreds of marks in cash received sentences ranging from two to six months hard labor. There is also reason to believe that youthful miscreants incarcerated for only a week or two in Kaiser-Ebersdorf reformatory suffered severe punishment. Unlike other cities in Hitler's realm, no teenage gangs roamed the cobblestone streets of Vienna, even though large groups had participated in outbursts of Nazi violence in 1938.

The second distinguishing feature of our survey is the relatively high number of youngsters apprehended for moral offences, most notably homosexual encounters. The percentage was higher than the official Viennese rate of 5.2 percent, though at 11 percent only marginally above that of 9.5 percent in 1936. The surviving records indicate that judges meted out some form of imprisonment to male homosexuals over the age of 16, but were inclined to subject younger adolescents to less severe punishment at Kaiser-Ebersdorf. As for cases of abortion, 17-year-old Theresia M. received a four-month jail sentence, while Franziska H. was found never to have been pregnant. The Nazis, as mentioned earlier, were obsessed with eradicating "unnatural sexual behavior," but had Hitler never invaded his Roman Catholic homeland the moral offences examined here would have been severely dealt with under existing statutes.

A third characteristic of those juveniles charged with criminal acts in the second half of 1938 was their age: sixty-one of the individuals were between 16 and 18 years of age. This surely puzzled the authorities because most members of this age cohort had been inducted into the Hitler Youth or the Wehrmacht, making them subject to different judicial procedures. With war clouds gathering on the horizon, criminologists, jurists, and Nazi officials feared a sharp rise in teenage crime such as had plagued Vienna and other great cities during the First World War. That youngsters over 16 should be tried as juveniles in wartime seemed unconscionable. Once war broke out, moreover, fathers, teachers, and HJ leaders would be conscripted into the armed forces, mothers would be compelled to work, blackouts would provide cover for mischief, and rationing would lead to black marketeering. Under these circumstances, it was argued, schoolchildren and younger adolescents would look to more mature teenagers as adult role models. Throughout 1938 and 1939, Austrian and German jurists worried that these older youngsters, as well as blue-collar workers and apprentices exempt from military service, would encourage pubescent misbehavior or subversive activities, much as unruly misfits were already doing in Leipzig, Cologne, Munich, and other cities in the "Altreich".[92] There was also pressure at the highest level in Berlin as Nazi jurists found their hands tied in planning to prosecute 17-year old Herschal Grynszpan for shooting the Third Secretary, Ernst von Rath, in the German embassy in Paris.[93]

Overall, the most striking aspect to emerge from this survey of prewar juvenile crime and punishment in Nazi Vienna is a pattern consistent with that of the of the authoritarian Dollfuss-Schuschnigg regime. This is not to suggest that the Austrian judicial order had avoided becoming an instrument of Nazi rule, particularly once the *Volksgerichtshof* and Special Courts became part of the system in mid-1938. Nor should it be forgotten that the head of the Vienna Gestapo Franz Josef Huber was a Reich German. Even so, most of the

Viennese police force stayed on the job while the Austrian judiciary remained largely intact, as we have already seen. Furthermore, both the types of juvenile offences committed and the sentences handed did not change significantly prior to the war. This generalization applies as well to nearly all the seventy-three adolescents charged with political crimes, as the Austro-Fascist regime had imprisoned or kept close surveillance on Socialist and Communists ever since 1934. What changed was the emergence in late 1938 of a network of youthful activists previously unknown to the security forces.

On October 4, 1939, an ordinance for Protection Against Dangerous Juvenile Criminals (*Verordnung zum Schutz gegen jügendliche Schwerverbrecher*) went into effect.[94] The new law was complex, as we shall see, but its key feature was to mandate the prosecution of minors over the age of 16 as adults, as stipulated by law today in the American states of North Carolina and New York. This meant that from now on those teenagers deemed to be "morally and intellectually mature" could be tried, convicted, and severely punished by Special Courts for a wide range of crimes ranging from felonies, violation of wartime ordinances, and even treason. As for younger offenders, they would be subjected to harsher punishment than in the past. To what extent the Ordinance for Protection Against Dangerous Juvenile Criminals combined with other wartime measures would alter the Austrian judicial system and preempt a juvenile crime wave will be discussed in the next chapter. Attention will also be paid to the efforts of the Gestapo to stamp out dissident or noncompliant behavior and brutally crush political resistance.

2

Nazification: The Impact of Wartime Ordinances on the Austrian Juvenile Penal Code, 1940–1944

In 1947, the International Committee of Criminal Police reported that juvenile crime had risen sharply throughout Europe, including the UK, during the Second World War. The dramatic increase varied from country to country. In Britain, for example, well over 1.5 million expectant mothers, infants, schoolchildren, and teachers were evacuated from London and other large cities to towns and villages in rural areas. Although safe from German bombs, roughly a million youngsters found themselves without schools, contributing to outbreaks of brawling, vandalism, and thefts. During the Blitz, teenage pickpockets stole purses, bags, and other belongings from refugees crowded in shelters or platforms of the London underground. Other adolescents took advantage of blackouts, particularly during the long winter months, to organize gangs that broke into homes or looted bombed-out stores, dwellings, and other public buildings, not only in London but in other cities such as Leeds and Sheffield. There were also cases of manslaughter and murder.[1] Across the Channel in occupied France, the number of minors tried in juvenile courts shot up to 192 percent between 1937 and 1942.[2]

Throughout Greater Germany, including incorporated Austria and the Sudetenland, the outbreak of war also had an enormous impact on juvenile justice. Even before the conflict Hitler's criminologists, jurists, SS officers, HJ leaders, officials in the home office of the NSDAP in Munich, and the Ministries of the Interior and Justice in Berlin had engaged in endless discussions and debates on measures to control juvenile crime. These included proposals to identify criminal types among wayward youth, to determine the "intellectual and moral maturity" of accused offenders, and to impose harsh juvenile detention as means of educative shock therapy. But because the competing parties failed to reach agreement and Hitler himself expressed little interest in legislative reform, the Juvenile Court Law of 1923 remained on the books. The reappearance of teenage gangs coupled with an upsurge of urban theft in 1936 admittedly came as a shock to the authorities, but juveniles continued to be sentenced under legislation passed in the Weimar Republic. However, between 1936 and 1939 a consensus did emerge that youthful malefactors should also be judged along racial-biological lines. Courts were to determine whether convicted adolescents were eligible to become members of the National Community through punitive education or to be expunged as parasites or criminal types.[3] Legal proceedings, in other words, came to reflect Fraenkel's notion of the "dual state."

In Vienna, as discussed in the previous chapter, continuity characterized juvenile justice in the eighteen months following the Anschluß. While it is true that the Juvenile Court was formally dissolved on April 13, 1939, it was reconstituted as a branch of the Higher Regional Court with seemingly little change in personnel. Of the thirteen judges known to be appointed to the bench thereafter, only four had been National Socialists prior to 1938.[4] Not only did the Austrian criminal code remain in place, but judges meted out sentences according to Austrian law, frequently taking into account mitigating circumstances. In at least one case a hardened Nazi judge saw no point in inflicting harsh punishment on a 15-year-old. According to official statistics, the percentage of juvenile misdemeanors, gross misdemeanors, and felonies increased some 12.8 percent between 1937 and 1939, though the actual numbers rose only by slightly over a hundred. Given the relatively harsh character of the Austrian criminal code as augmented and amended during the Dollfuss-Schuschnigg dictatorship, jurists in Hitler's homeland had good reason to argue that their more authoritarian and punitive precepts would enhance a "German Common Law."[5]

This is not to deny that significant changes were taking place. For one thing, state prosecutors were increasingly supplanting the authority of judges. For another, party, state, and municipal agencies were competing to extend control of the young in accordance with Hitler's aims. This meant mandatory enrollment of adolescents between 14 and 18 years of age in the Hitler Youth and League of German Girls. It also meant extending disciplinary control over wayward or neglected youngsters through local and municipal courts, the Higher Regional Court, and, above all, social workers of the Juvenile Welfare Board and the JLSA. The many single female members of the JLSA retained their positions throughout the Anschluß era, even though their agency was transferred from the Higher Regional Court to that of the NSV. Of the various political, judicial, and social agencies, the JSLA became the most influential in determining the fate of juvenile perpetrators. Indeed, evidence adduced by one historian reveals that inquests, reports, and recommendations of JSLA social workers significantly undermined the independence and sentencing power of juvenile judges during the Nazi era.[6]

Prior to the Anschluß, the personnel of the JSLA and other social agencies, including the Guardianship Authority, submitted pretrial assessments of juvenile offenders to the judicial authorities. The social workers based their reports on extensive investigation of previous conduct, home visits, and interviews of family members, a process similar to that institutionalized in France in 1912. Occasionally, they would mention medical abnormalities as contributing to deviant behavior. But, for the most part, the professional women avoided adjectives, reaching their conclusions on delinquency as rooted in the familial and social milieu of the minors. After the Nazi takeover, the social workers gradually embraced the pseudoscientific terminology of National Socialism, most likely as a means of keeping their jobs or advancing their own careers. Their reports did not ignore dysfunctional or impoverished living conditions, but increasingly focused on identifying juvenile types who were biologically "incorrigible," "deviant," "asocial," "psychopathic," "parasitic," or "socially undesirable." In considering these "social diagnoses" as part of the judicial process, the courts had to decide whether offenders should be subjected to harsh "corrective training" or excluded altogether from the National Community.[7]

Wartime Ordinances, 1939–1940

During the relatively stable period of Nazi rule between the Anschluß and Hitler's invasion of Poland, Viennese judges appear to have paid little attention to identifying biological or racial types in handing down sentences to juvenile offenders. This changed dramatically with the passage of wartime ordinances based on both Nazi ideology and the searing memory of adolescent delinquency during the First World War. Prior to the outbreak of hostilities, Hitler's regime had sought to "coordinate" Austrian private and public institutions, even though many of these were already aligned with the goals of the Third Reich. Notwithstanding the massive purge of Jewish and political opponents, the process was left incomplete in that judicial and professional institutions remained largely intact. The wartime ordinances, as discussed below, consolidated the process of Nazification by requiring courts to mete out justice according to social-biological diagnoses of the defendants. Juvenile judges, in other words, were to determine whether youthful malefactors were capable of remediation within the National Community or excluded altogether through imprisonment—or worse.[8]

The most significant of these measures was the Decree for Protection of Dangerous Juvenile Criminals passed on October 4, 1939.[9] Deliberately targeting teenagers over the age of 16, the ordinance can be interpreted as both prophylactic and punitive in nature. The law stipulated, as mentioned earlier, that youngsters between the ages of 16 and 18 could be prosecuted as adults if found intellectually and morally mature at the moment of committing a crime. Those indicted could be tried in a criminal or juvenile court, depending upon the decision of state prosecutors who also had the authority to change venues in the midst of a trial. Assessing the maturity of delinquents over age 16, as we shall see, would present the judicial authorities with innumerable challenges, ultimately enhancing the influence of social workers, criminologists, psychiatrists, and the police. The idea was to identify in advance what the foremost Nazi jurist Roland Freisler called "precocious juvenile criminals" so as to segregate them from the National Community. However reprehensible in ideology and practice, the notion of protecting society from "dangerous juvenile criminals" in wartime seemed a logical way to prevent or preempt the sort of teenage violence that had rocked German and Austrian cities between 1914 and 1918.[10]

More ominously, however, the new law enabled the courts to sentence juveniles to long terms in a penitentiary or even to death. And because Article 3 specifically abrogated § 52 and § 232 of the Austrian penal code, hundreds of adolescents would receive harsh prison sentences during the Anschluß era including the death penalty. In Vienna, for example, at least two 17-year-olds were convicted of high treason and beheaded within a year. In addition, six other minors, including a 16-year-old, were sentenced to death and executed as "dangerous habitual criminals" for multiple thefts, assault, and arson.[11] A month prior to issuing the Ordinance for the Protection of Dangerous Juvenile Criminals, the Ministry of Justice in Berlin had passed a number of measures that came to apply to juveniles over the age of 16. These included the War Economy Decree, an ordinance that banned listening to foreign radio broadcasts, and a Decree against National Parasites (*Volksschädlinge*). These measures were conceived to impose lengthy prison sentences on those convicted of taking advantage of wartime conditions to commit criminal acts, for example, during blackouts. The Parasite Decree adopted Nazi biological terminology requiring judicial officials to identify three criminal types: "plunderers, black-out exploiters, and anti-social saboteurs." Drafted to exclude or even exterminate "internal enemies," the new law gave judges enormous latitude in identifying "paracriminals" as well as the legal authority to condemn them to imprisonment or even execution. But the decree also contained a loophole giving state prosecutors and judges the right to decide whether juvenile offenders were biological criminal types or simply misguided youngsters who had taken advantage of blackouts or long winter nights to attend cinemas, hang out on street corners, or engage in petty theft.[12]

These measures combined to target juvenile delinquents by subjecting selected offenders between ages 16 and 18 to criminal prosecution. The ordinances were followed in early December by a Decree Against Violent Criminals mandating the death penalty for lawbreakers armed with a weapon and on March 9, 1940, by a Police Decree for the Protection of Youth (*Polizeiliche Verordnung zum Schutz der Jugend*). The Protection of Youth Decree constituted a reaction by the authorities to a perceived upsurge of juvenile petty theft and sexual promiscuity. It imposed an evening curfew that banned youngsters under 18 from smoking or dancing in public places, consuming alcoholic beverages, specifically brandy, attending movies after 9 p.m., or loitering in the streets. In coming years, judicial authorities in Vienna would prosecute youngsters under the Protection of Youth Decree, even though it differed little from a federal law passed in 1922. In this respect, it was redundant, constituting another thread of continuity in Austrian jurisprudence. Nevertheless, the new measure greatly enhanced the influence and power of the police. Between May and August, for example, over 600 youngsters had been warned or issued citations for loitering after dark, smoking in public places, or frequenting dance halls. The following year, the number rose to 818 in October alone, although it began to decline thereafter[13]

Exactly how these ordinances were to be carried out was not altogether clear, primarily because the regime's major goal was to redeem "racially valuable juveniles" to serve in the Wehrmacht or to work in the war effort. Furthermore, judicial officials and criminologists disagreed on defining or identifying the fewer number of "dangerous juvenile criminals" who should be tried as adults and expunged from the National Community. Franz Exner, for example, argued that only those adolescents whose violent or sociopathic behavior exceeded immaturity could be considered hardcore criminals. Roland Freisler, in contrast, took a racial-biological approach contending that heredity should be the determining factor. There was also much discussion regarding the sort of shock therapy to be imposed on nondangerous delinquents—debates that ranged from indefinite imprisonment to several months behind bars.

In late 1940, two decrees settled the matter. According to these measures, juvenile detention (*Jugendarrest*) was introduced as a means of punishing youthful malefactors without exposing them to the influence of adult criminals in jails or penitentiaries. This meant that the police or courts could impose detention on delinquents who might deserve a jail term but instead be incarcerated briefly in a court house, school, or other public facility. Indeed, judicial authorities in Vienna stressed that precisely because detainees were not to be punished as criminals or criminal types they should be confined in local facilities rather than reformatories such as Kaiser-Ebersdorf or Hirtenberg.[14] And because the principal objective of the measure was to maintain discipline in the workplace, those convicted would normally spend one to four weekends in isolation subsisting on bread and water, sleeping on the floor, and toiling long hours in menial work. Juvenile detention was thus designed both to chastise adolescent offenders and to make them aware of the dangers of their offence to the National Community.[15]

What sort of impact did Hitler's ordinances combined with the Austrian penal code have in curtailing teenage crime in wartime Vienna? Official statistics reveal that the total number of juvenile misdemeanors, gross misdemeanors, and felonies rose from 2,939 (12.8 percent of all offences) in 1939 to 3,247 (19.6 percent) in 1942, but declined to 2,142 (15.5 percent) the following year. The number of felonies including assaults, fraud, and theft remained relatively constant rising from 1,256 (14 percent) in 1939 to 1,404 (26 percent) in 1942, though falling to 1,135 (21 percent) in 1943. During this same period, the number of break-ins, robberies, and thefts remained high, constituting three-quarters of all juvenile felonies. The number of sex crimes, however, remained surprisingly low, ranging from 5 to 8 percent of juvenile convictions between 14 and 18 years of age.[16] Compared with other cities in Greater Germany such as Cologne, Leipzig, and Berlin, adolescent crime in Vienna appears not to have shot up during the Second World War. Nor did it skyrocket as in Nazi-occupied Paris.[17] (See Figures 1.1–1.4; 2.1–2.3.)

Examination of 171 surviving records of the Juvenile Division of the Higher Regional Court between January 1940 and December 1943 suggests that most youthful offenders acted as individuals, in teams, or as members of petty gangs in municipal parks such as the Prater. There appear to have been no massive street gangs such as the Edelweiß Pirates, whose members rambled and rumbled in the bombed-out cityscapes of the industrial Ruhr, roamed the countryside on weekends, and in late 1944 became involved in violence and shootings. Nor were there groups like the leftist Meuten, who operated in Leipzig and Dresden, or the "Al Capone gang," who assaulted pedestrians in Hanover.[18]

On the other hand, a large number of youngsters between ages 14 and 18 who had left school as 14-year-olds had been hanging out on street corners,

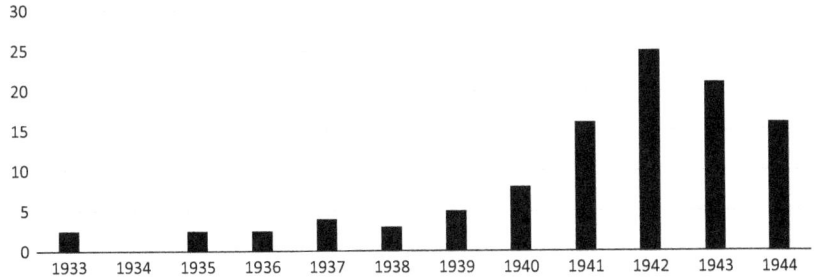

Figure 2.1 Increase in juvenile criminal offenses in Greater Germany, 1933–1944, by percentage.
Sources: Wolf, *Jugendliche vor Gericht*, 204.

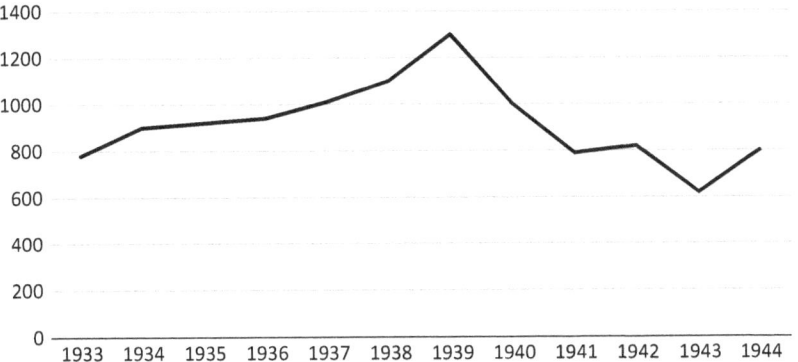

Figure 2.2 Juvenile indictments in Berlin, 1937–1944.
Sources: Wolf, *Jugendliche vor Gericht*, 279.

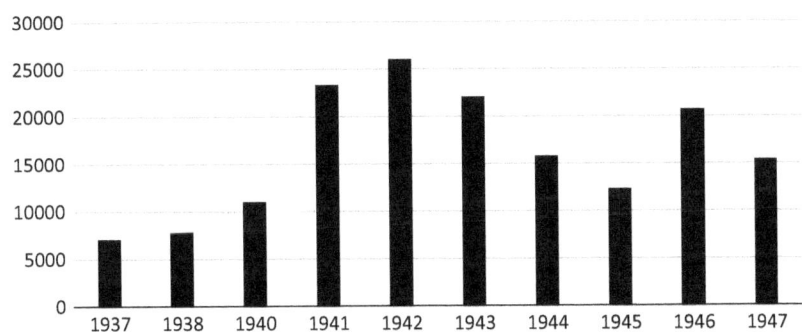

Figure 2.3 Number of juveniles charged with theft in the French courts, 1937–1947.
Sources: Fishman, *Battle for Children*, 84–85.

congregating in coffee houses, or spending summer evenings and weekends in the Prater since the early 1930s. By the time of the Anschluß, various groups of ten to fifteen boys and one or two girls had come to belong to a loosely organized band known as the Schlurfs, a subculture whose members resented the restrictive measures of the Christian Corporative dictatorship on their leisure time. Composed mostly of apprentices or part-time manual workers, the Schlurfs had no interest in joining the Hitler Youth or League of German Girls. This meant the Nazi regime considered them a threat, even though their nonconformist behavior was largely sartorial. In fashion-conscious Vienna, they sought to imitate the casual elegance of Hollywood by wearing flashy double-breasted jackets, thin neckties, and wide trousers. They also grew long, neatly combed hair and affected the sort of cool detachment associated with the postwar actor James Dean. In many ways, most notably in dress and nonconformist behavior, the Schlurfs resembled the teenage *"zazous"* in Nazi-occupied Paris more than other dissident groups in Hitler's Reich.[19] It is true that a few Schlurfs carried switchblades or knuckledusters and that some hustled on the black market or in a few cases congregated in small gangs. Most, however, preferred to pick up girls, strum guitars, and dance to jazz recordings. Until Himmler ordered a crackdown on dissident youth in 1941, most Schlurfs managed to stay out of trouble.[20] In March of that year, however, the Gestapo arrested a group of 12 to 15-year-olds who had pounced on a group of Hitler Youth in Alsergrund. One of them, 17-year-old Johann E., was held in custody until February 3, 1944, when the Juvenile Division of the Higher Regional Court sentenced him to two to four years in a juvenile detention center for "preparing high treason," most notably in "attacking and beating up members of the HJ."[21] Between 1941 and 1943, a number of Schlurfs became involved in scuffles with the Hitler Youth, detachments of the SA, and even the police. Nevertheless, the Schlurfs did not resist the Nazi regime as such. Rather they were criminalized as nonpolitical dissidents and misfits primarily because they refused to join the Hitler Youth, were attracted to American jazz, or merely wanted to be left alone.[22]

Juvenile Court Decisions, 1940–1944

This chapter examines to what extent Nazi ideology was translated into practice in Hitler's homeland. It will scrutinize and analyze surviving records of cases tried before the Juvenile Division of the Higher Regional Court between 1940 and January 1, 1944, the day on which a new comprehensive Reich Juvenile

Court Law went into force. It will be followed by a chapter scrutinizing the cases of those youngsters tried by the Viennese Special Court or the dreaded People's Court for politically motivated crimes including arson, sabotage, subversive behavior, and treason.

Structurally, the types of traditional transgressions committed by Viennese teenagers did not change dramatically between 1940 and 1944. Our imperfect sample indicates that 123 youngsters (74 percent) were found guilty of break-ins, theft, and robbery. These ranged from major crimes including the theft of automobiles, expensive jewelry, and cameras to petty misdemeanors such as pillaging cigarettes, sacks of wheat, and even apples and rabbits from municipal allotments (*Schrebergärten*). As before the war, some robberies were planned by small gangs, while others were undertaken spontaneously by one or two boys. In percentages, crimes against property approximated those committed in other cities of both Greater Germany and Vichy France, although those in Munich and Berlin appear to have been much higher.[23] The remaining juvenile offenses consisted of truancy or absenteeism, particularly after 1942 (12 percent), assault (7 percent), sexual immorality (4 percent), parasitic or mischievous behavior, and loitering (3 percent). Compared with official statistics, the number of sex crimes tried in juvenile court was strikingly low, not least because on October 30, 1942, the criminal police filed an official report warning that soaring teenage homosexuality constituted the root cause of habitual crime in Vienna.[24] Presumably most of the records of those convicted specifically for immoral offences were among those unintentionally shredded in 1998. Even so, it is likely that the sentences handed out were based on Austrian law.

With regard to maturation, three-quarters of those tried by the juvenile authorities in Vienna consisted of youngsters between 16 and 18 years of age. This had been the case before the war, though the remaining fourth tended to be 14 or 15 years old of whom a number were high-school pupils or dropouts. Overall, most of the miscreants were craftsmen apprentices, electrical or machinist trainees, domestics, or unskilled workers. This was also the case in Nazi-occupied Paris, where 87 percent of indicted minors came from working-class districts.[25] That nearly all the convicted apprentices and trainees in Vienna became involved in criminal behavior can be explained by two seemingly contradictory factors. In learning to do useful work outside impoverished or dysfunctional homes, many adolescents felt a sense of freedom and independence. As Christian Gerbel has demonstrated, most were paid sufficiently to make ends meet, but many concluded that the easiest way to become part of a perceived consumer society was through shoplifting and theft. Further, many resented the harsh discipline imposed by Nazi foremen and managers in the workplace. Joining fellow malcontents or a gang became a means of dissent and escape. Such groups even found it possible to operate as "competitive enterprises," taking advantage of blackouts to enrich themselves through break-ins, robberies, and theft.[26]

Although the pattern of teenage crime did not change significantly in wartime Vienna, the penalties imposed by the courts became increasingly harsh and draconian. In 1940, sentences handed out for felonies usually ranged from three to eight months in Kaiser-Ebersdorf. The following year these jumped from two months to several years in juvenile confinement. Between 1941 and 1944, the judges also ordered twenty-four youngsters to spend several days to a month in detention, most commonly for absenteeism. According to a report from Graz, weekend incarceration proved most effective, because the detainees were denied time off from their jobs.[27] The intensified severity of the penalties imposed by the Juvenile Division of the Higher Regional Court in Vienna may not have reflected a change in the judiciary. Of the four judges known to be appointed to the bench after 1940, only two had been "illegal" members of the NSDAP prior to the Anschluß. On the other hand, Dr. Anton Staininger, who presided over numerous cases between 1933 and 1945, was a hardened Nazi; after the war he was sentenced to eight years of hard labor for fraud, treason, and excessive cruelty.[28]

1. Juvenile Gangs

Between 1940 and 1944, at least two dozen youngsters belonging to gangs were found guilty of committing various felonies in Vienna. Nearly all of them were affiliated with bands of Schlurfs. Of these, only two or three resembled the well-organized gangs roaming the streets of Berlin, Munich, and industrial cities of the Ruhr. On June 4,1940, for example, the Juvenile Division of the Higher Regional Court convicted seven adolescents of multiple thefts that included skis and skiing equipment, a phonograph player, loudspeakers, a three-wheel motor vehicle, and an Austro-Daimler automobile. Four were sentenced to eight months in Kaiser-Ebersdorf, one to six months, and the last to four months. Judging from the trial record, it is by no means clear that the seven boys belonged to a single gang. In early February 1940, Johann S. and Heinrich W. appear to have spontaneously stolen skis from a repair shop, where the latter had taken his own snow gear to be repaired. Shortly thereafter, four other boys had gone on joyrides in purloined vehicles. The defendants appealed the sentences to the Supreme Court in Leipzig, where Hitler's judges let the verdicts of property theft stand but ruled that Articles 173 and 179 of the Austrian criminal code applied to larceny, not pleasure riding. The cases were ordered to be retried in Vienna, providing another example of judicial continuity.[29]

More typical of teenagers joining together as a small band of thieves was a gang of seven youngsters led by an 18-year-old manual worker, Anton Z. Throughout August and September 1940, he and his younger followers broke into twenty homes, offices, and shops making off with jewels, cash, edibles, a carbine and pistol, as well as an unspecified number of other valuables. The stolen goods were stored in a small flat in working-class Ottakring, where a middle-aged divorcee, Barbara K., agreed to fence them. The reports of court-appointed social workers revealed that four of the boys came from dysfunctional families, ranging from growing up in impoverished homes to suffering from abusive or alcoholic parents. Two had dropped out of school and taken up menial jobs. One had attempted to enlist in the armed forces but was already serving time for petty theft. When the case came to trial on October 2, Judge Peter Bogner, not yet a party member, singled out 16-year-olds Emmerich F. and Leopold T. for special punishment. Based on hard evidence and testimony, Bogner found both guilty of larceny under Articles 171–74 of the Austrian penal code. More seriously, he ruled that because they had undertaken at least three break-ins during blackouts, they had violated the Decree against National Parasites. Bogner thus sentenced Emmerich to fifteen months behind bars and Leopold to ten months.[30]

In an entirely different case, five Schlurfs, accustomed to loitering in the Prater, became involved in a spontaneous scuffle that led to lives of crime. Whether their delinquent behavior would have persisted in a more open society is difficult to say. On a glorious afternoon in September 1941, 18-year-old Josef P. and four younger pals went for a swim near the Prater. After drying off, they approached Herbert Hofmacher and his girlfriend to ask for a cigarette and five pennies. Refusal led to a fistfight, in which Hofmacher suffered a concussion, chest injury, and a bloody eye. After five months of interrogation and examination by social workers, Josef was sentenced to four months in solitary confinement.[31] Upon release from jail, Josef, now an adult, joined a looser though much larger gang, one which the police broke up within months. On April 13, 1943, the criminal division of the Higher Regional Court found him guilty of multiple thefts during blackouts as well as robberies that ranged from purse-snatching to stealing an expensive accordion. The state prosecutor also presented evidence that Josef had been involved in numerous homosexual encounters since 1940. The judge condemned him to seven years of imprisonment as a habitual criminal and national parasite (*Volksschädling*). In addition, he convicted two 17-year-old defendants on similar charges and meted out sentences of seven and six years respectively. As for Josef, he remained behind bars until after the war when he was cleared of violating the Parasite Decree but put on probation for five years.[32]

Among the juvenile gang members convicted with Josef P. on October 22, 1942, was 17-year-old Benno S., a high-school dropout who confessed to have joined Josef P. in breaking into a private home to steal articles of clothing, a jar of marmalade, 1 kilogram of sugar, a measuring stick, and a cigarette lighter. Evidence gathered by prosecutors demonstrated, however, that Benno had participated in multiple robberies from an early age and had already spent four months in detention. In addition, extensive investigation by court-appointed social workers suggests that Benno grew up in circumstances that might have led to delinquency even in a free society. Born an illegitimate child, he was reared by his grandmother and uncle in modest circumstances. Once the uncle was called up in 1939, the boy was left on his own. Disinterested in joining the Hitler Youth, he left school to help out in his elderly grandmother's tiny upholstering business. Like many teenagers he began staying up well beyond midnight, let his hair grow long, and associated with other youngsters who were Schlurfs. In reviewing Benno's record, social workers and a psychiatrist focused more on his character and "essence" than his criminal activities. Their diagnosis was that he was malicious, stubborn, impudent, cynical, undependable, and lazy, not least because he preferred to slouch into cinemas, loiter in coffee houses, and seduce willing girls. Although a three-judge panel declined to try Benno as an adult, its members sentenced him to three years of incarceration in Kaiser-Ebersdorf both for larceny and "dishonoring the race" as a national parasite.[33]

In the early years of the war, one of the largest teenage gangs arrested and tried in Vienna consisted of fourteen boys born between 1922 and 1925. The surviving documentation provides little information on their home lives or social background but does reveal that each and everyone was a craftsman apprentice or technician trainee. Better educated than other delinquents, the youngsters, like other Schlurfs, wore elegant clothes and congregated in a small park or around tables of a cafe in the heavily populated 7th District. Surviving trial records indicate that in early 1941 several of them spontaneously began a number of youthful pranks that emboldened the others to join them in carefully planned and coordinated operations that by October netted the group goods and cash worth RM 17,000. The lion's share of the loot consisted of bicycles, a golden bracelet, jewelry, diamonds, foodstuffs, wine, cigarettes, ration coupons, and other valuables. Once sold on the black market, the proceeds were divided equally among gang members. What struck the police and magistrates most about the delinquents was their sophisticated use of drills, wire-cutters, shears, and other tools to break into homes and shops. On October 22, 1942, Judge Anton Nirschl, a veteran National Socialist, found all the accused guilty of theft, but took into careful consideration the circumstances in which the crimes had been committed. He sentenced four youngsters who had acted under the cover of darkness to three to four years in a juvenile detention center both for larceny and for "dishonoring the race" as national parasites. Those not violating blackout regulations received lighter sentences ranging from seven months in jail to three weeks in detention.[34]

Shortly after Hitler's defeat in Stalingrad, three teenage gangs were rounded up in Vienna. Their members were tried on charges that ranged from petty theft, to robbery, assault, and dissident behavior. The fate of two of the teenage gangs hauled before the bench in 1943 is examined in great detail by Gerbel in his classic study of the Schlurfs. Two of the groups were active in the Prater, and the other, for which no court records have survived, in working-class Meidling. Most of the reports and transcripts of these bands have succumbed to the shredder, but some records have survived. Combined with Gerbel's findings, it is possible to reconstruct the social background of gang members as well as the interaction of delinquent behavior and political jurisprudence in Nazi Vienna.

The "Sandleiten" gang, as it was called, consisted of a dozen youngsters, half of whom were 17 years of age, three were 18, and the others slightly younger. Five were journeymen, four manual workers, one a crane operator, and the others jobless. The boys appear to have gotten to know each other in the Prater in late 1942, organizing as a gang shortly before Christmas. Between December 14, 1942, and late March 1943, they broke into numerous small shops, making off with shoes, apparel, cigarettes, wine, soap, razor blades, sugar, substantial amounts of cash, and even rabbits. Interestingly, most of the apprentice delinquents appear to have come from stable homes, whose fathers had been drafted into the armed forces, thus compelling their mothers to take low-paying menial jobs. By joining a gang, the boys were able to experience a sense of belonging to a group, enhance their own self-esteem, and even justify their criminal behavior as a means of supplementing family incomes. The ringleader of the "Sandleiten" gang, Josef W.,[35] had also lost his father, though as a result of an acrimonious divorce. While suffering from a chronic middle-ear infection, he had become a carpenter's apprentice and succeeded in passing his qualification examination, though with a lower grade than anticipated. By all accounts he took charge of the "Sandleiten" in February 1943 orchestrating a series of spectacular robberies that netted the group RM 880 in cash. Because the well-planned felonies had taken place during blackouts, the court threw the book at the defendants both as criminals and national parasites, sentencing Josef to imprisonment for a period of three to five years, two of his companions to terms of one to two years, and the others to four- to five-month confinement.[36] According to subsequent documentation, one of the convicted boys managed to enlist in the navy upon release and another in the Waffen SS. As for Josef W., he was drafted into a punishment battalion, survived Soviet captivity, and returned to Vienna in 1947. Still subject to serve out his sentence, he appealed for a pardon on March 12, 1947. Whether it was granted is unknown.[37]

A striking example of the impact of Nazi jurisprudence on the Austrian juvenile justice system can be seen in the treatment of the "Karo" gang, a group of teenagers arrested in May 1943 for multiple assaults in the Prater. According to police investigators, the youngsters had been congregating casually on Saturdays and Sundays in the Karo Coffeehouse where they tended to come and go on an informal basis. Like other teenagers, they liked to hang out, pick up girls, and dance to swing music. Now and then there would be rumbles with other groups, but the "Karos" never organized as a gang. What disturbed them was the appearance of young Czech and Polish workers whom they perceived as both rivals and enemies. In February 1943, a member of the League of German Girls incited the "Karos" to attack a company of Czechs who had refused demands to stop singing in their native tongue. In the following months, at least forty-two foreigners were roughed up or stabbed at by various locals in the Prater. As mentioned earlier, a police raid in early May led to the arrest and detention of a dozen troublemakers. When tried five months later, the court chastised the boys for belonging to a brawling juvenile gang (*Platte*), but imposed a penalty only on the principal ringleader. The judges sentenced him to spend eight months in Kaiser-Ebersdorf not for assault with a stiletto but for numerous homosexual encounters. In Nazi Vienna, "lewd behavior" as defined by § 129 of the Austrian penal code was considered more reprehensible than brutalizing strangers in a park.[38]

The "Tobogan" gang, organized in 1938, appears to have been made up more of countercultural dissidents than paracriminals. As paradigmatic Schlurfs they sported long slicked-down hair, wore fancy clothes, and enjoyed smoking, drinking, and listening to jazz records. Nearly all were underage workers and apprentices who simply wanted to spend their free time together as friends. They did not hang out in the Prater but around a carousel in a Meidling amusement center. The core of the group consisted of ten to fifteen boys and several girls who got together after work. Other youngsters came from nearby districts, but were not always welcome, particularly if suspected of making a pass at one of the Tobogan girls. Inevitably there were turf rumbles with other groups, such as the "Laaberg" gang in the 15th District, though more frequently with patrols of the Hitler Youth. On August 28, 1942, for example, the police took thirty-eight youngsters into custody, but released twenty-five of them almost immediately. How many belonged to the "Tobogans" is unknown. The same can be said of an assault on a Hitler Youth dormitory that took place the following summer in Wiener Neudorf. Years later, elderly Tobogans took pains to claim that lawbreakers had never belonged to their group. They acknowledged clashes with rival gangs and troops of the Hitler Youth, but in extensive interviews they dissociated themselves from the violent assaults and robberies undertaken by the "Karos" in the Prater. During the last years of the war, the Tobogans appear to have prided themselves in satisfying the sexual needs of lonely housewives and widows who had congregated at a local dance hall to meet them.[39]

Looking back, the bands of Schlurfs who joined together in the 1930s and 1940s constituted a juvenile counterculture opposed initially to the regimentation of the Dollfuss-Schuschnigg dictatorship and after March 1938 to mandatory service in the Hitler Youth. Refusal to enroll branded them and other dissident groups as a threat to the Nazi regime, not least because Hitler placed enormous faith in the loyalty of young Germans and Austrians to carry out his vast plans of conquest.[40] Technically nearly all Schlurfs belonged to gangs, even though the meaning of that term was and remains ambiguous. Historical scholarship and surviving evidence suggest that many, particularly wards of the state or children of impoverished homes, bonded together as an extended family. In Vienna, juvenile nonconformist behavior during the Anschluß era thus ranged from wearing outlandish costumes in public venues to listening to jazz music, picking up girls, or participating in various teenage high jinks that included turf wars and petty larceny. Of the six major gangs to come before the juvenile court between 1940 and 1944, only three were indicted as Schlurfs, although only the "Sandleiten" and "Karos" in the Prater were convicted of robbery and criminal assault. Other Schlurfs were later caught up in Gestapo crackdowns for black marketeering or pimping for prostitutes, but overall the dissidents did not organize violent street gangs, engage in massive theft, or become members of a political resistance group. Indeed, after investigating the arrest of sixty-five boys in October 1942 for disturbing the peace, the Gestapo concluded that "the deeds of the Schlurfs can in no way be characterized as politically motivated."[41] Overall, the Schlurfs are best understood as a nonconformist subculture or network opposed to the authoritarian order that prevailed in Austria between 1933 and 1945, first to the Dollfuss-Schuschnigg regime and later to the Nazi state. In this way, they constituted a distinctive Austrian phenomenon, similar and yet also different from other dissident groups in the "Altreich." Without exculpating those juveniles convicted of felonious offences, most Schlurfs did not engage in criminal behavior. And while they bitterly resented the regimentation of the Hitler Youth, they were for the most part nonpolitical. While some even dated members of the League of German Girls, others assaulted rival Czech youngsters. The Schlurfs, rather like the wealthy Swing Kids in Hamburg, simply wanted to be left alone. And yet their very existence represented such an affront to Hitler's National Community that in the eyes of the Nazis, most notably Himmler, they came to be considered opponents of the regime.[42]

2. Small Rings and Individuals

Most juvenile felons brought before the bench in Vienna between 1940 and 1944 for property crimes had operated in small groups or as individuals. Few of them belonged to gangs of Schlurfs. Their loot consisted of a wide range of items that included radios, gramophones, bicycles, jewelry, cameras, wrist watches, wearing apparel, typewriters, spare tires, auto parts, tools, and other consumer products or office equipment. Beginning in late 1941, targeted thefts included goods in short supply such as wine, cigarettes, eggs, fruit, flour, sugar, raisins, ration coupons, rabbits from allotments, and even restaurant food. That pilfering of staples and foodstuffs shot up in mid-1942 was hardly a coincidence. First, shortages of rationed food in a large city like Vienna had increased noticeably during the winter. Second, and more importantly, Hitler had delivered a blood-curdling speech to the Reichstag on April 26, 1942, both castigating the German judiciary and assuming chief appellate power for himself. Further, both official statistics and surviving judicial records reveal that, unlike the Schlurfs, three-quarters of the minors arraigned in Viennese courts for theft between 1940 and 1944 had been motivated to steal more frequently by deprivation rather than by opportunity. This was a pattern almost identical to that discerned by Roth in his study of crime and criminality in Cologne and Fishman in her study of juvenile crime in wartime Paris.[43] While there was little difference between transgressions committed by clusters of several boys and individuals in Vienna, their cases will be considered separately.

On June 19, 1940, 15-year-old Rudolf F. and 16-year-old Rudolf E. were found guilty of theft by the Juvenile Division of the Higher Regional Court. Both had left school to become manual workers in a small machinery plant. As the younger boy had gained access to a duplicate key to the firm's locker room, he persuaded the older to join him in a pilfering expedition. On April 23, the youngsters made off with several wallets, two pairs of gloves, a handful of photographs of female coworkers, and some cash. Their goal had been to accumulate enough money to attend as many movies as possible. Nowadays, their crime would be considered a misdemeanor, but Judge Peter Bogner invoked Articles 171 and 178 of the Austrian penal code to convict Rudolf F. of larceny. The judge sentenced him to fourteen days of harsh detention; however, only after three years of supervised probation was Rudolf E. placed on parole. Exactly what happened to Rudolf F. is not entirely clear. A military report filed on November 24, 1942, indicates that he was serving in the 177th division of the Wehrmacht. He obviously survived the war, for in 1948 the Viennese Juvenile Court expunged his record, ruling he was no longer liable to incarceration.[44]

In 1941, the number of felonies committed by small teams of two to five youngsters seems to have increased, or more precisely additional court records of such transgressions managed to survive the shredder for this study. A few examples should suffice. On October 2, 1941, four minors came before the court for having broken into an allotment garden near Seyss Inquart's home in 17th District. Once inside, they stole three bottles of wine, a half-liter of lemon juice, thirty to forty packages of sherbet powder, a block plane, a cutting knife, and 10 kilograms of fresh fruit. The owner, Johann M., estimated the worth of the loot at RM 50. According to reports by social workers, the ringleader, 16-year-old Johann S., had grown up in a single-room dwelling; he was the son of a widowed mother barely making ends meet as a housekeeper The boy had been considered indolent by his teachers, though following the Anschluß had enjoyed farming (*Landdienst*) in Saxony. Returning to Vienna, he had gone to work for Johann M. until his dismissal in September 1940. Another, Franz M., had also lost his father. Social workers indicated that he was both lazy and unintelligent. He too had dropped out of school and stayed out late, loitering in the streets and watching movies. Despite these negative assessments, the court ruled that all four youngsters could be redeemed for the National Community by imposing an educative penalty. Johann S. thus received a sentence of three weekend detentions, and the others a mere two.[45]

More severe were the sentences imposed by the court on May 15, 1941, on 15-year-old Walter N. and 14-year-old Friedrich T. During various long winter nights in early 1941, they had broken into 12 homes and firms taking tools, bicycle parts, books, toys, saws, knives, kitchen utensils, soap, detergents, and meat—altogether worth roughly RM 250. Their ages notwithstanding, the state prosecutor insisted that they be harshly punished. In a sense Judge Kurt Bamberger squared the circle. He sentenced Walter to three months severe imprisonment, primarily because § 180 of the Austrian penal code stipulated harsh punishment for offences committed under the cover of darkness. However, he declined to invoke the Parasite Decree and allowed the boy to remain free on supervised parole for three years before serving his sentence. Friedrich escaped incarceration, but was also placed on three-year probation. Whether either delinquent served time is unclear. A notation on the court record indicates that in 1948 Walter's conviction was effaced.[46]

In contrast, four teenagers convicted of larceny two months later received harsh sentences for a series of robberies committed in April. Their haul consisted of a typewriter, a briefcase, fountain pens, jewelry, postage stamps, and over RM 700 in cash. According to the Gestapo, 16-year-old Karl M. and 14-year-old Otto E. were also carrying Communist flysheets. For that reason the state prosecutor considered them "parasitic types," although too young to be prosecuted as habitual criminals. Nonetheless, the court sentenced Otto to eight months of harsh detention and Karl to five months behind bars. A third member received a sentence of five months and a marginal accomplice, still enrolled in school, two weekend detentions[47] Meanwhile, Otto had taken up with a 20-year-old streetwalker, with whom he fathered a child. After his release, presumably from Kaiser-Ebersdorf, he had trouble holding down a job. It was hardly a coincidence that he joined two other teenagers in prowling the Prater, where during blackouts they snatched purses and stole other items, including five rabbits from an allotment. After a lengthy process, the older boys were tried and sentenced as adults to six and seven years of imprisonment for larceny and "defiling the race." Otto was condemned to spend three to four years in indefinite imprisonment on the same charges, even though an appeal to the Reich Supreme Court overturned his conviction on the basis of age as a "precocious juvenile criminal." What mattered, the judges ruled, was neither maturity nor unlawful behavior but rather innate "moral degeneracy and reprehensible criminal disposition." With that in mind, there should be no possibility of parole or early release.[48]

A more conventional case involved four boys, two of whom were only 15 years of age, while the others 16 and 17 respectively. On October 10, 1942, the court convicted the youngsters of stealing no fewer than twelve bicycles as well as breaking into allotment huts where they made off with two wedding bands, a diamond ring, a pearl necklace, winter clothing, and food stuffs, including a rabbit. Tellingly, the judges imposed the harshest sentence on the youngest delinquent, Johannes J. Born on April 20, 1927, Johannes came from a dysfunctional impoverished family. His father had served in the French Foreign Legion but returned to Vienna suffering from a chronic illness, in effect leaving the mother to provide and care for him alone. Meanwhile, Johannes had done poorly in school and dropped out to do menial work. Considered unruly and unreliable, he became the ringleader of the small band of thieves, both instigating and committing the most number of crimes. The judges thus condemned him to serve educative incarceration of nine months to two years as stipulated by Paragraphs 171–5 of the Austrian penal code. His accomplices received sentences of one to six months in jail. Interestingly, none was found guilty of "dishonoring the race," according to the Parasite Decree. The court did, however, express doubt that Johannes could ever be reeducated.[49]

Other small groups convicted of larceny under the Austrian penal code included the following: two 17-year-olds sentenced to six months of harsh detention for bicycle theft and absenteeism; five younger boys to four weeks in detention for climbing over a garden fence, damaging property, and taking 50 kilograms of fruit; and three technician trainees who had stolen an expensive radio set, two boxes of tools, and substantial quantities of flour, bread, and raisins. The 15-year-old ringleader of the third group was condemned to spend three months in jail; his associates to two weeks in detention. As in other cases, the court followed the letter of Austrian law and did not invoke the Parasite Decree.[50] This approach appears to have continued well into the war. In April 1943, for example, three apprentices, ages 15, 16, and 17, were picked up by the police for breaking into a warehouse shortly before midnight. For stealing a motorcycle engine, tires, and other accessories, they were sentenced two months later to jail terms ranging from one to ten months, again according to Austrian law.[51] Significantly, in all these cases the convicted were compelled to pay court costs.

Records of thirty-three individuals convicted of property crimes by the Juvenile Division of the Higher Regional Court in Vienna between 1940 and 1944 have survived for this study. Many of the documents are fragmentary; others suggest that a number of the delinquents had not acted alone. In the aggregate, however, they provide significant information about the social background and motivation of those brought before the bench.

Bernhard H., born in 1925, is a good example of an adolescent who unwittingly went astray. According to a sympathetic diagnosis filed by a court-appointed social worker, Bernhard, the son of an overworked divorced mother, grew up in a one-room dwelling. The family received some assistance from the Guardianship Authority, enabling the boy to do well in the classroom; however, he would fall ill frequently. In 1939, he broke both his arm and leg, impelling him to drop out of high school. Having joined the Hitler Youth, he tried to survive as a lathe apprentice. Rather like Collodi's Pinocchio, however, he fell into bad company and between October and December 1940 stole RM 400 from his master. Shortly after the New Year, the court convicted him of five counts of larceny, though imposed a relatively mild sentence of three weeks suspended detention on the basis of his youth and "negligent education." Bernhard subsequently completed a probationary period and enlisted in the Waffen SS. In January 1945, his commanding officer sentenced him to four weeks of imprisonment for being absent without leave. His subsequent fate is unknown.[52]

Somewhat different was the fate of Albert F., an 18-year-old office trainee, who on January 24,1941, was condemned to spend two months of hard labor for stealing truck tires. The court acknowledged that he had not acted alone, but considered him incorrigible and likely to pursue a life of crime. Nevertheless, a personal appeal by Albert's mother to Gauleiter Schirach appears to have had some effect. Authorities in the Gauleitung supported amnesty upon completion of sentence, and so that by the end of the year Albert was serving in the Reich Labor Service[53] An entirely different and yet similar case reveals that Hitler's jurists believed educative punishment might save certain delinquents for the National Community. On October 25, 1940, the court sentenced an 18-year-old gaffer trainee to six months of suspended imprisonment for theft to be served following three years of probation. Reading between the lines, it is clear that the jurists wanted to make sure that the youngster would not evade military service. On April 28, 1944, a military judge informed the Higher Regional Court that he was serving a three-year sentence in a military penitentiary for absence without leave. Under these circumstances, the Luftwaffe official wrote, the civil sentence should either be legally effaced or reconsidered.[54]

In our imperfect sample of individual juvenile thieves only two adolescents—as opposed to gang members—were convicted of "dishonoring the race" as national parasites. There were, no doubt, others, but the juvenile judges appeared to have relied on Paragraphs 171–75 of the Austrian penal code to hand out stiff sentences for crimes against property. On September 15, 1941, for example, the court condemned a machinist trainee to a month of hard labor followed by two months in Kaiser-Ebersdorf for stealing hammers, levers, and various other tools during blackouts. Yet in the same decision they ruled that he had not "subjectively" violated the Parasite Decree.[55] The two known individuals to be sentenced to long prison terms for multiple thefts according to the Parasite Decree were 16-year-old Johann W. and Eugon T. Although both had belonged to gangs, each had committed robberies and assaults on his own.

Johann had grown up in Purgstall an der Erlach, apparently the son of a single mother. After completing elementary education, he moved in 1940 to Linz where the Labor Office assigned him to work as a trainee in the surveying division of the *Reichsbahn* and Hermann Göring Works. Ten months later, he returned to Lower Austria to live with his mother. Here the authorities ordered him to become a machinist apprentice in Simmering. Eugon had grown up in Hungary. But as his father had been an activist in the Hungarian branch of the Nazi Party, the family had fled to Vienna shortly before the Anschluß. Three years later, however, the boy's father had been called up and his mother had died of natural causes. Alone in the world, Eugon worked as an apprentice mechanic in the Floridsdorf locomotive factory and later for a Lufthansa branch near Aspern. Exactly when the two youngsters got know each other is unclear, although both were initially involved with Josef P.'s gang and occasionally cooperated as a team. When brought before the bench on April 13, 1943, however, they were convicted as individuals on seven counts of larceny that included bicycle theft, felonious assault, robbery, purse-snatching, indiscipline, and absenteeism.

According to the evidence, the court found Johann guilty of bicycle theft during his year in Linz as well as a series of daring nocturnal robberies two years later in the Kärtnerstraße. On one occasion, he had pursued the opera singer Josefine Stolz through the inner city to her room in the Hotel Excelsior. Here he slapped her in the face and made off with her purse. A month later, he assaulted another woman crossing University Square on the Wollzeile, throwing her to the ground and stealing her purse. As for Eugon, he was convicted of assailing fashionable women near the State Opera. In reaching their decisions, the judges took into account the numerous felonies committed by the youngsters both as gang members and as individuals. Because nearly all of the offences had been committed at night, often during blackouts, the justices sentenced Johann to seven years of imprisonment not only for violating seven articles of the Austrian penal code, but more significantly for "dishonoring the race" according to the Parasite Decree. Eugon was condemned to spend six years behind bars. Although his fate is unknown, postwar records reveal that Johann paid a bitter price for his teenage transgressions. Confined in Kaiser-Ebersdorf, he was released on March 30, 1945, to fight in a punishment battalion. He survived the last days of the war and Soviet captivity, but upon returning to Vienna the following year was dispatched to Stein penitentiary to complete his sentence. Not until 1948 could he resume his life as a free man.⁵⁶

According to official statistics, the number of juveniles convicted of crimes against property in Vienna rose significantly in 1942 but tapered off the following year. A number of those brought to trial were gang members, as we have already seen. Others, however, appear to have struck out on their own. Among them were two girls. Seventeen-year-old Klementine O. had grown up the lonely daughter of an abusive father and sickly mother, whose untimely death led her to drop out of school. Klementine then performed two months compulsory community service (*Pflichtjahr*), but was hospitalized and discharged for a serious hand infection. Upon release, her overbearing father insisted she care for him. Instead, she took a job in a malt factory and from June to December 1941 served as a housekeeper for a woman recovering from an illness. Thereafter, she appears to have done part-time work in two hotels, where she slept promiscuously with overnight guests and pilfered bed sheets, towels, and even curtains. When apprehended in April 1942, a routine examination revealed that she was suffering from a highly contagious venereal disease. On August 10, 1942, the court sentenced Klementine to five months in the female detention facility at Hirtenberg, south of Vienna, presumably to undergo "corrective education."⁵⁷

A similar fate befell Ernestine X., the teenage daughter of a divorced couple, whose father had been conscripted and mother remarried with two toddlers. Left in the care of a grandmother, Ernestine was apprehended in 1941 for stealing RM 20, which she used to purchase a purse and cigarettes. Investigation by court-appointed social workers indicated that she was also involved in black marketeering. Others filed conflicting reports, one stating that she was industrious and hardworking, another that she had become sexually promiscuous. That she might have been both seems not to have occurred to the prurient authorities. On February 22, 1941, the juvenile justices issued a stern warning, but did not impose a sentence. Thereafter, Ernestine took various jobs as a housekeeper only to taken into custody the following year for petty theft. On August 29, 1942, she was sentenced to six months behind bars in Hirtenberg.⁵⁸ In some ways, the fate of these two wayward girls may not have been as severe as that of their sisters in Vichy France. In 1943, French officials found girls incarcerated in state institutions for "premature sexuality" to have had their hair shorn short, compelled to wear black gowns, and forced to remain silent in "chicken wire" cells.⁵⁹

In surveying the records of other Viennese minors tried in 1942 for petty misdemeanors, the justices sometimes handed out relatively mild sentences, usually two weekend detentions or a few weeks in jail.⁶⁰ Even in 1943, the courts could demonstrate leniency as they did in sentencing an unskilled worker to three weeks in detention for stealing cherries from a municipal allotment.⁶¹ On the other hand, the judges did not hesitate to impose severe punishment for minor offences if a previous record or extenuating circumstances came to light during pretrial discovery. Late in the afternoon of August 20, 1942, 16-year-old machinist trainee Bernhard R. had persuaded two workmates to help him make off with 3 kilograms of sausage from a butcher shop in the Siccardsburggasse. Under Austrian law, the offense constituted a minor misdemeanor, but because Bernhard had been convicted for an unspecified sexual offense in 1940, the court sentenced him to three months in a juvenile correctional facility.⁶²

After Stalingrad, the Nazi regime's efforts to consolidate the war economy was accompanied by a crackdown on the home front in which the number of death sentences handed out increased dramatically, most notably in the case of Sophie Scholl and other members of Munich's White Rose Society. This was also true in war-torn Cologne, where death penalties increased exponentially, particularly for plundering and black marketeering.⁶³ In Vienna, minors convicted of theft appear to have received much harsher sentences than those brought to book for similar crimes in the past, even though our exiguous sample makes it difficult to generalize. In a number of instances, female social workers influenced judicial decisions by implying immoral behavior or characterizing the accused as a "criminal-biological type" immune to "corrective education." This was particularly striking in the case of Benno S., as we have already seen. Another example involved a 15-year-old locksmith apprentice who had come to know Benno in the Prater. Between June and August 1942, Gustav H., sometimes with accomplices, sometimes on his own, had stolen wrist watches, cash, marmalade, ration coupons, fountain pens, rubber boots, opera glasses, and other objects worth RM 7,000 on the black market. He was also accused of engaging in numerous acts of mutual masturbation. On June 8, 1943, the court sentenced Hermann to two to four years in a penitentiary. The judges conceded that juvenile detention was the stipulated penalty for acts committed under the age of 16, but ruled that Hermann's numerous crimes "dishonoring the race" as a national parasite justified his severe sentence.⁶⁴

Normally, teenage burglars and thieves seem to have been ordered to be confined for terms varying from six months to a year. On March 3, 1943, for example, 15-year-old Franz S. was found guilty of filching cigarettes, pipe tobacco, butter, cheese, eggs and margarine worth RM 276 from several small shops in Baden. As the break-ins had occurred after dark, Justice Hans

Mayer could have invoked the Parasite Decree to impose a long prison term. Instead, he sentenced Franz to six to twelve months in Kaiser-Ebersdorf as the most effective measure to "eradicate his dodgy predisposition."[65] Similarly, a 17-year-old manual worker, Paul L., was ordered to serve nine to fifteen months behind bars for having stolen rubber boots, various tools, a silver pocket watch, and some sweets. The lengthier sentence was imposed owing to a previous conviction.[66] Often judges seem to have assessed the worth of stolen goods in reaching a decision. Hildegard L. thus received a ten-week sentence for stealing a wrist watch, a gold fountain pen, a silver ring, and other valuables assessed at RM 300 from a private home, where she was completing a year of compulsory service as a maid. The trial record indicates that the worth of the stolen goods is what determined her punishment.[67] Assessed value was also decisive in the case of an unskilled worker, Karl S., sentenced to six months in Kaiser-Ebersdorf for stealing large quantities of cheese, rabbits, and a pig, that is, valuable foodstuffs in wartime. In contrast, two 13-year-old boys and their 15-year-old ringleader were compelled to spend three weekend detentions for making off with a dozen apples from a convent.[68]

3. Noncompliant Behavior, Indiscipline, Work Stoppages, Absenteeism

Shortly after the outbreak of war, on November 17, 1939, the Viennese Gestapo arrested a 17-year-old unskilled worker, Otto B., for being "work-shy." According to a decree passed on December 14, 1937, Himmler's police were authorized to send both "professional and habitual criminals" as well as those deemed "asocial" to concentration camps. Otto was thus fingerprinted, photographed, and dispatched to Sachsenhausen, where in 1943 he died of maltreatment.[69] Those classified as "asocials" were vagrants, beggars, gypsies, alcoholics, prostitutes, and nonconformists. However, individuals arrested under the law for walking off the job, work stoppages, or extended absenteeism might also find themselves facing charges of "asocial" behavior, particularly if deemed "criminal biological types" by social workers.[70] In 1943, nearly a third of those Viennese convicted of violating ordinances passed since the Anschluß had been hauled before the court for breach of contract, truancy, or other forms of insubordination in the workplace.[71] The figures do not reveal the number of adolescents, although our imperfect sample indicates that 12 percent had run afoul of their employers.

The sentences imposed by the Juvenile Division of the Higher Regional Court in Vienna on youngsters convicted of insubordination, malingering, or absence from the workplace appear to have varied widely from case to case. While some judicial decisions took into account age, gender, or parental negligence, others considered the biological character of the accused or the importance of his/her job for the war effort. Penalties thus ranged from weekend detentions to lengthy sentences. Normally, a proprietor or Nazi shop steward (*Betriebsobmann*) would file a complaint with the branch office of Reich Trustee of Labor, whose administrators would decide whether to bring charges. On October 3, 1941, for example, the shop steward of the Otto Lutzky Glass Factory reported that a 16-year-old manual apprentice had taken two weeks of leave in September, returned to work, but then walked off the job. The shop steward recommended internment in a work camp, but when tried and convicted in early December both the state prosecutor and presiding judge agreed to sentence the boy to two weeks in detention.[72]

Equally mild was a weekend detention imposed on 17-old Ferdinand M., who simply wanted to change jobs. This was also the case of 15-year-old Franz C., who on multiple occasions in May 1942 failed to report to work at the Achachy Iron Works. The court found Franz guilty of violating the Wage Structure Ordinance of 1938, but considering the boy's age and physical weakness sentenced him to spend a mere week in detention. In another instance, the justices imposed the same penalty on 17-year-old Adolf S., who had experienced difficulty finding protective overalls to work in a war production plant.[73] The judges also handed out brief detention sentences to nine other juveniles in our sample, though two were jailed for six months and three others conscripted before serving time.[74] During the last eighteen months of the war, as we shall see, the number of minors convicted of work stoppages and absenteeism rose exponentially. The reasons varied from case to case, but the records suggest that many of the youngsters may well have broken with the regime.

One type of delinquency that was common to all societies and that greatly annoyed the Nazi authorities was the alteration of identification papers. According to the state prosecutor, countless Viennese youngsters under 18 had updated or falsified various identity cards allowing them to enjoy the privileges of adults. These enabled them to leave home at night so as to attend movies, lounge in coffee houses, or simply hang out on street corners. To what extent such youthful malefactors were picked up by the police or disciplined does not appear in the judicial record, though it is likely they received little more than a reprimand or a brief detention.[75]

Analysis of the handful of surviving judicial records prior to 1944 should not exculpate Hitler's judges as merciful. The number is simply too small to draw firm conclusions. And as mentioned earlier, even those minors sentenced to brief periods of detention for work-related offences suffered considerable abuse. Indeed, one case analyzed in grim detail by Gerbel reveals the capricious brutality of the juvenile judicial system. The subject, Anton X., had been under the care of the Juvenile Welfare Board since early childhood. A social worker reported in 1927 that he was severely neglected, inhabiting a small room in a wartime barracks with his siblings and impoverished working mother. Shortly after the Anschluß, a second report indicated that Anton and his brother had spent ten days employed on a Rhine barge in Duisburg. On May 26, 1941, a third social worker wrote that Anton had run into serious trouble at his workplace in Vienna. Apprenticed as a machinist trainee, he had walked off the job so frequently, she wrote, it was imperative that the Juvenile Welfare Board intervene in order to impose "discipline and cleanliness." This recommendation made its way to the office of the Reich Trustee of Labor, which petitioned the Higher Regional Court to file a brief of indictment. By Christmas, Anton found himself in protective custody on charges of insubordination and moral indecency. Five months later the court sentenced him to one and one and a half years behind bars for insubordination and homosexuality as a "criminal-biological type." Thereafter, the director of Kaiser-Ebersdorf weighed in to recommend that Anton be transferred to the juvenile concentration camp in Moringen, near Northeim in Lower Saxony. This proposal was endorsed by a female social worker, who blamed Anton's mother for the sort of intentional negligence that had produced a "thoroughly squalid, primitive, and degenerate adolescent." The paper trail indicates that on April 8, 1944, he was dispatched to Moringen, where he appears to have perished.[76]

4. Violent Crimes

Very few adolescents committed violent crimes in wartime Vienna. Official statistics reveal that, between 1940 and 1943, fifteen boys were found guilty of homicide or attempted murder: five in 1940, nine in 1941, none in 1942, and one in 1943. During the same period, ninety-one were convicted of assault: twenty-two in 1940, thirty-nine in 1941, ten in 1942, and twenty in 1943.[77] The relatively low level of serious juvenile crimes committed in the Danubian metropolis stands in stark contrast to numerous cases of stabbings, beatings, and murders reported in other cities of Hitler's Reich, particularly in Cologne, the industrial Ruhr, and Hanover, though not in Vichy France.[78] As we have already seen, most adolescents arraigned or tried for violent crimes before the Viennese Higher Regional Court, though not in Special Courts, had been members of gangs, although a few had acted as individuals. Arthur S., for example, was sentenced to two months in Kaiser-Ebersdorf according to § 157 for his part in "inflicting severe bodily injury" on Herbert Hofmacher during the Prater incident discussed earlier in this chapter. In contrast, his accomplice, Alois S., was deemed a bystander and found not guilty[79] An altogether different case involved a scuffle on the shop floor, provoked by Josef D. when he refused to loan a drill to his 17-year-old coworker, Franz S. The youngster responded with a kick in the backside, which led to a brawl in which Josef was injured and hospitalized for thirty days. In reaching a decision, the court acknowledged Alois as the aggrieved party, but on May 13, 1941, sentenced him to two weekends of detention according to § 335 of the penal code for initiating the tussle. If the court believed in shock therapy, they were mistaken. A year later Alois was sentenced to four weeks of incarceration for his role in stealing fruits and vegetables from an allotment garden.[80]

5. Moral Offences and Homosexuality

As we have seen in the previous chapter, the Austrian Penal Code of 1852 remained in place in the years following the collapse of the Habsburg monarchy. No attempt was made prior to the Anschluß or thereafter to alter Articles 125–33 stipulating harsh penalties for moral offences, particularly "unnatural crimes" such as bestiality and homosexuality. Traditional Catholic doctrine, enshrined in law, that homosexual behavior was an abomination contrary to nature thus dovetailed with Nazism's paranoid dread of homosexuality as threat to the National Community. While the percentages of juveniles convicted of moral offences in Vienna remained comparatively steady between 1930 and 1943, fluctuating from between 6 and 8 percent, the total number of all Austrians sentenced for homosexuality rose sharply between 1938 and 1945.[81] On June 1, 1943, moreover, the state prosecutor lamented that destitute youngsters were congregating at the Roman Sauna seeking financial remuneration as juvenile prostitutes (*Strichjugend*).[82]

Only a handful of cases involving adolescents tried in Vienna specifically for moral offences, as opposed to those in gangs, have survived the shredder, making it impossible to generalize. Examination of the available records offer relatively few clues, although it is unlikely that the number of those apprehended by the Viennese vice squad would not have changed significantly had the Anschluß never taken place. On September 16, 1940, 14-year-old Eugen T. came before the bar accused of having molested an 8-year-old school girl the previous year in the

Augarten. The parties agreed that the girl had indeed exposed herself allowing Eugene to fondle her genitalia thus violating § 128 of the penal code. Conviction called for imprisonment of one to five years, but because Eugen had not yet reached the age of legal maturity he was allowed to go free. The following year, however, he was arrested as a member of Josef P.'s gang on multiple charges of vandalism and theft. This time his case was referred to a Special Court, which most likely did not let him off lightly.[83] In a similar case tried a fortnight later, two 17-year-olds were convicted of mutual masturbation in a bath house. They were fined but released on probation. The court apparently felt that a single act of sexual experimentation hardly warranted severe punishment.[84]

In late 1941, a 16-year-old machinist trainee, Walter S., was found guilty of statutory rape; the trial record revealed that he had engaged in sexual relations with 14-year-old Friedericke H. on a regular basis for six months in 1939–1940. According to a lengthy investigation by social workers and the criminal police, what began as an adolescent flirtation led to regular afternoon assignations in Friedericke's home while her parents were away at work. As both parties confessed, in one instance in prurient detail, the judges were inclined to be lenient, quite possibly because one case worker classified Friedericke as "sexually addicted to men." The court thus placed Walter on a three-year probation. Two years later, however, the police picked him up as a male prostitute in the Roman Sauna near the Praterstern. Desperate for money, he confessed to committing numerous acts of fellatio and masturbation. This time the judges sentenced him to three years of confinement. Having survived both incarceration and the war, Walter found a job as a porter first in the Roter Hahn Hotel and later in the more fashionable Regina. In 1951, however, he was convicted of theft and sentenced to serve eight months in prison to be followed by five months in harsh detention. In 1954, the police reported that he was working as a manual laborer in street construction.[85]

Equally grim was the fate of Franz H., a 17-year-old barber's apprentice, indicted for a single act of mutual masturbation in the Golden Unicorn Hotel. On October 25, 1941, the court found him guilty of indecency and immorality under § 129 and § 516 of the Austrian penal code, sentencing him to three months in confinement to be followed by three years on probation. Two years later, almost to the day, Franz came before the judges both for violating parole and for committing theft under the cover of darkness. This time the court imposed a prison sentence of six years of hard labor according to both Austrian law and § 2 of the Parasite Decree. After the war, the court expunged his conviction as a "national parasite," but required that he complete his sentence as stipulated by the Austrian penal code. Upon release, Franz was found guilty in 1952 of stealing toilet articles from his employer in Klagenfurt. He was again imprisoned and did not emerge from behind bars until 10 a.m. on January 7, 1956.[86]

Meanwhile, in late 1943 the Viennese vice squad stepped up raids on gay bath houses, most notably the Roman Sauna where a number of derelict teenagers were picked up as juvenile prostitutes. Exactly how many youngsters fell prey to the authorities is unknown, but a handful of court records reveal that those apprehended were severely punished. One outstanding culprit was an 18-year-old carpenter apprentice, who in mid-1942 began frequenting bath houses where he charged RM 10 for performing acts of fellatio, masturbation, and sodomy. The following year, he recruited two other boys to join him in his money-making activities. After several months, they were nabbed by the criminal police, along with thirty-four adults in the Roman Sauna, who remanded the minors to the juvenile division of the Higher Regional Court.

Surviving court records reveal that JSLA social workers spent considerable pretrial time and effort investigating the families, education, and prior conduct of the juveniles charged with "crimes contrary to nature." Unsurprisingly, the two principal offenders came from destitute, dysfunctional families. Erich B. for example, was born out of wedlock in 1927 to a divorced alcoholic mother. After the putative father committed suicide in 1933, the mother moved to Hüttelsdorf, remarried, but neglected her son. Erich completed two classes of high school, but was considered obstreperous and lazy. Apprenticed to a carpenter in 1942, he rarely showed up for work and for that reason was sentenced to several weeks in a reformatory. Following his release, he began his career as an adolescent gigolo and petty thief. On December 8, 1944, Judge Bamberger sentenced Erich to ten years in juvenile prison, noting that his criminal behavior and "injurious disposition" mandated severe punishment.[87]

One of Erich's recruits, 17-year-old Rudolf O., was also the offspring of a broken, dysfunctional family. Following his mother's death in 1934, Rudolf's insensitive father entrusted him to the care of the Guardianship Authority. Four years later the father remarried, allowing the boy to move back home. However, Rudolf could not abide his stepmother, who not only failed to win his affection but also threw him out of the household. Thereafter, the homeless boy fell into bad company, and in 1942 wound up in juvenile court, where he was sentenced to a month behind bars for theft and refusal to work. Shortly upon release, Rudolf met Erich B., who persuaded him to join him as a male prostitute. On December 2, 1942, the Higher Regional Court condemned him to serve eight months to two years in Kaiser-Ebersdorf. Assuming Erich and Rudolf survived the war, it is unlikely that either was released from a correctional facility prior to 1954 or 1955 as they had been convicted under § 129 of the Austrian penal code, an article that remained in place until 1971.[88]

In contrast, another 17-year-old convicted for indecency received a relatively mild sentence. The son of an impoverished widow, Johann K. had discovered that it was possible to acquire nonrationed cigarettes from elderly men living in a homeless shelter on the Wurlitzergasse. Here on January 9, 1942, he was caught in the act of masturbating a retired compositor in exchange for five cigarettes. Brought before the court two months later, he was sentenced to two months confinement instead of a much harsher penalty required by law. The court did not excuse Johann's transgression, but ruled that he had been seduced, albeit not against his will.[89]

One final case in our modest collection involved two 18-year-old lesbians. While judicial officials in Berlin sought to criminalize female homosexuality, they failed to pass legislation outlawing it in the "Altreich." In incorporated Austria, however, lesbianism was punishable under § 129 as a "sexual offence contrary to nature." Indeed, between 1940 and 1944, 35 Viennese women were convicted of lesbianism of whom seven were underage[90] On March 4, 1943, for example, two 18-year-old girls were convicted of mutual masturbation while sharing the same bed. As one was an office worker and the other a teacher trainee, the court may have considered their middle-class backgrounds in imposing a lenient sentence of two-week detention instead of the stipulated penalty of four to six years in prison. Judge Kurt Bamberger ruled that their favorable appearance and cooperative behavior ruled out harsher punishment.[91]

6. Subversive Behavior

Once Hitler had consolidated his power in Germany, as we have seen, his government passed a Law Against Subversive Attacks on the State and Party and for the Protection of Party Uniforms, popularly known as the "Subversion Law" (*Heimtückegesetz*). This legislation enabled the regime to prosecute individuals for seditious remarks or pre-treasonous behavior. During the Anschluß era, at least 10,000 Austrians, including minors, were brought before the bench for antiregime jokes, insulting Nazi officials, refusing to give the Hitler salute, or even spontaneous outbursts of frustration. Normally, those indicted for violating aspects of Hitler's speech code would be tried by Special Courts, whose judges regularly handed out draconian sentences.[92] Among the cases examined for this chapter, however, a 17-year-old crane operator was brought before juvenile justices, even though the Juvenile Criminals Act of October 4, 1939, classified him as an adult.

On February 11, 1943, Wilhelm M. was ushered into the chambers of Judge Anton Staininger, a hardened Nazi, known and even disdained by his colleagues for the harshness of sentences imposed on juvenile delinquents. Indicted for indiscipline, refusal to work, and subversive remarks, Wilhelm had every reason to expect the worst. According to the trial record, the young defendant was one of seven children of a widowed mother under the care of the Guardianship Authority. A member of the German Labor Front, he had completed compulsory service in an engineering firm. Taking a job as a crane operator in another plant, he had walked off the job and been hospitalized for psoriasis. In June 1942, he had entered the nursing station requesting additional salve to assuage his irritated skin. There he struck up a conversation with Erika A., a nurse belonging to the National Socialist Sisterhood. In the course of what became a heated discussion, he blurted out that while Hitler had constructed highways and provided work, the price exacted was war and bloodshed. Wilhelm also spoke out against the persecution of the Jews and even rejected the Anschluß. Other witnesses heard him state that the Führer was leading his people into the abyss.

Much to the astonishment of those present, Staininger sentenced Wilhelm to one month in detention instead of a lengthy term. The judge called attention to the boy's impoverished childhood and sound biological character, ruling that his outburst had not been intentionally "spiteful" or "incendiary" as defined in § 2 of the Subversion Law. Further, during three months in pretrial custody, social workers and Gestapo officials reported that Wilhelm had come to understand and appreciate the task and goals of National Socialism. For that reason Staininger saw no reason to inflict further punishment on a young man likely to become a valuable member of the National Community.[93]

Conclusions

The total number of juveniles convicted in Vienna for misdemeanors, gross misdemeanors, and felonies remained relatively constant between 1940 and the implementation of a comprehensive Reich Juvenile Code on January 1, 1944. As mentioned earlier, the figures rose from 12.8 percent in 1939 to 19.6 percent in 1942, though declined to 15.5 percent the following year. This was particularly true of felonies against property, constituting three-quarters of all juvenile convictions. Interestingly, this percentage corresponded almost exactly to the cases considered in our imperfect sample. As we have also seen, the sentences meted out by Juvenile Division of the Higher Regional Court were increasingly harsh after 1942, ranging from six months incarceration to six or seven years in an adolescent correctional facility with hard labor. What remains puzzling are the guidelines utilized by the justices in imposing sanctions. Fifty-four youngsters were found guilty of various acts of robbery and theft committed during blackouts. Of these, over half were sentenced to lengthy prison terms for "dishonoring the race" according to the Parasite Decree. In contrast, twenty-five others received stiff sentences according to Austrian law, most notably § 180 which explicitly required severe punishment for felonies committed at night. Insofar as differences can be discerned, it appears that gang members were more likely to be condemned as "national parasites," than as individual offenders. Investigative reports by social workers undoubtedly shaped decisions, for example, in the case of a machinist trainee who was sentenced to three months of hard labor but had not "subjectively" violated the Parasite Decree. In another case, two minors were considered too young to have "dishonored the race."

Also inconsistent and difficult to explain are the sentences imposed on youngsters for petty offences such as refusal to work or absenteeism. For the most part, the justices tended to sentence minors convicted of work-related offences to one or two weekend detentions, often against the insistence of Nazi shop stewards who demanded severe punishment. The fragmentary evidence suggests that careful attention was paid to the age and motivation of those who had walked off the job, seeking to return them to work after undergoing relatively mild educative punishment. It was also in the interest of the war economy to return these detainees to the shop floor as soon as possible. Here the evidence suggests that Austrian jurists may have been more pragmatic than those in the Old Reich. In Munich, for example, the judiciary paid little heed to ordinances introducing "indefinite imprisonment" or weekend detentions. According to a report filed by an official in the Ministry of Justice, magistrates in the Bavarian city considered the new measures far too lenient and mild. Throughout the war, they regularly imposed sanctions ranging from three months to one year in jail thus stigmatizing the juveniles as convicted felons.[94] And yet, Viennese judges could also be brutal, as in the case of Anton X., who was dispatched to Moringen.

Other example of inconsistencies appear in the records of those tried for moral offences. Because the authorities in Vienna considered homosexuality a major cause of juvenile criminal behavior, the sentences handed out could be draconian, particularly for minors convicted as gang members. At the same time, the age of the defendant and the nature of the sexual act appear to have been taken into consideration. Masturbation for those under 16, for example, normally warranted only a brief jail sentence. Similar inconsistencies appear in the handful of other cases examined in this study.

In many ways, both the pattern and treatment of juvenile delinquents between 1940 and 1944 in Vienna did not differ dramatically from that prior to the outbreak of Hitler's war. And yet while the Juvenile Division of the Higher Regional Court handed out much harsher sentences for serious crimes according to ordinances passed in between 1939 and 1942, the overall juvenile crime rate did *not* soar as it did in other cities of the Greater German Reich. In 1943, for example, the Reich Statistical Agency reported that teenage robberies and assaults had risen 40 percent during the first half of that year. In Vienna, however, the figures indicate a slight decline.[95] Judging from the numerous debates involving the police, psychiatrists, criminologists, jurists, party officials, Hitler Youth leaders, and members of the Interior Ministry, pressure mounted to resolve the differences between the Austrian and German juvenile codes. The result was the Reich Juvenile Court Law, a comprehensive measure, promulgated on November 6, 1943, that became law on January 1, 1944. As we shall see, the new juvenile code incorporated features of the Austrian criminal code such as the "personality principle" and "indefinite imprisonment." It also stipulated more precisely the conditions under which a juvenile offender could be tried as an adult based both on the number and types of crimes committed and careful scrutiny of the defendant's character.[96] Before examining the impact of the new law in Vienna, however, it is necessary to scrutinize case histories of those youngsters hauled before Hitler's tribunals for politically motivated acts of resistance including "radio crimes," subversion, high treason, and other offences undermining the morale or the martial spirit of the National Community.

3

Juveniles Tried by Hitler's Special Courts, 1940–1945

This chapter examines surviving files of young adults tried by Special Courts (*Sondergerichte*) in Vienna and Lower Danube between 1940 and 1945, nearly all of whom were under the age of 21. As these irregular benches had been established in Germany by the Nazi regime in 1933–1934, their enactment in Austria following the Anschluß constituted a major breach in the existing legal system. The Special Courts were to try those accused of crimes enumerated in the Reichstag Fire Decree, specifically the Decree to Protect the Government of the National Socialist Revolution from Treacherous Attacks proclaimed on March 21, 1933. This ordinance was followed in October by a measure to Guarantee Peace Based on Law, and in December 1934 by a Law Against Insidious Attacks upon the State and Party and the Party Uniform. Defendants brought before Special Courts faced a panel of three professional judges reassigned from district courts. They were represented by a court-appointed counsel, but not entitled to pretrial investigative evidence. Once convicted, the defendants had no right to appeal verdicts and were usually subjected to immediate punishment. Overall, judicial decisions made by Special Courts, rather like those in the Soviet Union, were expected to match the expectations of Hitler's regime. As an official in the Reich Ministry of Justice noted, "A member of the *Volk* does not expect judges to provide detailed and learned commentaries on the law, nor is he interested in the numerous minor points which they have taken into consideration in reaching their opinion. He would like to be told, in a few words, understandable to the general public, the decisive reason for his being right or wrong."[1]

With the outbreak of the Second World War, as we have already seen, the Ministry of Justice issued a so-called Simplification Decree, a measure designed to prevent a collapse on the home front. This meant streamlining legal proceedings and expanding the jurisdiction of Special Courts to prosecute radio crimes, acts of subversion (*Heimtücke*), "undermining military strength," asocial behavior, excessive violence, and "gangsterism." According to Roland Freisler, the Special Courts were to act as both the "armored troops of the legal profession" and the "courts martial of the domestic front." During the first years of the war, the judiciary panel of a Special Court usually assessed the evidence presented by the prosecution before deciding whether the case should be tried. But on August 13, 1942, an ordinance required the judges to accept the state prosecutor's indictment without question. In other words, the state prosecutor became both judge and jury.[2]

In November and December 1938, two decrees had established Special Courts in incorporated Austria. Between 1938 and 1945, Special Courts in Vienna and Lower Danube tried at least 14,500 cases of which 10,000 records have survived. Unlike members of the Senate of the dreaded People's Court (*Volksgerichtshof*), the judges and prosecutors of the Special Courts were professional jurists trained in Austrian law. Even so, they did not always follow established legal procedures, at times handing out capricious or summary verdicts. In Vienna and Lower Danube alone, the Special Courts handed out 565 death sentences during the period of Nazi rule. To what extent their decisions were shaped by ideology or the rule of law will be scrutinized in our study of the trials of youthful defendants.[3]

Exhaustive investigation of legal records elsewhere in Hitler's realm reveal that those remanded to Special Courts were charged with exceptionally severe crimes. Foremost among them were lawbreakers with extensive criminal records, gang members, persons apprehended for mail theft or looting, prostitutes, and foreign workers accused of "racial defilement," or misdemeanors involving food. Petty offences perceived as a threat to the National Community were often elevated to the status of capital crimes. Given these guidelines, relatively few juveniles were tried in Special Courts. In Cologne, judicial officials were even instructed to try "precocious juvenile criminals" in the Higher Regional Court.[4]

In Vienna, the number of youngsters tried by Special Courts between 1940 and 1945 was also comparatively small. Of ninety-one young adults known to be convicted by the tribunal, three-fifths were minors, ranging in age from 14 to 18 years. The average age of the adolescent offenders was 17.3, a figure almost identical to that of those convicted by the Juvenile Division of the Higher Regional Court between 1939 and 1944. Structurally, the kinds of crimes brought before the Special Courts differed noticeably from those adjudicated by the traditional courts, even though the largest number of sentences (48 percent) handed out continued to be for crimes against property. These included break-ins and thefts of bicycles, sporting goods, radios, gramophones, tobacco products, but also pilfering of sausage, butter, margarine, bread, fruits, vegetables, and other items in short supply such as shoe leather. There were also a number of juveniles sentenced to long terms for postal theft. As might be expected, roughly a fourth of those minors brought before the Special Courts were convicted of political offenses, particularly for subversion (*Heimtücke*), listening to foreign radio broadcasts, insulting the Führer or the party, undermining military strength, or fraternizing with prisoners of war. Another tenth were found guilty of sex crimes. The remaining individuals were convicted of forgery, murder, assault, vandalism, arson, or in one case, belonging to the Jehovah's Witnesses.

Because Hitler's Special Courts intended to identify "criminal types" and protect the National Community from the "enemy within," judges relied largely on biological-racial diagnoses, particularly in cases involving foreign defendants. Sentences handed out were thus exceptionally harsh. Four youngsters convicted of multiple thefts during blackouts, for example, were condemned to death as felons, "national parasites," and "precocious juvenile criminals." Fifteen others received sentences ranging from two and a half to eight years in prison, the longest for postal theft. Each and every one was also found guilty of violating the Parasite Decree and that of the Protection of Dangerous Criminals. Surprisingly, as we shall see, those convicted of political crimes were not as severely punished. Sentences usually ranged from four to fourteen months in a juvenile detention facility, as compared with the lengthy prison terms or death penalties meted out by the Higher Regional Court and the People's Court. On the other hand, youngsters indicted for sexual offences by Special Courts could expect little mercy. Five girls were sentenced to lengthy terms for sleeping with French prisoners of war; however, one 15-year-old mother was ordered to spend only eight months in a reformatory. Of the remaining offenders considered here, a 16-year-old girl was sentenced to two and a half years in prison for forging and marketing food coupons. A 17-year-old housemaid was condemned to death for arson as were two Polish farmworkers for murder and assault. All of those convicted were compelled to pay court costs as well as a heavy fine.

Magistrates of the Special Courts

Who were the judges who presided over the Special Court in Vienna? Thanks to the efforts of researchers in the Documentation Archives of the Austrian Resistance, information is available on eleven of the justices. Contrary to the findings of Ingo Müller, the judges assigned to the Special Court in Vienna and

Lower Danube were not youthful barristers educated in the Third Reich. Eight of judges were born between 1877 and 1895 with an average age (in 1940) of 50.5. Only two came into the world in the twentieth century: one in 1906 the other in 1907. Six of the magistrates had been affiliated with the Nazi movement either as "illegal" members prior to the Anschluß or as associates of Franz Langoth's Austrian Refugee's Society, an umbrella organization that had funneled money to Nazi sympathizers between 1934 and 1938. The other judges subsequently joined the NSDAP, though one not until 1940. The imposition of Special Courts in Hitler's homeland indisputably constituted a rupture in the Austrian legal system. Nevertheless, each and every one of the justices was a native Austrian, as the following brief biographical sketches reveal.

The oldest of the justices, Dr. Friedrich Frauenberger, had been born in November 1877 in Upper Austria. He was admitted to the bar in 1902, became a judge in 1908, and by 1934 had risen to become President of the Higher Regional Court in Linz. In that year, he was transferred to Vienna, where he served as a justice on the Higher Regional Court until retirement in April 1943. A veteran National Socialist, active since 1931, he continued his career as the party's district legal advisor until the collapse of the regime in 1945. Exactly when he served on the Special Court is not revealed in the surviving documentation.[5]

According to a commission of the postwar Austrian Ministry of Justice, the most ruthless members of the Special Courts in Vienna and its branch in St. Pölten were Alois Wotawa, Hans Watzek, Otto Hesch, and Georg Zednik.

Alois Wotawa was born in 1896 in Vienna and served in a mountain division of the Austro-Hungarian army during the Great War. After passing the bar examination in 1923, he rose through the prosecutorial ranks to become Chief Prosecutor of the Higher Regional Court on October 1, 1939. His Nazi superiors considered him "somewhat nervous," though exceptionally intelligent, well-educated, and adept in reaching politically sound judicial decisions. On May 28, 1940, he was appointed Chief Justice of the Special Court, a position he held until 1944 when the District Office of the NSDAP promoted him Vice President of the Higher Regional Court. As we shall see, Wotawa did not hesitate in sentencing minors to death.[6]

Hans Watzek, born in 1895, pursued a slightly different career trajectory. Admitted to the bar in 1921, he received a judicial appointment six years later. At the time of the Anschluß, he had been serving on the bench of the Viennese commercial court since 1935. In October 1938, he was transferred to the Higher Regional Court, where he was assigned to preside over cases coming before the Special Court. Called up in 1942, he served in the Wehrmacht until the end of the war. Thereafter, he resumed his duties in the criminal division of the Higher Regional Court, but on April 24, 1946 was dismissed by the Allies. Six months later, Austrian judicial officials affirmed the dismissal, noting that Watzek had been an "extremely harsh chief justice." Despite repeated appeals extending into the 1970s, he was never again permitted to practice law.[7]

Otto Hesch, though slightly older, belonged to the same age cohort. He too had risen through the judicial ranks to preside over criminal cases in the Higher Regional Court. On September 22, 1939, he was promoted to associate justice of the Special Court, a position he held until the Russian conquest of Vienna. On May 24, 1945, Soviet authorities placed him under arrest, tried him in Moscow, and sentenced him to twenty-five years in prison. Released in 1955, he returned to Vienna, where he was granted a modest pension.[8]

Georg Zednik, born in 1885, had entered the legal profession in 1910. He became a judge in 1917 and served in the district court at St. Pölten as an associate justice from 1931 until 1938. A member of the Fatherland Front Youth Organization (ÖJV; Österreichisches Jungvolk), he presided over the trial of defeated workers in the 1934 civil war, sentencing two of them to death. Zednik did not apply to join the NSDAP until some months after the Anschluß, though between 1939 and 1942 he was commissioned to serve as a criminal judge in the St. Pölten branch of the Special Court. During his tenure, he handed out twelve death sentences, though none for "political reasons." Arrested and tried after the war, he was found to have been "rude and cynical" in interrogating defendants and to have violated established judicial procedures. But as he had not been an "illegal" Nazi prior to Hitler's takeover, he was released and forced into early retirement.[9]

Of the other judges known to have presided over Special Court proceedings in Vienna and Lower Danube, all had been Nazi activists. The career trajectory of Hans Urbanek, in particular, may be considered both paradigmatic and representative of Austrian jurists in the twentieth century. Born in 1906 the son of a Privy Councilor, Urbanek had joined the Nazi Party as a student in 1924. He entered the legal profession in 1930 as judicial law clerk, becoming an official in a rural county court in Lower Austria. On April 15, 1938, he was appointed a criminal judge in Vienna. By that time, he had been active as an SA man, an official of the National Socialist League of Jurists, and a District Leader in Horn. Based on his judicial performance and distinguished Nazi career, he was assigned to the third bench of the Special Court in October 1943, a position he held until the collapse of the Third Reich. Disbarred in July 1946, Urbanek had already moved with his family to Krefeld in West Germany, where he remained until 1952. Allowed to reenter the Austrian legal profession, he returned home to become a legal clerk in Gmünd. After a "refresher course" and brief Stint in Schärding, the Federal Ministry of Justice (BJM; Bundesjustizministerium) appointed him to the criminal bench in Krems. Upon retirement in 1971, the erstwhile holder of Hitler's Golden Party Badge received the title Privy Councilor for his distinguished contributions to Austrian jurisprudence.[10]

Felonies Committed against Property

1. Austrian Juveniles

Between 1940 and 1945, no fewer than twenty-seven adolescents were handed over to Special Courts in Vienna, Krems, and St. Pölten for committing crimes of robbery and theft. Exactly why these minors were remanded to these tribunals instead of the Juvenile Division of the Higher Regional Court is not entirely clear; although Hitler's angry denunciation of the legal profession on April 26, 1942, surely accelerated the crackdown. Even so, the first known case of a juvenile to be tried by a Special Court took place on March 13, 1940, in Krems. On that date, a 17-year-old Reich German, Horst B., was found guilty of having broken into a tobacco shop after dark. As the owner, Johanna Mies, had not left for home, Horst hit her in the face before fleeing into the night. Because the defendant had violated both § 190 of the Austrian penal code for "using violence against a person in order to seize an object belonging to that person" as well as the Parasite Decree, Judge Lahajnar, a non-Nazi, sentenced Horst to a year in jail, a relatively mild penalty based on the existing law.[11]

Two months later, 15-year-old Alfred B. and 16-year-old Erwin W. faced Judge Alois Wotawa in the chambers of the Special Court, both charged with multiple break-ins and thefts. According to the diagnosis of a quasi-sympathetic social worker, Alfred had lived with his maternal grandmother following his parents' divorce at age 4. He had dropped out of school and become an apprentice for a book dealer. Although a member of the Hitler Youth, the report continued, he had little grasp of history, literature, or the principles of National Socialism. Further, he had become a fanatical moviegoer. Although lacking in intelligence, Alfred recognized the difference between right and wrong in wartime. His sense of ethics, however, was clearly deficient: "He counts as that sort of youngster who feels no sense or obligation to duty, but only the basic instincts of life."

Erwin was also the son of divorced parents, but had been reared by his mother, a trained physician. Like his codefendant, Erwin had dropped out of middle school, though had managed to transfer to an engineering training academy. According the court-appointed social worker, Erwin was physically mature, though of mediocre intelligence. He had no knowledge of Kant and could not even grasp the fundamental principles of energy. Owing to the professional demands of his mother, the social worker concluded, he too had no sense of duty, even though both boys were members of the Hitler Youth.

In the early months of 1940, Alfred and Erwin had joined another youngster, Otto S., in undertaking a number of daring nocturnal robberies. Using a motorcycle belonging to Erwin's mother, they had stolen a gramophone, radio, and various sporting goods. On Sunday, March 14, they proceeded to break into their own Hitler Youth quarters, where they trashed the furniture and made off with three BB pistols, an air rifle, and ink blotter, a letter box, and three HJ golden badges.

Unsurprisingly, Wotawa threw the book at the accused, convicting them of theft, grand larceny, and violation of the Parasite Decree. His opinion expressed a desire to impose long prison terms, but in accordance with the Austrian juvenile penal code, he sentenced Alfred to eighteen months in a juvenile correctional facility and Erwin to fifteen months. In each case, the convicted were to pay all court costs. According to surviving documentation, Erwin served eleven months and was thereafter conscripted into the Luftwaffe. On November 16, 1943, a Stuttgart military tribunal found him guilty of trafficking in morphine and imposed a penalty of six months in prison.[12]

During the first year of the war, three juveniles were convicted of postal theft. Considering the gravity of the offence, there was good reason that each would be remanded to a Special Court, as was usually the case in Cologne.[13] The most egregious case was that of Friedrich K., a 17-year-old postal worker in St. Pölten. Born and reared in nearby Spratzen, Friedrich had left school to work in Autobahn construction. Spending the winter of 1938–1939 fulfilling compulsory service in Wilhelmshafen, he returned home just before Christmas to work as a manual laborer for the Luftwaffe. In January 1940, he landed a job as a postal worker in St. Pölten. Available evidence reveals no record of deviant behavior in Friedrich's upbringing or background, but in April or May he began pilfering military parcels sent from soldiers stationed in Western Europe. Initially, Friedrich stole only small quantities of cigarettes, candy, and other sweets, but as the summer wore on he took bundles of grapes, apples, pears, and packages of chocolates. When apprehended on November 5, postal authorities and the police concluded he had stolen goods from no fewer than sixty parcels. Retribution was not long in coming. Five days later, Justice Zednik sentenced Friedrich to seven years in a penitentiary at hard labor. In his opinion, the judge found him guilty of breaching his oath of loyalty to the Führer, grand larceny, and violation of the Parasite Decree. Zednik acknowledged that Friedrich was under 18 years of age, but contended in keeping with Nazi biological diagnostics that his offence demonstrated "a particularly reprehensible, criminal disposition" that warranted harsh punishment as a "precocious juvenile criminal."[14]

Equally grim were the fates of 16-year-old Friedrich B. and 20-year-old Josef S. Both were indicted for stealing a great many cigarette packages from military parcels throughout 1940. After attempting to flee to the "Altreich," presumably to sell looted tobacco products on the black market, they were apprehended and tried by a Special Court in Krems. Friedrich claimed that he had been misled by the older Josef, but Justices Lahajnar and Christelbauer remained unpersuaded. Convicting both defendants of disloyalty, larceny, and "dishonoring the race" according to Parasite Decree, the judges sentenced each of them to five years in a juvenile jail[15] In a similar case, the Viennese Special Court condemned a 19-year-old butcher's assistant, Karl J., to spend one and a half years in prison at hard labor for stealing RM 700 in postal savings stamps. The judges acknowledged that Karl had committed the crime as a juvenile in 1941, but on March 11, 1942, sentenced him as an adult.[16]

Less severe was the penalty imposed several months later on another underage postal thief, Karl S. The son of a market supervisor, Karl had grown up in a modest family in Vienna. After completing eight years of schooling, he went to work for two years as a commercial apprentice. In May 1940, he was conscripted by the Reich Labor Service and spent six months on the Western Front. Discharged in October, he entered the postal service, took an oath of loyalty to Hitler, and became a mailman in the 15th District. Beginning in January 1941, he began pilfering cigarettes from military parcels. Unlike Friedrich K., he took little else, but when apprehended was nonetheless remanded to a Special Court. On March 31, Judge Hans Watzek sentenced Karl to fourteen months in prison at hard labor for abusing his governmental position as stipulated by § 101 of the Austrian penal code and for "dishonoring the race" according to § 4 of the Parasite Decree. Like Zednik, Watzek conceded that Karl had committed his crime as a minor, but possessed the "intellectual and moral maturity of an adult." Further, the reprehensible nature of the offence constituted a threat to "healthy national sentiment," thus warranting severe punishment. Josef's ultimate fate is unknown, but his record was effaced in 1946, suggesting he survived both imprisonment and the war.[17]

Much more fortunate was the fate of 16-year-old Franz W., a youngster who never should have been brought before a Special Court. The fact that he was tried in Krems suggests that it may have been easier to undertake legal proceedings in that town rather than transport him to the juvenile court in Vienna. Born illegitimate in Weiden, Franz was reared by a stepfather with four stepchildren. School authorities characterized him as "angry, impudent, and reluctant to work," although once apprenticed to an electrician his attitude seems to have improved. Further investigation revealed that Franz had been abused by a stepmother and was so impoverished that he could not make ends meet. On the evening of December 12, 1940, he stole a bundle of clothes from an attic of the local hospital. Soon apprehended, Franz was indicted for larceny and "dishonoring the race" as a "national parasite." Three months later he stood before the judges of the Special Court, who had carefully reviewed the reports of court-appointed social workers. On February 20, 1940, Justices Lahajnar and Christelbauer ruled that Franz was too immature to be tried as an adult or convicted as a "precocious juvenile criminal." Instead, they considered him worthy of "improvement," sentencing him to fourteen days in detention, to be followed by three months on probation. This appears to have been a wise decision. Franz survived the war and in 1950 had his criminal record expunged.[18]

Following Hitler's angry speech of April 26, 1942, as we have seen, juveniles convicted of property crimes faced longer prison terms than in the past. And those brought before a Special Court could expect little mercy, particularly those with a criminal record such as 16-year-old Josef F. In December 1941, he had been sentenced to five months of detention for having stolen roughly RM 1,000 in various shops and guest houses in Carinthia and Styria. Upon completing his sentence, he was assigned a position as manual laborer in a porcelain plant in Simmering. At the end of June, Josef and another youngster, Karl P., broke into a barracks where they made off with 30 kilograms of chocolate, margarine, and buttered lard. The following day they fenced their loot on the black market for RM 160. Two weeks later, the boys hooked up with 24-year-old Karl J. to begin a spree of nocturnal robberies from Viennese bakeries, tobacco shops, workers' billets, small industrial firms, clothing warehouses, and even garden allotments. Their loot consisted of cigarettes, tobacco, foodstuffs, wearing apparel, driving belts, leather goods, as well as six rabbits and two chickens, amounting to thousands of marks on the black market. Not until September 1, 1942, were they apprehended by the police.

Held in custody throughout the winter, the delinquents were tried on March 26, 1943, in a Special Court. Based on extensive investigation and overwhelming evidence, the justices found the defendants guilty of grand larceny according to §§ 171, 173, and 174 of the Austrian penal code and culpable of violating § 176 as habitual thieves. Each was also convicted of "dishonoring the race" as national parasites. The justices sentenced Karl P. to four years in confinement as an accessory and the older Karl J. to six years in prison as a "national parasite and dangerous habitual criminal." As for Josef F., the judges concluded that he should be "eliminated" altogether from the National Community. They conceded that Josef F. was only 16 years old, but as a ringleader with a criminal record he possessed the intellectual and mental maturity of an adult. The court then proceeded to condemn him to death as a "national parasite, hardened offender, and dangerous habitual criminal."[19]

One month later, eleven individuals were ordered tried by the Special Court for a series of robberies and thefts committed during the first half of 1942. Of these, seven were teenagers who belonged to what appears to have been a larger group that included adult gangsters. According to a thick but incomplete file, the members were unskilled workers or apprentices who operated as teams. The ringleaders were Franz K., a construction worker, and his 17-year old son Karl. On April 10, 1942, father and son had stolen 15 kilograms of ersatz coffee from a warehouse. In the weeks that followed, they and their accomplices proceeded to break into coffee houses, tobacco shops, warehouses, and various stores, making off with substantial amounts of coffee, butter, margarine, an automobile radio, ninety-four pairs of gloves, twenty pairs of underwear, bolts of fabric, ration coupons, and over 8,000 cigars and cigarettes worth thousands of marks on the black market. While a transcript of the legal proceedings of July 17, 1942, has not survived, court records reveal the verdicts and sentences handed down by the Special Court on that day. Each and every one of the defendants was found guilty of grand larceny according to §§ 171–9 of the Austrian penal code. They were also convicted of "dishonoring the race" as both national parasites and dangerous habitual criminals. Both Franz and his 17-year-old son Karl were condemned to death. One of the youngsters, 17-year-old Franz B., was sentenced to six years in a juvenile correctional facility at hard labor as Karl's principal accomplice; the others were sentenced to terms ranging from six months to several years' incarceration. Four of the adults, including a 30-year-old woman, received long prison sentences, while a bystander was acquitted. Six weeks later, the Reich Ministry of Justice rejected clemency appeals, ordering the immediate execution of Franz K. and Karl to be carried out in secret. At 6:32 p.m. October 8, 1943, both father and son went to the guillotine.[20]

One of the last-known nonforeign adolescents to be tried by a Special Court in Vienna was a 17-year-old Reich German, Ewald R. Born in 1925 in Hamburg to an impoverished family with six siblings, he had moved by way of Berlin to Vienna in December 1942. Arriving virtually penniless in the Northern Train Station, he had stolen a clothing bag from a soldier who had left it on a bench while in the washroom. Ewald then moved to the Eastern Depot, where he fenced the contents, beginning a career of petty theft on railroad platforms and other public places such as the Prater until apprehended in early May. After thorough investigation by police and social workers, he was brought to bench in a Special Court. Here on July 21, 1943, Judge Wotawa found Ewald guilty of multiple offences that included theft, embezzlement, forgery, and behavior "contrary to nature" with a member of the naval shore patrol. According to Austrian law, the Ordinance for the Protection of Dangerous Juvenile, and the Parasite Decree, Wotawa sentenced him to seven years in strict confinement as a dangerous habitual criminal.[21]

In one unusual case, a minor was tried and convicted twice by a Viennese Special Court, both times for stealing and trafficking in ration coupons. During the winter of 1941–1942, 17-year-old Gerhard S. had sought to purchase a phonograph console from Dr. Albert B., a prosperous real estate agent and property manager, who had once practiced law and belonged to the SS. Unlike most juvenile offenders, Gerhard grew up in a middle-class family, the son of the owner of a printing establishment. He was employed by his father, though received a payment allowance of only RM 7 weekly. Without sufficient cash to pay for the console, Gerhard persuaded two other boys to join him in purloining ration coupons from his parents and another print shop that produced them for the government. According to court records, Dr. B. was not only willing to accept the coupons as payment for the phonograph player, but encouraged the boys to pilfer additional meat and tobacco stamps to sell on the black market.

On August 16, 1942, the Special Court found Dr. B., Gerhard, and two other boys guilty of violating the War Economy Ordinance of September 1, 1939. The judges sentenced Dr. B. to five years in prison at hard labor, young Gerhard to one and a half years in juvenile confinement, and his two accomplices to three months. Three months later, however, Gerhard was called up and sent to the Eastern Front. Here he served until September 1943, when he fell ill and was transferred to a military hospital in Preßbaum outside Vienna. Allowed to come and go on furlough, he met a longtime friend in Vienna, who possessed keys to an official printing house. During the night of February 7–8, 1944, the two stole into the office building, making off with over sixty sheets of food and tobacco ration stamps. Caught almost on the spot, the two were convicted by a Special Court on April 5, 1944. Gerhard was sentenced to three years in prison at hard labor, and his accomplice to two years. Exactly how much time Gerhard spent behind bars is unclear, although on October 15, 1948, the Higher Regional Court ruled that both felons had completed their sentences.[22]

2. Foreign Juveniles

On December 4, 1941, a Council of Ministers in Berlin had issued a "Decree on Criminal Justice Regarding Poles and Jews in Incorporated Eastern Territories." The ordinance made Poles living in annexed or occupied territories subject to German law, stipulating that those committing offences injurious to "German prestige" should be tried by Special Courts and if found guilty sentenced to death. As more than 100,000 Polish prisoners of war and civilian workers had been employed since 1940 as laborers in the "Ostmark," the law applied to them as well. Exactly how many Poles and other foreign workers were brought before Hitler's irregular tribunals in Vienna and Lower Danube has not been calculated, but the surviving records of juvenile cases indicates that no fewer than twenty individuals found themselves subject to such legal proceedings. Of these, a Belgian and seven adolescent Poles were convicted of crimes against property.

Léon Bourgeois, born in Mons, was the son of an electrician. Only 15 years old upon Belgium's capitulation to Nazi Germany in 1940, he was subsequently inspired to join Léon De Grelle Rexist movement, hoping to fight on the Eastern Front as a member of the 28th SS Walloon Division. Although too young to enlist, Léon volunteered to work in the German Reich. In September 1942, he landed a position as a mechanic apprentice in Wiener Neustadt, where he also served as a translator. He then moved on to a light metal plant in Ennesdorf, where he fell ill and received word that he was unfit to serve in the armed forces. Depressed and dissatisfied with his job, in March and April 1943 Léon began stealing cash, photographs, and ration cards from locker rooms, kitchens, and purses. He also acquired a HJ uniform, which he wore with an Iron Cross First Class claiming that he had been wounded in Russia. On November 11, 1943, the Special Court convicted this confused youngster of theft and impersonation. The justices concurred that the normal penalty for such criminal behavior should be six months to a year at hard labor, but taking into account his age and dedication to the principles of National Socialism, they sentenced him to spend ten months in juvenile confinement. According to an orange document in his file, Léon was released from Kaiser-Ebersdorf on March 13, 1944, but handed over to the Gestapo in Wiener Neustadt.[23]

The ultimate fate of Léon Bourgeois is unknown. That of four Polish and Ukrainian workers is not. In July 1944, they broke into a canteen in Wiener Neustadt stealing shoe leather to repair their worn-out soles. Arrested by the Gestapo, the four boys were sentenced to death by the Special Court on August 11 and executed shortly thereafter. Three years earlier, a 17-year-old Czech agricultural worker, Paul G., had severely beaten a middle-aged farm wife after stealing RM 420 from her home. A Special Court in Znaim proceeded to find him guilty as a "precocious juvenile criminal" and sentenced him to fifteen years at hard labor. However, the Supreme Court in Leipzig intervened to overrule the decision, demanding that Paul be retried as an adult habitual criminal. On May 5, 1942, the Special Court complied by condemning him to death. Paul avoided the executioner by dying of tuberculosis four weeks later.[24]

Political Offences

By 1942, some seventy-four Special Courts had been established in Greater Germany. Their remit was wide-ranging, as legal scholars have emphasized. But in 1940 the Ministry of Justice urged the justices to root out political enemies of the state, asocial groups, vicious outsiders, and economic and social parasites.[25] As we have just seen, the Special Courts in Vienna and Lower Danube followed this directive by severely punishing juveniles found guilty of crimes against property. Strange as it may seem, those youngsters convicted for subversion were treated with relative leniency.[26] The most famous group of adolescents and young people tried by the Viennese Special Court were members of Friedrich Theiss's Austrian Movement. On December 17, 1941, as previously discussed, the Special Court convicted Theiss and fifteen members for violating the Law Against the Formation of New Parties, but handed out relatively mild sentences ranging from four weeks of jail to two years of confinement at hard labor.[27]

The first known minor tried by a Special Court in Lower Danube for subversion was Franz R., a 15-year-old farm boy. The son of a deeply religious family, he had joined a Catholic youth movement in late 1937, choosing not to enroll in the Hitler Youth after the Anschluß. Like the future Christian martyr Franz Jägerstätter, young Franz had only a rudimentary education, but appears to have been intelligent and well informed. On September 13, 1939, he had spent the day harvesting grain in a field near Kirchberg. Over supper, during which he gulped down considerable quantities of hard cider, he shocked nearly two dozen diners by speaking out against German atrocities in Poland. He claimed that soldiers were torturing Polish children in accordance with Hitler's orders. He continued by passing on several anti-Nazi jokes, sardonically concluding that while the Führer claimed to have helped Austrians to their feet he had actually seized them by their throats.

Three days later, Franz was taken into custody, jailed, and on January 4, 1940, tried before a Special Court in St. Pölten. Allowed to speak in his own defense, he claimed no recollection of his remarks in what had been a drunken stupor. Justice Zednik expressed a degree of sympathy for the defendant. He expressed the view that Franz had confused German with Polish atrocities and that however "hateful and incendiary," his wisecracks constituted no threat to the German people. Zednik and his associates proceeded to convict Franz of subversion, but taking his age into account sentenced him to four months in a juvenile detention facility with time off for time served.[28]

Three other adolescents convicted of subversion by Special Courts also received relatively lenient treatment. On November 22, 1940, a 17-year-old market trader, Siegfried V., was ushered into Judge Lahajnar's judicial chambers in Krems. Accused by the Kreisleiter of passing on anti-Nazi jokes, insulting the Führer, and making defeatist remarks, the court found Siegfried guilty of violating the Subversion Law. However, the judges took into account his age and the fact that his remarks had been made only to individuals, thus sentencing him to six months in juvenile jail instead of imposing a lengthy prison sentence. Happily, Siegfried survived the Third Reich to have his record expunged in 1949.[29]

The second case involved a 17-year-old motor mechanic, Adolf P., employed in the Messerschmitt plant in Wiener Neustadt. During the summer of 1940, Adolf made no secret of his hostility to the Nazi regime. In numerous conversations with coworkers on the shop floor, he questioned the war effort, argued that Britain would hold out against Germany, and predicted that the Soviet Union would soon enter the conflict. He also denounced party bosses, refused to listen to Hitler speeches, and startled a female colleague, by exclaiming that the Führer could kiss his ass. On April 26, 1941, the Special Court in Vienna convicted Adolf of subversion, sentencing him to three months in juvenile confinement. Like Franz R., Adolf survived the war, managing to have his record effaced, although not until 1958.[30]

The third juvenile receiving a relatively mild sentence—though more severe than what others had received—was a 17-year-old Belgian student,

Hermann G. He was a Flemish National Socialist, who had volunteered to work for the German Reich. In May 1941, Hermann was stationed in a training camp of the German Labor Front when news arrived of Rudolf Hess's bizarre flight to England. According to a Gestapo report, Hermann had burst into his dormitory room claiming that Hess had been shot as a British spy, but that a "swine" like Hitler still remained among the living. When brought before Judge Wotawa, Hermann found himself charged with questioning the veracity of the German news service and insulting the Führer. In the course of six hours of testimony and cross-examination, Hermann denied he had affronted Hitler, but was nevertheless found guilty of violating § 2 of the Subversion Law. Wotawa clearly wished to impose a heavy prison term. But he took into account Hermann's age and political views, sentencing him to ten months in Kaiser-Ebersdorf.[31]

Given the fact that Special Courts frequently sentenced adults to prison or even death for trivial violations of the Subversion Law, age appears to have played a role in decisions to mete out comparatively mild sentences to juveniles.[32] Equally significant may have been the fact that the offences were committed by individuals rather than organized political groups perceived as endangering the "enemy within." On November 15, 1943, for example, a 17-year-old Czech farm laborer, Kvetoslava D., was brought before the Special Court in Vienna. He had quarreled with his parents in early June, deciding to slip over the border from nearby Cejkove in the "Protectorate" to take a job as a farmhand in Lower Danube. He seems to have enjoyed his work, but made no secret of his Czech patriotism, freely speaking out that Germany was doomed to lose the war and belting out Czech songs. In reaching judgment, Justice Otto Hesch convicted young Kvetoslava of illegal border-crossing and violation of the Subversion Law. But following the Austrian penal code, he took into account his integrity and age to pronounce a sentence of ten months in juvenile detention[33]

That same month another 17-year-old, Friedrich W., was convicted of violating both paragraphs of the Radio Ordinance of September 1, 1939. Like so many juveniles arrested by the Gestapo, Friedrich grew up in a deprived working-class family. He had done poorly in school, having to repeat a grade before dropping out altogether. But he had completed his year of compulsory service as an agricultural worker and thereafter taken a steady job as a manual laborer. According to the court transcript, in November 1942 Friedrich had listened to a BBC radio broadcast reporting the fate of 80,000 German troops surrounded in Stalingrad. Worse, he had spread this news to his coworkers. When brought before the Viennese Special Court on November 19, 1943, Friedrich had been in protective custody since April. Over the summer, he had suffered from a severe lung infection, and appeared pale and weak. Justice Dölz cryptically noted Friedrich's dull and "mentally awkward" temperament and suggested that he had not fully understood the confession he had made to the authorities. With that in mind, Dölz found Friedrich guilty as charged, sentenced him to a month in Kaiser-Ebersdorf, but allowed him to walk out of the courtroom on the basis of time served. In 1948, Friedrich's "criminal record" was effaced.[34]

In several other cases, even toward the end of the war, Special Courts continued to hand out relatively mild sentences to adolescents accused of subversion. In one instance, the judges even acquitted a 17-year-old boy who bore the stigma of "Mischling of the First Degree." On April 26, 1943, Friedrich K. had rudely elbowed his way past a baby carriage clamoring aboard a crowded trolley at the Westbahnhof. As the mother made her way to the back of the tram, an indignant officer's wife chastised Friedrich to his face. He responded with a brash remark about "oafs wearing two-star shoulder boards." This, in turn, led to a charge that Friedrich had insulted the uniform of the Führer, which caused Captain Julius Gregor to file charges with the Gestapo. Two months later, Friedrich found himself before the judges of a Special Court. Based largely on reports and testimony on Friedrich's outstanding record in the Hitler Youth, the court reprimanded him for offending Captain Gregor, but cleared him of all charges of subversion.[35] Toward the very end of the war, on November 12, 1944, the Special Court in Vienna tried a 17-year-old manual worker, Friedrich R. for failing to register for the draft on his sixteenth birthday. Social workers reported that Friedrich had been confined for theft in a corrective facility between November 1941 and April 1943 and upon release worked briefly on a farm and later in a Krupp plant. Because the boy then volunteered to serve in the SS, the judges imposed what they considered to be a mild sentence of ten months behind bars. Friedrich appears to have walked free in July 1945 and had his record effaced four years later.[36]

Surprisingly, Hitler's justices also tended to impose comparatively mild penalties on adolescent foreign workers charged with subversion, most likely because their labor was considered essential to the war effort. These included a 17-year-old French factory worker, sentenced to one-year confinement for spitting on a picture of the Führer and a Polish farmhand for expressing hostility to the German people. The latter was also sentenced to a year in jail, but soon released to return to work. Two other Polish farmworkers were tried for writing subversive letters to relatives, but ordered to be confined for only four weeks. One of them, Josef H., was let go at the request of a dairy farmer in order to assist his wife in meeting the required milk quota. Four months of incarceration was also the sentence imposed on a Slovakian seasonal worker who in 1941 had quipped that Hitler had been wounded and lay dying. On the other hand, a 17-year-old Czech machinist trainee was condemned to spend thirteen months in jail for listening to a foreign radio broadcast, even though his offence had been committed early in the war.[37]

Sexual Offences

Much has been written about teenage sexuality in the Third Reich, not least about the regime's unease with promiscuity and its obsession with ferreting out, deprogramming, or eliminating homosexuality. As mentioned above, roughly one-tenth of those youngsters prosecuted by Special Courts in Vienna between 1940 and 1944 were found guilty of moral offences, a figure slightly above the official percentages that ranged between 5.1 and 8.3 percent. Without exception those convicted were teenage girls who had been caught in sexual liaisons with foreigners. While the record is by no means complete, this suggests that the more serious infractions of juvenile "crimes contrary to nature" or "racial defilement" (*Rassenschande*) were tried by separate divisions of the Higher Regional Court.[38] Of course, it should not be forgotten that in 1940 Himmler had ordered the instantaneous punishment of Germans caught in intimate relations with Polish prisoners of war or workers, a command that had led to a rash of lynch justice throughout the "Ostmark." However, popular outrage at the sight of Nazi thugs sadistically pillorying adulterous housewives or farm girls was so intense that in late 1941 Hitler himself intervened to order an end to such barbaric practices. The directive did not apply to Polish paramours, who were usually lynched on the spot.[39]

Those teenage girls brought before the Special Court in Vienna for sexual liaisons with foreigners usually received exceptionally harsh treatment. On July 20, 1942, the Gestapo arrested Elfriede K. for a romantic affair with a French prisoner of war. Elfriede came from a middle-class family. She had completed her secondary education at age 16, excelled in French, and performed eight months of compulsory farm work near Ried. At age 17 she took a job as a stenographer in the Schrack and Ericsson telephone company in Vienna. Shortly thereafter, she fell in love with a French prisoner of war. At first the two exchanged letters in French, but in mid-May, 1942 the couple had sex in a meadow. After prurient interrogation and scrutiny of her correspondence, the court on November 13, 1942 convicted Elfriede of undermining the military strength of the German people.⁴⁰ The justices sentenced her to eight months in jail detention, denying her an appeal for clemency by her parents on New Year's Eve.⁴¹

Two years later, the penalties imposed on teenage girls apprehended for sexual relationships with foreigners had become more severe. On May 5, 1944, a servant girl, Maria E., and a housekeeper, Maria B., were ushered into the chambers of the Special Court. Both had been arrested in January for having slept with French prisoners of war. The older, Maria E., admitted to multiple affairs but put up an odd defense that she had retained her Aryan virginity by engaging only in fellatio. Judge Dölz was not impressed; he sentenced Maria to three years in a juvenile facility at hard labor. Maria B. was more fortunate. As she was already pregnant, the court sentenced her to one year and three months in a reformatory. On December 13, 1949, both records were effaced.⁴² Equally harsh were the sentences imposed on two lowly working girls, Josefine Z. and Margarete H. Although pregnant, the former was condemned to two years in confinement, while the latter to one and half years behind bars. In 1948, both "criminal records" were also expunged.⁴³

Violence and Assault Felonies

Comparatively few youngsters under the age of 18 were convicted by Special Courts in Vienna and Lower Danube for crimes of violence or felonious assault. Most juveniles accused of attempted murder or muggings appear to have been tried by the Juvenile Division of the Higher Regional Court. Surviving records reveal one dramatic exception. Shortly after midnight on January 8, 1944, three youngsters incarcerated in Kaiser-Ebersdorf overpowered their guards and in the course of a bloody struggle severely wounded two of them. After rushing through the cell block and down two flights of stairs, 16-year-old Franz K. was captured, but 18-year-old Karl P. and 17-year-old Alfred K. escaped into the night. The two boys made it to the Danubian Canal, clad only in their underwear. Here they ducked into a coal cellar to keep warm. The following morning, Alfred and Karl persuaded a young maid to provide them with some larded bread as well as hand-me-down clothing and shoes to make it back to what they claimed was an athletic club. From there they proceeded to the home of a housekeeper acquaintance, Erika O., who provided them with winter coats and agreed to help them make their way to her grandmother in Wiener Neustadt. On the night of the January 10, however, all three were arrested and placed in protective custody.

Exhaustive investigation by court-appointed social workers revealed that the three boys came from broken or dysfunctional homes. Franz had been living with an abusive stepmother while his father was serving in the Wehrmacht. Following an altercation with teenage girls, he had been incarcerated in Kaiser-Ebersdorf, where he came under the malignant influence of both Karl and Alfred. Arguing that Franz was confused, at times suicidal, and victimized by a "wicked stepmother," the social worker concluded that he was too immature to be condemned as a habitual criminal despite a "demonstrable deformity of character." This was not the official assessment of Karl's background. Instead, the social worker emphasized a long record of criminal behavior, concluding that, although underage, Karl was "predestined" to lead a life of crime. The same official indicated that Alfred, who had been jailed for petty theft, was too immature to be judged a habitual criminal and could with time be made to recognize the errors of his ways.

On July 12, 1944, the Special Court found both Karl and Alfred guilty of mutiny and theft, sentencing each to eight years of imprisonment as "precocious juvenile criminals." Six months later the Fourth Senate of the Reich Supreme Court intervened to overturn the convictions as too lenient. Hitler's justices ruled that the evidence presented in court demonstrated that while both Karl and Alfred were underage, they should have been condemned as "serious dangerous criminals" and "national parasites" owing to their "loathsome personalities and deeds" as well as the professional assessments of social workers. Karl, in particular, had a lengthy record of previous convictions for theft and indecency that had been overlooked or discounted by the Viennese Special Court. As for Alfred, the justices considered him "sophisticated," but also "violent, devious, and repugnant with no sense of honor." On February 5, 1945, the Reich Supreme Court sentenced Karl to death and branded Alfred a "national parasite." The ultimate fate of the two juveniles is unknown.[44]

Other adolescents known to have been convicted by Special Courts in Vienna and Lower Danube for violent crimes or vandalism appear to have been Polish farmhands working in Lower Danube. One of the first to be tried was 16-year-old Jan W. In August 1940, he had been forced to work for Johann B. on a family farm north of Klosterneuburg. From the outset, Johann considered Jan "uncooperative and negligent," while Jan resented what amounted to unrequited servitude. On January 22, 1941, Jan simply refused to work unless paid for his labor. Johann and his wife proceeded to lock Jan in a stable, after which Jan threatened them with a pitchfork. As a consequence, on September 12 a Special

Court convicted Jan for subversion, sentencing him to three years in harsh confinement.[45] Two months later, 17-year-old Eduard S. was sentenced to three years in a penal camp for having punched a dairy farmer in a drunken stupor on a Sunday afternoon.[46] In contrast, a Special Court in St. Pölten extended remarkable leniency to a Polish farm girl, who had deliberately urinated on several bushels of harvested grain. The justices found her guilty of malicious destruction of property, but sentenced her to a mere three weeks of detention.[47]

A much grimmer fate awaited 17-year-old Jan B., tried on January 30, 1943, for having beaten to death a Ukrainian electrician near Waidhofen. Interrogation of coworkers and testimony by one Anna K. revealed that he been frequently chastised for stealing bread and milk and was known to be generally uncooperative. On September 10, 1943, Justice Wotawa showed no hesitation sentencing Jan to death as an adult "habitual criminal."[48] In a different case, a 17-year-old Pole was brought to book for threatening behavior. In late January 1943, Tadeusz Z. was cleaning out a cowshed with Mariana R., presumably a native farm woman. When asked why Mariana's pitchfork was broken, Tadeusz snatched it from her hands and hurled a feed basket in her face. Mariana reported the incident immediately to the local constable, who took him into custody. On May 22, 1943, the Special Court convicted Tadeusz of violating the Decree on Criminal Justice Regarding Poles and Jews. The judge stressed that he was a "disgustingly insolent Pole," who made a point of calling local girls whores. With these words, he sentenced him to eight months in a penal camp.[49] As the war drew toward a conclusion, sentences imposed by Special Courts and military tribunals became more draconian. Josefa G., an illiterate Polish peasant, had been dispatched to work in Vienna in 1941. Only 15 years old at the time, she had been assigned to a metal factory but then became a domestic for an innkeeper. In September 1944, a fire broke out in a storage barn that took the lives of two cows, two calves, three goats, and thirty rabbits. The flames also destroyed three automobiles, a small truck, and 25,000 kilograms of straw. Accused of arson, Josefa was tried by a Special Court on March 1, 1945. The judges found her guilty of arson and according to § 167 sentenced her to death.[50]

Conclusions

What conclusions can be drawn about those juveniles convicted by Special Courts in Vienna and Lower Danube between 1940 and 1945? First, and obviously, the penalties imposed tended to be much more severe than those sentenced by the

Juvenile Division of the Higher Regional Court, particularly for crimes against property. Of those found guilty of break-ins and theft, nine were sentenced to six months in a reformatory or six to eight years in jail, seven to hard labor in a penitentiary for terms ranging from two to eight years, and at least five to death. As we have seen, the harshest sentences were handed down as part of the regime's crackdown following Hitler's Reichstag address of April 26, 1942. This was also true of six girls convicted of sexual affairs with prisoners of war. While a highly educated stenographer received a sentence of eight months in jail, a housekeeper in Haag was condemned to five years in prison for engaging in "disgusting acts" with twenty French prisoners of war; three others were condemned to two to three years in penitentiary, and one to fifteen months in a juvenile jail. Oddly, those few youngsters brought to book for subversive remarks or gestures were let off lightly, including a "Mischling of the First Degree" who was acquitted on charges of insulting the Führer.

In one important respect, the social profile of those minors known to have been convicted by Special Courts in Vienna and Lower Danube differed notably from those tried by the Juvenile Division of the Higher Regional Court. Whereas most of the youngsters brought before juvenile judges tended to have been apprentices or trainees from impoverished or dysfunctional families, those facing the justices of Special Courts came from more divergent backgrounds. Excluding the sixteen well-educated members of the Austrian Movement who were tried and sentenced as young adults, the most numerous underage perpetrators were Polish or Ukrainian agricultural laborers; they constituted 22 percent of the total. Another fifth were Austrian manual workers while only 16 percent were journeymen or trainees. As for the rest, nearly 15 percent were skilled workers or factory hands. Numerically, the other juvenile perpetrators consisted of five postal clerks, six housekeepers, three students, and a salesgirl. The rest appear to have been either drifters or unemployed.

Exactly why the juveniles examined in this sample were consigned to be tried by Special Courts is not altogether clear. That members of the Austrian Movement or Polish workers should have been be brought before Hitler's irregular tribunals corresponded to Nazi jurisprudence, in the first instance for breaking the Law Against the Formation of New Parties, in the second for violating the Polish decree of December 1941. What remains difficult to understand is why some youngsters were brought to book for property crimes in Special Courts prior to 1943 rather than in the Juvenile Division of the Higher Regional Court. As suggested above, locality may have played a role in that arraigning youthful perpetrators in St. Pölten or Krems was certainly easier than transporting them to the Gray House in Vienna. Another explanation may be that some juveniles had been involved in felonies committed by adults, such as Kurt K. who belonged to a gang of thieves run by his father Franz or Gerhard S. who fenced ration coupons for Dr. Albert B. While the reasons for trying minors in different judicial venues requires further investigation, that of formulating a comprehensive juvenile criminal code for the Greater German Reich has been thoroughly explored. That story and the impact of its introduction on January 1, 1944, in Vienna constitutes the substance of a subsequent chapter.

4

Juvenile Political Crimes, 1940–1944

During the Second World War, the Viennese Gestapo arrested no fewer than 293 minors for politically conscious acts of defiance. Of these, 13 percent were girls or young women. Roughly 40 percent of the youthful militants belonged to the KJV, to other cells of the KPÖ, or to small groups of Revolutionary Socialists. Approximately 13 percent belonged to Catholic conservative or legitimist movements; 2 percent were Jehovah's Witnesses. The remaining, surprisingly large number of individual adolescents picked up for defying Nazi rule acted for a variety of reasons. These ranged from moral or religious opposition to concern for persecuted friends, or in a number of cases to resentment of totalitarian demands at the workplace or intrusions into everyday life. Although difficult to generalize, the archival evidence scrutinized for this study reveals that a great many, indeed a majority, appear to have been motivated by a sense of Austrian patriotism. The remaining 148 individuals were arrested for "Jewish-related" offences, homosexuality, illicit intercourse, walking off their jobs, or other transgressions criminalized by the Gestapo. Their cases will be considered at the end of this chapter.

Once arraigned, political militants, including minors, were remanded to the office of the Viennese state prosecutor. The magistrates then examined the charges and assigned each case to one of the three courts of law. According to the findings of Ursula Schwarz, most of the 4,163 persons tried by the Higher Regional Court usually received prison sentences, although fifteen were condemned to death while 10 percent were acquitted. How many of these were minors is unknown. Those charged with more serious political offences were consigned to Special Courts, whose remit, as we have seen, covered such transgressions as insulting the party and its uniform, listening to foreign radio broadcasts, subversion, undermining the war effort, and "gangsterism." As we have already seen, these guidelines were followed haphazardly in Vienna, since most of the minors convicted in Special Courts were found guilty of aggravated assault, grand larceny, and arson. A much smaller number were punished for politically motivated crimes. Finally, those accused of state treason, high treason, espionage, attempted treason, or undermining the war effort were brought before Hitler's dreaded revolutionary tribunal, the VGH. Between 1939 and 1945, some 2,137 Austrians were tried by the VGH in Vienna of whom 814 were sentenced to death and 451 executed. Although exact figures have yet to be tabulated, a substantial number of adolescent militants were convicted by the tribunal, of whom ten received the death penalty.[1] And because those indicted spent three to five months in protective custody, or in some cases a year or longer, an unknown number of minors may have been tried as adults once they reached adulthood.

Prior to the outbreak of Hitler's war, the vast majority of juvenile militants arrested by the Gestapo were members of the Communist Youth. The youngsters engaged in penetrating the ranks of the Hitler Youth, the League of German Girls, and various sporting associations; they also distributed fly sheets and other duplicated materials. Because they had been largely unknown to the police, it was not until 1939 that thirty-two of them fell prey to the security organs. In August 1939, the signing of the Hitler-Stalin Pact followed by the Nazi-Soviet conquest and division of Poland threw the KPÖ into great confusion. Unlike their comrades in other European countries and the United States, however, the Communists in incorporated Austria continued to post anti-Nazi graffiti, distribute leaflets, and agitate in factories.[2] In early October, for example, the Gestapo picked up 16-year-old Erna W. for possessing thirty-four copies of the *Austrian Communist Newsletter*. In blistering prose, the pamphlet condemned Hitler's order as a criminal enterprise, decried mass murders reported by Austrian soldiers in Poland, and implored Catholics, Communists, and Socialists to join the Austrian people in an uprising for independence. After a year in custody, Erna was sentenced by the Higher Regional Court to one year and four months behind bars.[3] Whether she was later released or consigned to a concentration camp is unknown. In November and December 1939, the Gestapo broke up a student group in Starnersdorf that included two boys, ages 16 and 17, wearing red arm bands marked with hammers and sickles. Several days later, 14-year-old Kurt B. was arrested in Alten for shouting "We are and remain Communists! Hail Moscow! The Illegals (Austrian Nazis) are absolute scoundrels!" Just before Christmas, the police arrested two Hitler Youth members in Lillienfeld for tearing down Hitler's portrait in a pub with the words "Hail Moscow! Down with Hitler!"[4]

Throughout the early months of 1940, the Security Police continued to apprehend youthful Communists, most of whom had belonged to the KJV and been active prior to the war. On February 23, for example, a house search led to the arrest in the 3rd District of 18-year-old Franz X., who in June 1939 had typed fly sheets appealing to youngsters to dodge conscription into the Wehrmacht. Other minors appear to have resisted spontaneously as "lone wolves." In late June 1940, two 16-year-old maids tore down a Führer poster in the Juchgasse youth center, also in the 3rd District, replacing it with a handwoven hammer and sickle, inscribed "Hail Moscow."[5] These and other arrests notwithstanding, the combination of Gestapo terror and fissures within the KPÖ had led to a decline in clandestine activities. Indeed, as the foremost authorities on the Austrian Resistance concur, the first six months of 1940 represented a "nadir" both in Communist agitation and arrests.[6]

Although the Communists would reemerge as the most numerous and prominent movement resisting Nazi rule in Austria, the first year of the war saw the arrest of a number of middle-class youngsters who had belonged to the Christian Corporative Youth Group (Österreichisches Jungvolk) or to fraternal (bündisch) associations affiliated with Catholic conservative or legitimist circles. Immediately following the Anschluß, scores of young men and boys had joined various organizations opposed to the new order, particularly in the Tyrol but also in Vienna. Lacking underground experience, they tended to be poorly organized and dedicated to utopian goals such as the restoration of the Habsburg monarchy. Curiously, the Gestapo appears to have paid little attention to these cliques of youthful opponents, even though the huge anti-Nazi demonstration on October 7, 1938, in St. Stephan's Square should have provided ample warning of adolescent discontent. A year later, in December 1939, a deserter confessed that he had belonged to an "Austrian Movement," made up of thirty Catholic boys, many of whom were 15 to 18 years old. Their program, Luza explains, was largely incoherent, calling for a defense of Christianity against Bolshevism, Nazism, and the Jews.[7]

In mid-February 1940, the Gestapo swept up sixteen members of another cell of the Austrian Movement, headed by Friedrich Theiss, a 21-year-old law student. The others were 18 to 20 years of age, including seven young women recruited by Theiss. Organized in 1938, the group had held monthly meetings, collected dues, and spread propaganda calling for an independent Austria opposed to Communism, National Socialism, and Judaism "in all its forms." According to the postwar testimony of a survivor, Camillo Heger (1921–1998), the organization even maintained contact with the British embassy in Budapest. Once picked up by the Gestapo, the conspirators were charged with attempted treason and jailed in Rossauer Lände immediately above the execution chamber.

After extensive interrogation, an investigating judge, Dr. Silvio Marius, persuaded the state prosecutor to change the charge from attempted treason to violation of the Law Against the Formation of New Parties. This meant a change of venue from the People's Court to a Special Court. On December 17, 1941, Hitler's Austrian judges handed down sentences ranging from four weeks behind bars to two years in prison at hard labor without time served. Compared to the many death sentences handed down to members of the KJV, Neugebauer argues, the sentences were relatively mild. And yet upon completion, the convicted Catholic resisters were drafted into the Wehrmacht and sent immediately to the Eastern Front.[8]

Following the arrest of the Theiss group, the Viennese Gestapo paid closer attention to members of Catholic fraternal associations who had joined the Hitler Youth, particularly a group of forty-eight youngsters headed by a former Scout leader and young soldier, Otto Arlow. The boys made a point of attending concerts by émigré Russian choirs, loudly applauding performances of the famous Don Cossack "Platov Chorus" celebrating General Matvei Platov's deeds in defeating Napoleon's Grand Army. On May 20, 1940, the Gestapo broke up a performance in the Konzerthaus, arresting Arlow and four 18-year-old ringleaders, presumably for subtly demonstrating against Hitler's war. On October 18, 1941, a Special Court sentenced Arlow to one and one half years in Kaiser-Ebersdorf, but released the other boys.[9]

Another group of youngsters opposed to the regime was founded by an 18-year-old "quarter-Jewish" student, Otto Haan. Shortly after the outbreak of war, he recruited ten other boys between 14 and 19 years of age who had belonged to the ÖJV or Boy Scouts and gotten to know each other fencing or playing table tennis. The group met Sunday evenings in the 9th District's municipal driving school, pledging "to fight together under one flag and one leadership against our sworn enemy, Adolf Hitler, and his Nazi band of murderers." It was not until mid-October that the Gestapo arrested the boys and jailed them in protective custody. A year later, the Special Court convicted them of breaking the Law Against the Formation of New Parties, imposing comparatively mild sentences from six to nine months behind bars.[10]

Much more severe were the punishments meted out to four underage members of Karl Roman Scholz's Austrian Freedom Movement, an underground organization characterized by Luza as "the most important non-Communist network in the early phase of the Resistance."[11] Scholz, an illegitimate child reared in Mährisch-Schönberg, had left Czechoslovakia in 1930 to enter an Augustinian monastery at Klosterneuburg. Four years later at age 24 he was ordained a priest. Much like another Augustinian monk Martin Luther, Scholz appears to have been torn by complex and contradictory emotions. Like Luther, he was a fiery German nationalist who had joined the Nazi Party in 1935. He served as a curate in Heiligenstadt until 1938 when he returned to Klosterneuburg to teach theology. Known as an inspirational lecturer, Scholz initially welcomed the Anschluß, but gradually turned against the Nazi regime in reaction to its ban on religious instruction. In the autumn of 1938, he and Victor Reimann founded what is acknowledged as the first organized Resistance group in incorporated Austria. The Austrian Freedom Movement, as it came to be known, collected dues, established contacts abroad, and reached out to two other like-minded groups led by Jakob Kastelic and Karl Lederer. Comprising roughly a hundred members, including a women's group, the Austrian Freedom Movement distributed patriotic leaflets calling for the restoration of Austrian independence and began gathering weapons and ammunition to be used in sabotage.[12]

Those familiar with Austrian history know that in June 1940 Scholz was betrayed by an actor, Otto Hartmann, and on July 22, 1940, along with 121 Catholic activists was rounded up by the Gestapo. After years of torture and imprisonment, Scholz was convicted by the People's Court on February 23, 1944, of treason, was sentenced to death, and on March 10 was beheaded. His last words were "For Jesus Christ and Austria."[13] Scholz, Kastelic, and Lederer had headed Catholic resistance movements of young adults. However, four boys and two girls between the ages of 13 and 18 had also been members. Unlike those youngsters affiliated with fraternal resistance groups, the state prosecutor indicted Scholz's followers as juvenile criminals, incarcerating the four boys in protective custody for three years before trying them in the chambers of the Higher Regional Court. The sentences handed out, as mentioned earlier, were harsh. On December 6, 1943, the judges condemned 14-year-old Arthur Reis to four years behind bars. Two months later they sentenced two 18-year gymnasial students, Herbert Goller and Herbert Cramer, to five years of imprisonment. Another, Franz Martin, was ordered to serve one and a half years in a reformatory, presumably Kaiser-Ebersdorf.[14]

One of the most courageous groups of middle-class youngsters to oppose Nazi rule in Vienna consisted of four ninth-grade pupils at the prestigious 3rd District gymnasium on the Kundmanngasse. The leader of the clique was Josef Landgraf, 14 years old at the time of the Anschluß. The son of a prosperous pub keeper, Landgraf excelled in the classroom, had learned English, and was exceptionally fond of music. Like many boys his age, he enrolled in the Hitler

Youth but grew weary of its compulsory drills and meetings. He also resented the expulsion of Jewish classmates and the Nazi ban of jazz, which he had enjoyed listening to on the radio. Long before the outbreak of war, Landgraf began tuning into BBC shortwave broadcasts, both in English and in German. He took copious notes and collected photographs of Roosevelt, Churchill, and Eden, which he carefully filed on his desk. In early September 1941, Landgraf began typing anti-Nazi fly sheets based on British news reports. With the aid of three other schoolmates, Anton Brunner, Ludwig Jgalffy, and Friedrich Fexner, he managed to produce seventy well-written handbills, which according to the Gestapo "contain very strong attacks on the Führer and National Socialism as well as extremely venomous enemy propaganda." One leaflet aimed at farmers asked, "Do you want to deliver your crops to market so that Göring and his cronies can become even fatter?" Another called for a "victory army" to rise up against Hitler and his war. Throughout September, Landgraf and his friends managed to distribute their leaflets through the mail, pasting them on front doors and telephone booths, and even placing smaller ones in the pockets of other schoolmates.[15]

In retrospect, Landgraf's efforts must be judged naïve, careless, and recklessly courageous. As he had made little secret of his hatred of the Nazi regime, the gymnasial director, Dr. Ferdinand Walter, showed little hesitation in reporting his seditious pupil to the Security Police. On September 28, 1942, Landgraf was taken to Gestapo headquarters on Morzin Square, where he was interrogated, grilled, and repeatedly beaten for a month until moved to a juvenile detention center in the Rödengasse. The following summer, Landgraf along with Brunner, Jgalffy, and Fexner, who had been apprehended in January, were transported to Berlin to stand trial for high treason before the People's Court. During the proceedings, which lasted seven hours, Landgraf recklessly stood his ground. When Dr. Lorenz, the presiding judge, asked the bespectacled youth if he held by the Latin motto "Fiat pax et pereat Germania," Landgraf defiantly responded, "Fiat pax et pereat Hitler!" ("Let there be peace when Hitler is destroyed!"). Shortly before 5 p.m. on August 28, 1942, the People's Court sentenced Landgraf and Brunner to death, Jgalffy and Fexner to eight and six years of imprisonment, respectively.[16]

Both Landgraf and Brunner were returned to Vienna to await execution. Confined to death row, the boys lived in terror as they witnessed 300 men and women being dragged to the guillotine. Meanwhile, Landgraf's parents raised considerable sums of money to persuade the warden's wife to petition Göring's wife for clemency. On September 21, 1943, the Reich Ministry of Justice issued a reprieve, changing the sentences to five to seven years in prison.[17] Thereafter, the boys were transferred to Kaiser-Ebersdorf; however, in 1944 Brunner and Fexner were drafted into the Wehrmacht to fight in a punishment company. Landgraf, Fexner, and Brunner all survived the collapse of the Anschluß regime, although each experienced difficult days in the immediate postwar period. Unable to find a job, Landgraf played in various jazz bands while petitioning the police to have his conviction effaced, an effort that fell on deaf ears until October 26, 1949. Thereafter, he became an official in the Viennese health insurance office. Fexner became a teacher; Brunner spent a year as a French prisoner of war and in 1950 took holy orders. Between 1956 and 1987, he served as a rector and spiritual counselor for wayward boys confined in a reformatory in Stein. After retirement, he became a priest in a remote village, where he spent the rest of his days cohabiting with his longtime housekeeper.[18]

The Landgraf case represented the high-water mark of organized opposition by traditional, legitimist, and Catholic youngsters to Nazi rule in Vienna, at least until the last year of the war. While it is true that a few girls and boys were arrested now and then for distributing legitimist fly sheets,[19] Gestapo arrest lists reveal a huge upsurge of resistance by Communist Youth following Hitler's invasion of the Soviet Union as well as a striking number of political crimes committed by individuals. The story of the Communist resistance in incorporated Austria is both well documented and well known. Unlike legitimist or Catholic groups, the KPÖ had developed an underground movement opposed to the Dollfuss-Schuschnigg dictatorship while espousing the cause of Austrian independence. And as mentioned earlier, 85 percent of all Communist activists had been Social Democrats. By April 1940, as we have also seen, the underground movement appeared to have come close to dissolution. Luza's research reveals that thereafter Moscow curriers and functionaries reorganized various cells, primarily in Viennese factories and industrial regions in Styria; otherwise they kept a low profile. In late January 1941, the police undertook a number of successful raids in Vienna, though only a few members of the Communist Youth were involved.[20] On April 19, the Gestapo picked up two youngsters, 16 and 17 years old, in a 3rd District park. The boys had used an Underwood typewriter, which they had stolen from a shoe factory, to print several fly sheets stating "Dear Comrades. Hail Moscow. The party calls. Be prepared at any time." As the police also found a handgun, a pair of shoes, and a ream of paper, it is likely that "The Bad Guys," as they called themselves, were self-styled Marxists rather than members of the KJV.[21]

In early July, the Gestapo stepped up mass arrests. Once apprehended, those indicted as Communists were to be tried by the People's Court. According to a directive from the Reich Ministry of Justice, convicted culprits were to be sentenced to death, and individuals marginally affiliated with the KPÖ might be tried by the Higher Regional Court, although not to be let off lightly.[22] Among those minors swept up were a 17-year-old clerk, Leopoldine Morawitz, charged with using the office copy machine to reproduce Communist leaflets. Held in protective custody for twenty months, she was sentenced to three years of imprisonment on April 2, 1943.[23] Another youngster, 17-year-old Johann Mithlinger, was more fortunate. Arrested for distributing Communist pamphlets, he was sentenced in October 1942 to a year in jail without time served.[24]

Shortly before the Wehrmacht launched Operation Barbarossa, the KJV had followed Moscow's dictate in establishing a centralized command structure in Vienna. The new cadre was led by four highly educated, middle-class militants, Alfred Fenz, Friedrich Mastny, Walter Kämpf, and Elfriede Hartmann—all underage at the time of the Anschluß and now in their early twenties. Their goal was to infiltrate Nazi youth organizations, to foster industrial sabotage, and to distribute anti-Nazi literature directed at Wehrmacht recruits. Fenz, Mastny, and Kämpf proceeded to assemble several fire bombs and other incendiary devices to be set off in railroad marshaling yards. These seem to have little effect, as by September the Gestapo reported no fewer than forty arson attacks. Meanwhile Hartmann, racially classified as "half-Jewish," began printing an underground newspaper, *Der Soldatenrat*, urging soldiers to desert to the Red Army. Between October 1941 and February 1942, she mailed over 2,000 copies to a 1,000 servicemen through her lover, Rudolf Masl, a corporal who had discovered the recipients' army postal numbers. Arrested on February 24, Hartmann was charged with high treason as well as aiding and abetting the enemy. On September 22, 1943, she was condemned to death by the People's Court, and on November 2, 1943, decapitated at 6 p.m. As for Masl, he had been executed on August 27. Mastny was arrested on May 13, 1942, condemned to death on September 22, 1943, and sent to the guillotine shortly after Hartmann six weeks later. Apprehended a month earlier than Mastny, Kämpf was sentenced to death by the People's Court on February 17, 1943, and executed at 6:15 p.m. on November 2, 1943.

Fenz met with a similar fate. Arrested on April 23, 1942, he was indicted on August 8 for high treason, specifically for recruiting younger members, distributing printed materials, planning sabotage, and aiding and abetting the enemy. On September 25, he was condemned to death by the People's Court and on November 2, 1943, executed along with Kämpf. Interestingly, Hitler's judges had taken pity on one of Fenz's co-defendant, 20-year-old Valarie Sassmann.

In their view, she had posted flysheets in telephone booths two years before as a minor solely out of love for a fellow traveler. Considering her immature "psychological dependence," they sentenced her to eighteen months in jail.[25]

It was not only KJV functionaries who were swept up by Hitler's terror apparatus, but also a great many local activists, including minors. Between 1941 and 1943, the Security Police apprehended 3,561 Communists in Vienna and Lower Austria of whom Gestapo records reveal at least fifty-one were 18 years of age or younger.[26] The information is often sparse, but it does indicate that thirty-four were boys and seventeen were girls. It also suggests that nearly all were held in custody until they could be tried as adults. Seventeen-year-old Ernst Mischek, for example, was arrested in October 1941 for spreading an estimated 150 rubber-stamped hammer and sickle handbills in Hietzing. The following February, just before his eighteenth birthday, the Higher Regional Court convicted him of high treason and imposed a three-year prison sentence.[27] Between October and December 1941 alone, twenty-two young Communists received lengthy terms ranging from two to three years behind bars. Of these, eighteen were 21-year-old adults; the remaining four juveniles were 18 years of age or younger.[28]

The following year the number of juvenile arrests declined. But the punishments meted out were draconian, indisputably in response to Hitler's savage attack on the judiciary on April 26, 1942.[29] Several notable examples prove the point. In mid-May, the Gestapo arrested seven members of a cell operating in "Region I," an area consisting of the contiguous 9th, 16th, 20th, and 21st Districts. All but one of the activists was 19 years old; the youngest, Friedrich Lachnitt, had been born on February 22, 1925. According to the Gestapo, the young Communists had committed high treason and undermined the war effort by continuing the distribution of *Der Soldatenrat* in factories and working-class neighborhoods. They had sent fifty copies through the mail and distributed just under a thousand handbills throughout the four districts. Although a latecomer, Lachhnitt was charged with founding a new cell. Arrested on May 14, the accused were indicted on August 4, 1943, condemned to death by the People's Court on November 13, and executed shortly after 6 p.m. on January 11, 1944. In the view of one authority, the judicial authorities adhered to the "letter of the law" by waiting until Lachnitt had turned 19 before sending him to the guillotine.[30]

Arguably more egregious was the condemnation of a 17-year-old seamstress, Anna Gräf. Reared in working-class Favoriten, Gräf had joined the League of German Girls and two other affiliated groups shortly after the Anschluß. In mid-summer 1940, however, she became acquainted with a group of boys and girls on a swimming trip, all of whom were wearing red kerchiefs. Within months she befriended one of them, Leopoldine Sicka, a KJV activist associated with the Hartmann-Mastny cadre. Gräf then proceeded to post anti-Nazi flyers in telephone booths, collect dues, and mail copies of *Der Soldatenrat* to servicemen urging them to desert. In late autumn 1941, she received various explosives, hotplates, and fuses to be used in the 5th District. Thereafter, while working as a seamstress, she continued distributing copies of *Der Soldatenrat* and *Die Rote Jugend*. On November 14, 1942, she was picked up by the Gestapo, charged with aiding and abetting the enemy, undermining the fighting spirit of the German people, sabotage, and high treason. After a year in custody, she was convicted by the 5th Senate of the People's Court and along with three close associates, Leopoldine Sicka, Franz Sikuta, and Heinrich Mann, was condemned to death. In imposing the ultimate penalty, the judges, including Franz Langoth, one of Hitler's childhood educators, acknowledged that the young Communists had been minors while engaged in subversive and treasonable activities; they also conceded that Gräf and Mann were still underage. Under normal circumstances, the tribunal continued, juvenile indiscretions might be taken into consideration. However, Gräf and Mann had acted as "intellectually and morally mature" adults. As "precocious juvenile criminals," it followed that they had to be extirpated from the National Community. On January 11, 1944, shortly after 6 p.m., Gräf, Sicka, and Sikuta were decapitated. Two months later, on March 13, Mann was also dragged to the guillotine.[31]

At least three other minors are known to have been sentenced to death by the People's Court as Communist activists. These included Karl Budin, an 18-year-old carpet weaver who fell prey to the Gestapo on November 28, 1942. According to the formal bill of indictment, Budin had enrolled in the Hitler Youth in 1939, risen to a leadership position, and sought to win his juniors to the Marxist-Leninist cause. Further, he had served as a liaison between KJV cells in Ebergassig and Lanzendorf. Unsurprisingly, the People's Court showed no mercy. On November 5, 1943, Budin received the death sentence and was executed two months later. Meanwhile, two other minors, Emil Fröch, an engineering student, and Emil Ifkovic, an assistant upholsterer, had been picked up in Felixdorf, a market town near Wiener Neustadt. Both had received explosives and anti-Nazi leaflets from Fenz in late 1941. On November 11, the anniversary of the founding of the First Republic in 1918, they distributed 400 hundred well-written fly sheets denouncing Hitler, capitalism, the Nazi war effort, and calling for the restoration of Austrian independence. Convicted by the People's Court for treason as well as aiding and abetting the enemy, the youngsters had the dubious distinction of being sentenced twice to death. On June 25, 1943, Ifkovic accepted a pardon in return for service at the front. But the following year, both were found guilty of desertion by a court of the 177th Division in Moravia. Ifkovic was executed by firing squad on December 12, 1944; Fröch had the good luck to escape from a military hospital and survived the war.[32]

Strikingly different was the fate of Katharina (Käthe) Smudits. Born in 1926 to a Croatian family in the Burgenland, she vividly recalled childhood memories of the 1934 civil war and her parents' detestation of the Dollfuss-Schuschnigg dictatorship. Following the Nazi takeover, her sense of injustice was reinforced by her teachers' visceral persecution of fellow Jewish classmates. Exactly when Käthe became involved in the Communist underground is unclear, though at the time of her mother's death in 1941 she had been engaged in spreading anti-Nazi leaflets and flyers in the 10th District. On August 24, 1942, an informer betrayed her to the Gestapo. Thrown into solitary confinement in the Rossauer Lände, Käthe underwent months of intense interrogation and physical abuse until transferred to a holding cell on death row in the Gray House. Here she subsisted on bread and water, witnessing an endless succession of prisoners being spirited away to the guillotine. On April 21, 1944, almost without warning, she was brought to trial by the 8th Senate of the Higher Regional Court and found guilty of high treason. Remarkably, Judge Erwin Wintersberger made a point of sentencing her to one and a half years in a juvenile detention center, a relatively mild punishment, he explained, owing to Käthe's age and naiveté. Shortly before the leaves began to fall, however, Käthe was shipped off to Ravensbrück, where she miraculously survived both the winter and death marches at the end of March 1945. Upon returning to Vienna, she was thrown off a trolley car for not purchasing a ticket.[33]

Among the nearly 2,000 Communists swept up by the Viennese Gestapo in 1942–1944, at least thirty were minors at the time of their arrest. Because the records are incomplete, the pattern of punishment is difficult to discern. Age may have played some role in the sanctions imposed, particularly by the Higher Regional Court. Those over the age of 19 usually received long prison sentences or worse. Otto Fresinger, for example, was arrested in May 1942, charged with spreading word-of-mouth propaganda and distributing over a thousand handbills in the 5th and 6th Districts. The following year, shortly before his twentieth birthday, he was sentenced to five years in prison at hard labor. In contrast, on September 14, 1943, 17-year-old Rudolf Lutz received a one-year juvenile detention sentence, while his older codefendants were condemned to spend six to seven years in prison.[34] Another minor, Norbert Bures, also received a relatively mild sentence of three years in juvenile confinement, even though he had been a member of Lachhnitt's cell.[35] The absence of trial records and other judicial documents makes it impossible to discern the fate of the remaining two dozen minors arrested as Communist activists by the Gestapo between 1940 and 1944. This includes that of Karl Singer, born in 1925, apprehended for sabotage in a munitions factory in Simmering or Karl Franz Vadiva, handed over to the People's Court for trial.[36] Based on exiguous evidence, there is little reason to believe that they evaded harsh treatment at the hands of the Nazi judicial system. Indeed, Neugebauer is surely correct that Communist activists, including minors, were more severely punished than other resistance groups.[37]

The third largest group of juveniles arrested by the Gestapo for political offences (8.4 percent) consisted of youngsters who had committed "Jewish-related" transgressions. These included boys and girls who had concealed their "racial" identity, been caught in hiding, or attempted to flee abroad. It was, of course, the Nazis who had criminalized Vienna's large Jewish population, but those "non-Aryans" who had failed to emigrate sought to oppose the regime primarily through noncompliance, refusal to obey orders, or other more subtle acts. Between September and October 1940, the Gestapo fined 106 Jews for curfew violations or attending movies. The Security Police also apprehended twelve individuals for listening to foreign radio broadcasts. The following year another thirty-nine were picked up for subversive remarks and sixteen others for Communist activities. Thereafter, the SS rounded up nearly all of Vienna's remaining Jews to be exterminated in the East.[38]

According to the Gestapo arrest lists, only one minor, an 18-year-old "half-Jew" Ernst Thomas Fraenkel, was apprehended in 1940. The previous year he had served two weeks in detention for petty theft. In November 1940, he was charged with committing the "radio crime" of listening to the BBC. Remanded to a Special Court, he was sentenced on February 14, 1941, to spend one year behind bars in juvenile confinement.[39] A month later 17-year-old Malvina "Sara" Z. was convicted of "racial defilement" for sleeping with a German soldier, a crime for which she received a fifteen-month sentence. And in May, Karl "Israel" Feuer was remanded to a Special Court for "spreading rumors" that Jews rounded up in collection centers were doomed to be slaughtered.[40]

Once mass deportations of Viennese Jews to the East resumed in January 1942, the number of Jewish minors arrested for political offences increased dramatically. Anna "Sara" Jaml was shipped off for insulting Aryans. Others were deported for refusing to wear the Star of David. These included Alfred "Israel" Schirene, Alfred "Israel" Glaser, Kurt "Israel" Scholder, Emil "Israel"

Fokschaner. Monika "Sara" Heinsheimer, and Ella "Sara" Hirschmann. Of these, Scholder and Fokschaner are known to have been murdered in Auschwitz. It is unlikely the others survived. Also targeted by the Gestapo were Jewish minors who had misrepresented their "racial" identity. One particularly tragic case was that of Walter Nowak, the 16-year-old adopted son of "German-blooded" parents. According to the Gestapo arrest list, Nowak refused to wear the star, frequently neglected to report for work, and spent most evenings with "German-blooded" girls hanging out in "disreputable pubs." Following his arrest on October 29, 1942, the authorities cold-bloodedly informed Nowak's parents that their son was a "full Jew" and for that reason was being moved to a collection center. Two months later, Nowak was deported to Theresianstadt and from there to Auschwitz. Toward the end of the war, he was transferred to Dachau/Flossenbürg, where he perished on January 7, 1945.[41]

In 1943, the Nazis set their sights on partial Jews, most notably the offspring of Jewish-Gentile parents who had been enrolled in the Jewish Religious Community and thus "counted as Jews" (*Geltungsjuden*). We know that 1,621 Viennese *Geltungsjuden* were swept up in the Holocaust of whom about a dozen were youngsters between 14 and 18 years of age.[42] Usually, the teenagers were arrested for minor infractions such as absenteeism or labor indiscipline. In early March, for example, 16-year-old Edith "Sara" Langberg was picked up for refusing to work as a menial wage earner. Seven months later, she was deported to Auschwitz and from there to Ravensbrück, where she died on March 4, 1945[43]. In May, Elisabeth "Sara" Kölnberger, born in 1926, was picked up for having walked off the job shortly after New Year and failing to return to the workplace. Even earlier, Margarethe Steiner was arrested for not wearing the six-pointed star. Seventeen-year-old Ernst "Israel" Weiss fell prey to the Gestapo for refusing to wear the star and deserting his job. Another, 14-year-old Gertrude Mloch, was apprehended for unspecified "asocial behavior."[44] Unlike Edith Langberg, the fate of these individuals is unknown, although the Gestapo arrest lists indicate they were to be dispatched to concentration camps. This was the lot of 15-year-old Hermann "Israel" Spitzer, a *Geltungsjude* who survived as an inmate only to perish in an air raid at the end of the war.[45]

Of the eleven other minors known to have been persecuted for "Jewish-related" offences, five were caught attempting to flee abroad or escape deportation. Seventeen-year-old Brunhilde "Sara" Silber had been deported with her older brother in February 1941 to Opole, but had managed to break out and return to Vienna. Both apparently thought they could avoid detection by living with their father who had been classified as a "half-Jew" or "Mischling of the First Degree." But under the Nuremberg Laws, brother and sister had been stigmatized as "full-Jews." Picked by the Gestapo in mid-April 1943, all three were shipped off to Auschwitz in September and from there to Ravensbrück. In 1958, Brunhilde was declared officially dead. Two other "non-Aryan" teenagers suffered a similar fate. In April 1942, Paul "Israel" Rosenthal was apprehended attempting to flee abroad. On June 6, he was deported to Maly Trostinetz, where he was shot upon arrival. In late October, Valerie "Sara" Margulies was picked up in Eisenstadt, close to the Hungarian border. She was immediately shipped off to Theresianstadt, where she survived for eighteen months until dispatched to Auschwitz to go into the gas.[46] The fate of the other minors arrested for "Jewish-related" offences is not recorded in the surviving documentary evidence, although one case is suggestive. On October 8, 1943, the Higher Regional Court sentenced Lilli "Sara" Zach, a *Geltungsjudin*, to three years of imprisonment for Communist agitation. As a political prisoner it is conceivable she survived.[47]

Little is known about juveniles prosecuted by the courts for belonging to the Jehovah's Witnesses. The International Association of Bible Students had been banned by the Dollfuss-Schuschnigg dictatorship in 1935–1936, most likely for doctrinal hostility to Roman Catholicism. The small, millenarian sect placed emphasis in the inerrancy of biblical scripture, opposed the taking of oaths, and refused to salute the flag or pledge allegiance to Hitler. Its members also stood firmly against military service including work in munitions plants. In June 1940, the Reich Main Security Office (RSHA; Reichssicherheitsdiensthauptamt) ordered the incarceration of all Jehovah's Witnesses, which in Vienna took place overnight. In the years that followed, 145 Austrian members of the Jehovah's Witness were executed of whom fifty-four refused to serve in the Wehrmacht.[48]

The record of one youngster prosecuted as a Jehovah's Witness has survived. On November 11, 1941, 17-year-old Kurt Melzer was picked up by the Gestapo. Four months later, he was ushered into the chambers of the Special Court presided over by Justice Wotawa. Unlike most juvenile defendants, Melzer was the son of a prosperous music teacher and his wife. Pretrial investigation revealed that upon completing secondary school he had been enrolled in as a student in the Reich Conservatory of Music and belonged to the National Socialist Student League. He also suffered from scoliosis. Under oath, Melzer confessed that in July 1941 he had participated in a Bible study session, but after giving the Hitler salute, he affirmed his allegiance to the German Reich, and expressed his willingness to take up arms if called to duty. In reaching judgment, Wotawa found Melzer guilty of having belonged to the Jehovah's Witnesses, which called for a heavy prison sentence. But the judge took into account parental influence, age, and

Melzer's proven loyalty to order him confined four months in jail, presumably in Kaiser-Ebersdorf.[49]

After the Communists, the largest numbers of Viennese minors arrested for political crimes between 1940 and 1944 consisted of seventy-one individuals charged with anti-Nazi outbursts, "radio crimes," subversion, undermining the war effort, work stoppage, and even espionage. In 1940, two boys were charged with telling anti-Hitler jokes, one for insulting the regime, two others for listening to foreign radio broadcasts, and one for throwing three stink bombs into the Apollo Theater in St. Pölten.[50] The following year, 17-year-old Gertrude Wärfl, a "Mischling of the First Degree" was arrested for spreading a "false rumor," that was in fact true. In November 1941, Reich Marshal Göring's wife had been mocked in the State Opera for "wearing an expensive evening dress and tiara." Although Wärfl claimed to have been among the audience, the authorities remanded her to a Special Court for trial as an adult.[51] In mid-July, another 17-year-old, Johann Cernoch, was picked up for indiscriminately telling listeners in taverns, parks and other public places that Austria and Bavaria should be united as an independent country.[52] Even earlier, Hermann Gabriel had blurted out that Hess had been shot down over Scotland, regretting that the "swine Hitler still lives."[53] On October 22, 15-year-old Friedrich Seidl and 15-year-old Victor Glück were apprehended for placing explosives in a telephone booth in the 3rd District. Their motives, however, are not revealed in the record.[54] According to the daily Gestapo arrest lists, the number of nonforeign teenagers arrested for indiscipline and work stoppages shot up dramatically during the second half of 1941. One minor went so far as to throw a crowbar into a lumber sawing machine, destroying its teeth[55] Whether these cases of labor indiscipline constituted political defiance during Hitler's years of triumph is unlikely, although open to question.

In 1942, oppositional crimes committed by adolescents rose substantially. On February 2, 1942, 17-year-old Erich K. was arrested for socializing with a Bulgarian gardener and a French Legionnaire seeking news about the progress of the war.[56] On February 11, 1942, a Special Court sentenced a salesgirl to two years in prison for violating § 3 of the Law for the Protection of the Military Strength of the German People, presumably for associating with perceived enemies of the regime.[57] A month later, an 18-year-old seamstress received a four-month jail term for fraternizing with prisoners of war. Much more serious was the fate of an office clerk, Alois F., who at age 18 had been caught listening to foreign radio broadcasts. On May 2, 1942, the Higher Regional Court sentenced him to five years in prison.[58] Exceptionally revealing was the case of 18-year-old Maria

Aloisa P. On April 21, 1942, she was arrested for posting "insulting letters" to her brother on the Eastern Front. One of them stated "the city of Vienna should be paved with Nazi skulls. For in Russia the Germans are digging graves, shoving in Jews, and once filled, shooting them whether living or dead."[59] This letter suggests that awareness of the Final Solution may have been well known, even among young people. At least three 16-year-old non-Jewish boys were arraigned for aiding Jews seeking to cross the frontier into Hungary or attempting to do so themselves.[60]

Two additional patterns of juvenile opposition emerged in 1942: industrial sabotage and assaults on groups of Hitler Youth and the League of German Girls. Whether the perpetrators aimed at undermining the Nazi regime is unclear, although they certainly had no use for Hitler's ever tightening capricious and arbitrary demands. On January 21, three 17-year-old boys were apprehended for breaking into the Semperit Rubber Works and slashing a fair number of tires. Gestapo investigators could not decide whether the youngsters were politically motivated or simply youthful vandals.[61] A fortnight later, 17-year-old Emmerich U. was accused of cutting cables and damaging antennas in Wiener Neustadt, though later cleared of charges and released.[62] Less ambiguous appear to have been the motives of four other "saboteurs": 18-year-old Karl W., charged with deliberately damaging war material, Egon S. for destroying thirteen clay pipes in a munitions plant, and 18-year-old Karl R. for maliciously damaging a rolling machine in a Viennese metal factory. Even more strikingly, 17-year-old Karl D. was caught red-handed sabotaging Wehrmacht radios produced in a municipal factory. Given the absence of trial transcripts, the fate of the boys is unknown, although it is likely they were sentenced to prison, dispatched to concentration camps, or conscripted into the Wehrmacht.[63]

Attacks on Hitler Youth groups and their lodges by working-class youngsters in their mid-teens were not unique to Vienna.[64] However, they increased in 1941 and accelerated rapidly the following year. According to one Gestapo report, "In recent days we have received various reports of members of the Hitler Youth being picked on by adolescent boys and in part also being maltreated. On 13 March 1941, for instance, a group of HJ members were attacked and maltreated in Vienna-Alsergrund [9th District] with a shot being fired from an unknown gun."[65] Thereafter, attackers between 12 and 15 years old were gradually identified and arrested. In April 1942, Walter H., a 16-year-old machinist trainee, and 15-year-old Karl Franz W. were caught beating up two Hitler Youths under the cover of darkness in the 18th District. As both delinquents had previously spent time behind bars for petty theft, their motivation may not be considered political. The same observation may be made regarding mass arrests for dust-ups in late September, discussed in the previous chapter, although not for three boys aged 12 to 14 apprehended in early December. They had jumped a member of the League of German girls, shorn her impeccably plaited hair, and insulted her as a Nazi.[66] In another incident, three other boys, also in the early teens, broke into a BDM (Bund Deutsche Mädchen) lodge in the 12th District and sexually "mishandled" two girls, though to what extent was not explained in the official report.[67] Earlier in 1943, the police reported that unknown assailants had vandalized Hitler Youth lodges in the 10th and 19th Districts.[68] These various assaults, Ernst Hanisch has argued convincingly, may not have been overtly political, but they indisputably "constituted a form of recalcitrance that the Nazi authorities saw as a definite threat."[69]

Following Hitler's defeat at Stalingrad, shock, disenchantment, and discontent spread throughout Viennese society. The security organs noted an upsurge of anti-Nazi outbursts and, here and there, shouts of "Hail Austria!" While it is doubtful that a majority of the municipal populace had broken with Nazi rule, large numbers of citizens were beginning to express misgivings.[70] Even members of the Hitler Youth were not immune. On March 18, 1943, a roll call in working-class Meidling (12th District) provoked an uproar in the local lodge. Instead of following orders to line up, ten mid-teenage boys unscrewed an electrical fuse, ripped up chairs, broke them apart, and trashed the meeting room. Once in police custody, several of the boys freely admitted that they had deliberately planned to "wallop" an insufferable leader for whom they had no respect.[71] Two months later, nearly an entire troop of Hitler Youth were arrested by the Gestapo in Drosendorf, north of Vienna. Here 17 members had organized a cell called "Freischar Ostmark," an organization dedicated to the restoration of the Habsburg monarchy.[72]

Even more remarkably, shortly before Christmas, the Viennese Gestapo arrested three Hitler Youths, who were members of a patriotic resistance group in Pulkau, a village north of Vienna. They and a dozen other minors had joined an underground movement "Always Faithful Austria," a cell organized by Anna Goldsteiner, a middle-aged wife and mother. Influenced by Allied leaflets strewn by aircraft in northern Germany as well as soldiers who were home on leave, she and her young followers gathered arms and explosives in a scheme to overthrow the despised local establishment and somehow assist the British in liberating Austria. Arrested by the Gestapo on November 1, 1943, Goldsteiner was convicted by the 5th Senate of the People's Court on April 17, 1944, for undermining the war effort and high treason. She was sentenced to death and on July 5 executed in Vienna. Two minors, Johann Zajlbruckner and Franz Frischauf, were ordered to be confined in a juvenile penitentiary for eight years and five years, respectively. Five other young conspirators were more fortunate. Convicted by the Higher Regional Court, they received sentences of ten to twelve months in jail.[73]

The year 1943 saw a recrudescence of Communist agitation and sabotage in which 1,173 individuals were apprehended in Vienna and Lower Austria.[74] Most were young or seasoned adults; only about two dozen minors appear on the Gestapo arrest list.[75] The available evidence offers no clues to their fate, although each was most certainly severely punished. There were also arrests of a few minors affiliated with Catholic resistance groups.[76] Perhaps most remarkable were acts of sabotage committed by a 17-year-old member of the Hitler Youth, Walter S. On March 19, he used a night key to open a brake clutch on a trolley car, forcing it to derail. Under interrogation he freely admitted that for over a year he had thrown cinders into street tracks, bringing at least nine trams to a stop, proudly disrupting urban traffic. Whether Walter deliberately sought to undermine the Nazi regime or was simply a hooligan must remain an open question. Gestapo officials, however, indisputably considered him a threat to the National Community.[77]

Between 1940 and 1944, some 300 Viennese minors were convicted of crimes "contrary to nature." Of these, only five were girls.[78] Given the loss of court records, little is known about the fate of adolescent homosexuals in Vienna during wartime, not least because the accused were arrested by the criminal police. Between 1938 and 1945, the Vienna Gestapo arrested only 207 homosexuals, of whom fewer than a dozen were minors.[79] This relatively small number suggests that in the eyes of the authorities homosexual behavior was considered more traditionally deviant than political.[80] Only scant information can be gleaned from daily Gestapo reports. In several cases, for example, the agents simply remanded offenders to the juvenile court. However, other instances were more ambivalent. In one, the Gestapo stressed that a 19-year-old detainee had a long record of encounters with no fewer than fifty adults, and in another that an 18-year-old aircraft mechanic trainee had been involved with Russian prisoners of war. These two cases may have had political overtones, though one cannot say for sure. On the other hand, the police sought the advice of the RSHA on how to proceed against a 15-year-old schoolboy picked up in November 1943.[81]

Less oblique was the Gestapo approach to underage girls caught sleeping with prisoners of war or foreign workers. This was because Nazi regulations prohibiting sexual relationships with Jews and non-Aryans categorized as "racial defilement" had been extended during the war to include foreigners, particularly Poles and other *Ostarbeiter*. Illicit intercourse, in other words, was criminalized as a political offense. Between 1941 and 1942 alone, sixteen Viennese girls in their late teens were arrested and remanded to the judiciary for trial.[82] As we shall see in a subsequent chapter, sentences handed down by judges in a handful of surviving court records varied considerably, but tended to be much harsher toward the end of the war. But in 1941, as mentioned before, a Gestapo report indicates that 17-year-old Malvina Z. was convicted of "racial defilement" for sleeping with a German soldier and sentenced to fifteen months in a detention center.[83]

On January 30, 1943, State Prosecutor Dr. Johann Karl Stich submitted a situation report to the Reich Ministry of Justice. In it he wrote that Viennese walls and kiosks plastered with scarlet posters of numerous executions had provoked a spate of anonymous threats aimed at the judiciary. He also stressed a sharp rise in arrests for subversion, defeatism, and undermining the war effort. Most revealing for this study, he indicated that juvenile offenses had risen 24 percent in recent months, most alarmingly for labor indiscipline and work stoppages. Between September 1 and December 31, he concluded, no fewer than 525 such cases were pending adjudication.[84] To what extent these cases of work stoppages or absenteeism constituted a form of youthful indigenous opposition is problematic, at least until late 1944. For one thing, meticulous research by Timothy Kirk has revealed that between January and June 1941 only 126 (7.6 percent) of 1,667 adult individuals arrested for labor indiscipline in Vienna and Lower Danube were German-Austrians. The rest were overwhelmingly Polish or other Eastern European workers. Even more striking were the figures for February 1943 to March 1944. Of the 21,555 persons charged with work stoppages in Vienna and Lower Danube, a mere 589 (3 percent) were indigenous wage earners. As in the past, the overwhelming majority were *Ostarbeiter*. The Gestapo knew fully well that most industrial discontent was based on appalling labor conditions or hatred of Germany, but shied away from mass arrests for the fear of undermining the war economy. As for the ethnic Germans or Austrians, patriotic resistance may have played some role, but, as Kirk concludes, "the motives and the degree of political intention ... are difficult to assess."[85]

As we have already seen in Chapter 2, those youngsters known to have been convicted by the courts for labor indiscipline or work stoppages prior to 1944 were by no means politically motivated. Further, the judges tended to take into consideration age and working conditions while handing out mild sentences. The data recorded on Gestapo arrest lists are exiguous, consisting primarily of the name and date of birth of a dozen adolescents taken into custody between 1939 and 1944. There were a few exceptions. In mid-October 1939, 18-year-old Johann H. walked off the job in a metal factory because the presses were too hot and he was considered too weak for the job.[86] While Johann's fate is unknown, he most likely did not suffer severe sanctions. In April 1940, for example, 17-year-old Walter A. was given a "severe warning" for refusal to work.[87] Thereafter few arrests were recorded until summer 1941. Between March and August, ten Austrian boys in their late teens were among a large number of foreign workers taken into custody for work stoppages. One was identified as an office worker, another as a stone mason, and the rest as day laborers. There is little reason to believe that they refused for political reasons.[88] One arguable exception was the case of 18-year-old Friedrich "Israel" Braun, a "half-Jew," who had managed to survive as a day laborer. In late October, the Gestapo picked him up for absenteeism and black marketeering. Without trial, he was deported to Auschwitz, where he was murdered on January 22, 1944.[89]

Conclusions

Were those youngsters arrested and tried for political misconduct in Vienna during the Anschluß era juvenile delinquents? Or were they youthful opponents of the Nazi regime? The question is difficult to address, as this chapter has attempted to demonstrate. Of the 293 youngsters arrested for political transgressions, approximately 40 percent belonged to the Communist Youth or other leftist groups, and 13 percent to Catholic conservative or monarchist associations. Examination of the available evidence makes it unmistakably clear that over half of those apprehended for political crimes in Vienna and Lower Danube acted as Austrian patriots opposed to both the Anschluß and National Socialism. The same applies to the two dozen minors picked up for "Jewish-related" offences, although in these cases resistance usually meant refusal to wear the star, attempting to avoid detection, or seeking to flee over the border to Hungary. As for the seventy-one minors arrested for acts of individual opposition, motives appear to have been mixed, ranging from telling harmless jokes, to listening to foreign radio broadcasts, socializing with foreign workers, publicly insulting the regime or deliberately committing acts of industrial sabotage. In at least one case the Gestapo could not decide whether three boys who broke into the Semper Rubber Works sought to disrupt the Nazi war machine or acted as vandals.

After Stalingrad, the Gestapo arrest lists reveal an upsurge of youthful discontent, most notably in attacks on members of the Hitler Youth and League of the German girls. These assaults no doubt reflected dissent and disillusionment, but did not differ much from the noncompliant behavior of the Schlurfs. On the other hand, the utopian revolt of the Hitler Youth in Pulkau indisputably constituted a form of patriotic suicidal resistance. In the view of the state prosecutor, however, the most dangerous threat to the regime came from adults and youngsters downing tools or refusing to work. The surviving evidence reveals that these fears were misplaced, at least with regard to native Viennese minors. Whether youthful work stoppages constituted a form of political opposition during the last year of the war will be considered in the next chapter that is devoted to the impact on youthful malefactors of the Reich Juvenile Court Law that went into effect on January 1, 1944.

5

Impact of the Juvenile Court Act, 1944–1945

On November 6, 1943, Berlin announced the introduction of a comprehensive Juvenile Court Law, an ordinance agreed upon after years of numerous meetings and conferences. The new measure was to go into effect on January 1, 1944. Shortly after the first of the year, Reich Minister of Justice Otto Thierack explained that the substance of the law constituted a new approach to the corrective education of young people that corresponded to the fundamental principles of National Socialism. In a sense, he was not disingenuous. The objective of the new penal code was to extend control of delinquents and wayward youth throughout Greater Germany by closing loopholes in juvenile law that had led to inconsistent sentencing by magistrates, for example, in Munich and Vienna. In such a way, Wolff has argued, adolescents would be more inclined to conform to the legal system of the Nazi state. Furthermore, the enhanced power of the Hitler Youth in arresting youthful offenders as well as that of school officials, social workers, and psychologists in reaching judicial decisions further undermined the independence of the judiciary.[1]

We have already seen that following the Anschluß ministerial bureaucrats, party officials, SS officers, Hitler Youth leaders, jurists, and criminologists failed to combine the legal systems of Germany and the "Ostmark," thus leaving the Austrian civil and penal codes in place. Thereafter, a series of conferences in Munich, Goslar, Salzburg, Bad Aussee, and Semmering attempted to formulate a common juvenile code, but were unable to reach consensus. Himmler, for example, refused to countenance the introduction of short-term detention centers, arguing that convicted youngsters should serve time in a juvenile concentration camp such as Moringen. There were also disputes on the efficacy of "indefinite imprisonment," the "personality principle," the right to appeal, and coordinating legal procedures among the ministries, the Wehrmacht, and the SS. Above all, there was disagreement on age, not least because some benches were trying adolescents as juveniles, others as adults. This meant that although hundreds of wartime ordinances were invoked to convict wayward youth and juvenile delinquents, only one, the Decree for Protection of Dangerous Juvenile Criminals, was passed specifically to deal with adolescent crime.[2]

That an all-embracing juvenile criminal code was not promulgated in Hitler's Reich until late 1943 can be explained by the exigencies of the German war effort. While it is true that all parties had concurred on the necessity of juvenile reform, their discussions never gave pride of place to that issue. The major goal of the conferences mentioned above was to bolster the German war effort, not to reform the juvenile penal code. By mid-July 1943, nearly all male Germans and Austrians were serving in the Wehrmacht and hundreds of thousands of civilians succumbing to Allied bombing. The manpower shortage suddenly became so acute that not even the millions of foreign workers, prisoners of war, and concentration camp inmates could meet the soaring demands of Hitler's industrial war machine. Under these circumstances, even Himmler conceded that an entirely new penal code was needed in order to integrate wayward youngsters and juvenile delinquents following minimal educative punishment into the workforce.[3]

This is not to suggest that other factors played inconsequential roles in the formulation of the Juvenile Court Law of November 6, 1943. Long ago, Bruno Blau demonstrated in his meticulous study of criminality in wartime Greater Germany that whereas the overall number of punishable offences, particularly theft, had declined by 20 percent between 1937 and 1943, those of juveniles had risen by 140 percent. Further, the upsurge of serious juvenile transgressions particularly in 1942 and 1943 both confounded and alarmed party officials and judicial authorities, not least because harsh sentences meted out failed to stem a rising crime rate. Between July 1, 1942, and June 30, 1943, for example, twenty-seven "precocious juvenile criminals" were condemned to death and sixty-four others sentenced to long prison terms.[4] During that same period, the number of property offences, particularly break-ins and thefts, continued to constitute over two-thirds of juvenile offences. In a number of towns, there was also an upsurge of violent felonies by youngsters under the age of 16, particularly in the bombed-out cityscapes in the Ruhr, Hamburg, and Munich.[5] As Vienna remained untouched by Allied air raids until September 1944, the number of such felonies did *not* shoot up. On June 1, 1943, as we have already seen, the state prosecutor, Dr. Johann Karl Stich, lamented a sharp rise in absenteeism, a trend that had begun the previous summer. He conceded that the number of robberies remained high, and took pains to stress that too many youngsters under 18 were forging personal identification papers in order to attend movies, hang out in coffee houses, or loiter in the streets after dark as adults.[6]

The 1943 Juvenile Court Law constituted a revised approach in the judicial treatment of wayward and delinquent youngsters. Its most distinctive feature, much applauded by jurists and criminologists, was to categorize minors as members of a distinctive group between 14 and 18 years of age. This meant, as Waite stresses, that juveniles would no longer be regarded as children or tried as "small adults."[7] The law thus abolished the German Welfare and Juvenile Court Act of 1922 and 1923 as well as the 1928 Austrian Juvenile Court Law. It also negated the 1939 Decree for the Protection of Dangerous Juvenile Criminals and sixteen other wartime ordinances that had been applied, often inconsistently or capriciously, to underage offenders. The legislation specifically stipulated that, aside from certain egregious cases, teenage lawbreakers should serve time in a juvenile a confinement facility, not prison. Even so, judges were directed to avoid handing out harsh sentences unless the deed revealed an "injurious predisposition" on the part of the delinquent. Instead, justices were encouraged to sentence underage miscreants to short-term detentions, special tasks, or simple warnings. The court was also empowered to impose pedagogical measures. Here the intent of the new legislation was clearly to reintegrate youthful wrongdoers into the National Community by keeping them at work in Hitler's war machine.[8]

Overall, the Reich Juvenile Court Law was anything but benign. The official commentary published by Dr. Heinz Kümmerlein, Councilor for Juvenile Issues in the Reich Ministry of Justice, made this brutally clear. "Today it is axiomatic," he wrote, "that the prosecution of adolescents must take into account biological character in the determination and choice of sanctions." Wartime ordinances, he continued, necessitated the promulgation of a comprehensive juvenile code, not least in the Alpine and Danubian districts, where the implantation of various decrees had been at variance with the Austrian penal code or as in the case of detentions (*Jugendarrest*) difficult to enforce. Above all, "the principal goal of the new law is to ensure that criminal justice be firmly embedded in the National Socialist state. The requisite education of the young must be fulfilled in an orderly manner for the protection of the National Community. Even so, safeguarding criminal law relating to young offenders must not overlook the chilling impact of judicial punishment."[9]

Paragraph 20, for example, laid down precise guidelines for sentencing "precocious juvenile criminals." It stated:

1. If the juvenile, at the time of the offence, was as morally and intellectually developed as an 18-year-old, the judge can order the use of the general criminal code, or if the healthy sensitivity of the people demand it

because of his serious criminal intentions or because of the seriousness of the crime.
2. The same applies if the juvenile's moral and intellectual development at the time of the crime is equal to that of an adult, but the assessment of his total personality and the offense show that he is, as a result of his deficient character, a serious offender, and that the protection of the people demand this action.[10]

Looking back, the 1943 Juvenile Court Law formalized two major objectives shared by most juvenile justice systems in Europe and the Western world. The first was to rehabilitate, educate, or resocialize youngsters found guilty of minor offences, and the second was to identify and punish those who had committed ruthless or violent crimes. This helps to explain why the code was retained largely intact after 1945 in the Federal Republic of Germany, though not in Austria. Until the collapse of Hitler's Reich, however, the first rationale was to keep wayward youngsters toiling in munition plants, foundries, or other war-related enterprises under the strict supervision of Nazi shop stewards.

The second purpose of the law was to discern and categorize the personality of those delinquents whose deeds were egregiously odious, who threatened the "healthy sensitivity" of the people or were themselves destined to become incorrigible criminals. This was no easy task, as it required extensive pretrial investigation by Hitler Youth officials, the Youth Welfare Office, school authorities, shop stewards, and even physicians. Paragraph 28, for example, stipulated that the judicial authorities could order criminal-biological examinations as a means of diagnosing "precocious juvenile criminals." Those identified as such were to be delivered to the psychiatric division of a correctional facility.[11]

The new penal code empowered state prosecutors to monitor the implementation of penalties, particularly sentences of "indefinite imprisonment." Paragraph 58 mandated that terms of "indefinite imprisonment" should range between two to five years behind bars, though even in exceptional cases those convicted could not be released or paroled until serving their full sentence.[12] Even worse, § 60 stipulated that if enforcement officials concluded that their wards were "character deficient serious criminals," the delinquents were to be dispatched to a juvenile concentration camp.[13] Finally, § 76 authorized state prosecutors to remand adolescent malefactors to Special Courts for trial as adults, which meant that even 14-year-olds could be sentenced to long prison terms or even death[14]

Just how seriously the regime took its comprehensive carrot and stick approach to juvenile crime appears evident in a lengthy pamphlet published by Himmler's

SS on January 3, 1944.[15] The booklet begins on a cautionary note. It stresses that abnormal or deviant behavior should not be considered unusual during puberty, even among wayward or delinquent adolescents. In assessing specific cases, trained officials were instructed to understand the age, personality, and genetic makeup of youthful offenders in order to decide whether they were "internally wholesome" or genetically disposed to lead a life of crime. Judges were also urged to take into account the maturity of defendants in deciding whether they should be punished or placed under close supervision of the Guardianship Authority.[16]

The pamphlet continues by stipulating specific guidelines for police interrogations. Trained personnel were to undertake initial questioning outside the home or school. They were to put the accused at ease by avoiding slights or threats, to take careful notes, and to file a report weighing the individual's maturity. The SS brochure next authorized authorities from the HJ, the NSV, or the Youth Welfare Office to make additional inquiries in order to determine whether the accused had grown up in a criminal environment. Once indicted and placed under arrest, the police were to keep defendants isolated from hardened criminals. They were to be tried by a judge and if convicted sentenced to detention in a public facility or locked up in a juvenile jail. The pamphlet concluded that nearly all habitual criminals had committed offences as children or teenagers. In some cases, early intervention might head off a life of crime, though childhood negligence usually made that next to impossible. Even so, the attempt should be made.[17]

How effective was the new Juvenile Court Law in stemming adolescent crime? Waite speculates that it had little impact, but the absence of municipal or national statistics makes it impossible to say. In Vienna, however, numerous documents have survived that provide substantial information on juvenile offences between January 1944 and the collapse of Hitler's regime. These include the daily arrest lists of the Viennese Gestapo as well as forty-one records of indictments and trial transcripts brought before the magistrates of the Higher Regional Court in 1944. Finally, a complete collection of court records from January to December 1945 has been preserved in the city's municipal archives, most of which consist of arrests, indictments, and trial transcripts made prior to the end of Nazi rule.

Judicial Reports

On July 4, 1944, the president of the Higher Regional Court expressed concern about the impact of sudden American air raids on industrial centers near

Vienna. Although general confidence in the war effort remained steady, he continued, "hostile propaganda and various rumors" were having a deleterious impact on morale. Further, the massive influx of foreign workers, particularly from the Balkans, had contributed to an upsurge on the black market, most notably in cigarettes and tobacco products. Five months later, the Justice was more precise. While over 30,000 foreigners were engaged in heavy industry and the construction of earthworks, underage girls were being assigned tasks in munitions plants that were beyond their physical strength. And on November 4, Allied bombs had destroyed a detention center and damaged other judicial facilities.[18]

A month earlier, on October 1, 1944, State Prosecutor Dr. Johann Karl Stich dealt more explicitly with the impact of Allied bombing and the Reich's deteriorating military situation. The raids in Vienna and Lower Danube, he wrote, had led to an upsurge of Communist word-of-mouth propaganda and rumormongering as well as renewed legitimist agitation. Further, he had received a number of personal threats characterizing him as a "blood hound." Within a year, the crime rate had shot up 33 percent, most notably in the number of break-ins and thefts of foodstuffs. The result led to a thriving black market in staples, tobacco, and clothing. For the purposes of this study, Stich provided data on juvenile crime. Between May 1 and August 31, 1944, some 1,048 individuals had been indicted for felonies of whom 924 (88 percent) were minors. Given the composition of the largely foreign adult workforce, it is likely that most of the adolescent malefactors were Austrians. The principal charges levied against girls were for work stoppages or prostitution. In addition, twenty-four others were convicted of socializing or sleeping with prisoners of war. As for male youngsters, some twenty-four had been sentenced to "indefinite imprisonment," of whom eight were to serve a minimum of four years behind bars.[19]

While it is difficult to draw conclusions about the impact of the new Juvenile Court Law from these reports, those from judicial officials in Linz and Graz suggest a similar pattern. Writing on February 29, 1944, Dr. Leo Sturma, the newly appointed president of the Higher Regional Court in Linz, explained that juvenile court judges welcomed the new legislation, not least because the region lacked the facilities to house short-term detainees. Presumably, he considered jail sentences of "indefinite imprisonment" more salutary. On the other hand, Sturma seemed confounded by a sharp increase of arrests for break-ins and shoplifting from tobacco stores. Ten months later, the president of the Higher Regional Court in Graz reported an alarming rise in juvenile theft and numerous cases of local girls sleeping with prisoners of war.[20]

Gestapo Reports

The surviving Gestapo arrest lists during the last year and a half of Nazi rule provide more specific information on juvenile crime in Vienna and Lower Danube than those of the judicial officials. While it is difficult to gauge the impact of the 1943 Juvenile Court Law on youthful malefactors from these documents, the Gestapo records do reveal that economic and social tensions contributed to an alarming surge in teenage work stoppages and sexual promiscuity, particularly during the last months of the war.[21] In addition, the arrest lists include cases of forty-six boys and twelve girls charged with traditional offences as well as political crimes. These admittedly constitute only a fraction of overall indictments, but they do offer some clues.

The most numerous arrests were, as might be expected, for political crimes. Of these a majority belonged to Communist cells. Between April and June 1944, the SD picked up twelve boys in their mid-teens in Eisenstadt and Wiener Neustadt. The documents do not reveal the fate of the youngsters, although Gestapo officials indicated that six of the boys in Wiener Neustadt had done little more than pay small weekly dues.[22] The remaining adolescents arrested for political crimes appear to have acted as individuals, although two salesmen trainees, Karl W. and Ernst W., had been taken into custody for distributing handmade Social Democratic fly sheets on New Year's Eve.[23] Another, 18-year-old Heinrich K., was loosely affiliated with the Austrian Freedom Movement. Others included 18-year-old Herbert F., for listening to foreign radio broadcasts; 15-year-old Anton P., for composing and distributing hostile flyers derived from Allied wireless news to French prisoners of war; and 17-year-old Hildegard B., a "Mischling of the First Degree," for politically motivated theft.[24]

One of the most unusual cases of a juvenile charged with committing a political crime took place on January 23, 1945. On that date, Gestapo agents picked up 18-year-old Herbert Hans Eduard P. in his home in prosperous Hietzing. There they found manometers, various brake parts, electrical bulbs, and a number of casings stolen from the Viennese municipal rail line (*Stadtbahn*). Exactly why young Herbert had made off with so many purloined devices is unclear, but the authorities charged him with sabotage.[25]

Between 1938 and 1945, as we have seen, the Viennese Gestapo refrained from reporting traditional crimes and misdemeanors committed by adults or juveniles. During the last year of the war, however, agents arrested a great many foreign workers for a variety of offences, though usually for sabotage, work stoppages, or other acts that were considered undermining the war effort. Among those charged were several Viennese youngsters who were picked up for traditional offences. On March 1, 1944, for example, a 15-year-old glazier apprentice was apprehended for walking off the job. That he was "half-Jewish" may explain why he fell prey to the Gestapo. But in following months, other boys were arrested for break-ins and theft. These included a 16-year-old precision engineer trainee and two other boys in their mid-teens who succeeded in breaking into a tobacco shop in the 12th District. Here they stole 15,000 cigarettes, a fair number of cigars, and other tobacco products, which they intended to sell to foreign workers on the black market. It is perhaps not without significance that the Gestapo remanded them to the Higher Regional Court to be tried as juveniles.[26]

Throughout the spring and summer, the Gestapo continued to arrest juveniles for absenteeism and theft, particularly of foodstuffs, tobacco, and other necessities in short supply. In April and May, for example, Hitler's agents picked up two 18-year-old SA members for stealing goods from the local "Feldernhalle" lodge. They also arrested two members of the Hitler Youth, Friedrich N. and Erwin S., both in their mid-teens, for grand theft on a countryside outing. The loot consisted of stocks of children's clothing and dental supplies that they intended to fence on the Hungarian border. For some odd reason, the boys were let off with a severe warning, quite possibly because they came from middle-class backgrounds or enjoyed the protection of Nazi officials.[27] Less fortunate was the fate of 18-year-old Willi B., who was expelled from the SA and charged with undermining the war effort.[28] In retrospect, the specific cases cited here do not reveal a pattern of juvenile crime significantly different from that discerned between September 1939 and December 31, 1943. What the arrest lists do suggest is that the personnel of the Viennese Gestapo came to consider traditional juvenile offences as dangerous to the Nazi regime.

Court Records

As mentioned above, a large number of juvenile court records have survived for this part of our study. These include forty-one cases involving fifty-eight minors tried by the Higher Regional Court in 1944 as well as arrest lists, indictments, and trial transcripts of 171 youngsters picked up before the end of the Nazi regime. Structurally, the types of offences committed by Viennese adolescents mutated as the war drew to its conclusion, particularly in the last six months of the conflict. Crimes against property remained high constituting 65 percent of all transgressions. However, there was a notable difference. Fifty-two boys

(30 percent) were arrested for breaking, entering, and theft, primarily in tobacco shops (*Tabaktrafik*) making off with thousands of cigarettes, cigars, and ration coupons, items that were supplanting currency in a developing black market. More dramatic was an upsurge of hold-ups and robberies, largely by individuals, of bicycles, purses, jewelry, cash, clothing, fur coats, watches, rings, gloves, and even entire suitcases. Added to the list were instances of petty theft that included pillaging municipal allotments for fruit, potatoes, ducks, geese, bottles of wine, and even Christmas trees. All in all, hold-ups and robberies represented 35 percent of property crimes. Equally dramatic was a sharp rise in work stoppages and absenteeism (*Arbeitsvertragsbruch*) as predicted by the state prosecutor in mid-1943. The rate grew incrementally throughout 1944, but shot up between Advent of that year and March 1945. Overall, seventy-seven boys and girls (31 percent) were charged with refusal to work by their employers, who insisted that they be severely punished. The remaining juvenile transgressions consisted of vandalism, sexual immorality, firearms violations, assault, and several unspecified charges.

In terms of age, nearly all of the youngsters remanded to the Higher Regional Court were between 16 and 18 years old at the time of their arrest; only nineteen were younger. Of the total, 85.5 percent were boys, and 14.5 percent were girls. As in the past, over half were listed as apprentices, machinist trainees, domestics, or manual laborers. However, the occupation of 49 percent of the juveniles arrested or brought before the bench was not recorded. At the same time, the documentation makes it clear that, aside from four high-school pupils, nearly all came from impoverished families desperately seeking to make ends meet.

Scrutiny of a number of trial transcripts in 1944 suggests the persistence of largely female social workers in shaping judicial decisions. Friedrich X., for example, had been under the supervision of the Juvenile Welfare Board since infancy. As his impoverished parents were both chronically ill and estranged, members of the board recommended in 1937 that he be briefly confined in a Czech correctional facility. Three years later they filed a positive report that Friedrich had found productive work as a tailor's apprentice. However, in early 1942 Friedrich and two other youngsters were tried and sentenced to four months of strict detention for stealing eggs, liquor, cigarettes, bicycle tires, and a typewriter. After completing his sentence, Friedrich resumed his duties as a journeyman, but in 1944 was arrested for stealing wearing apparel from his master's home. This time the social worker undertook an extensive investigation, determining that the accused had spent too much time drinking, picking up girls, and attending movies. She concluded that his "criminal-biological" nature required a psychiatric examination, clearly hoping that Friedrich be judged morally and intellectually mature to stand trial as an adult. Investigators reached the opposite conclusion, even though they reported that Friedrich was "congenitally tainted." The court then sentenced him to spend ten months in jail to be followed by one to three years in Kaiser-Ebersdorf. How long he spent behind bars is unknown. On May 19, 1947, a welfare worker grudgingly reported that while Friedrich had landed a position as a journeyman, his demeanor remained that of a "Schlurf."[29]

Another youngster, Johann X., had also been under the care of the Juvenile Welfare Board since the death of his father in 1935. The family was so impoverished that the board provided occasional assistance, including, for example, a pair of shoes. A 1942 report indicated that Johann had failed as an electrical apprentice, dropped out of the Hitler Youth, and was hanging out in coffee houses. In January 1942, he was sentenced to three weeks in detention for involvement with the Karo gang in the Prater. After his release, Johann went to work first as an unskilled worker for an electrician and next as a stoker in a military hospital. However, NSV supervisors considered him lazy, indifferent, and disrespectful. In May 1944, they filed charges, recommending Johann be dispatched to Moringen. The court rejected this request, finding the boy innocent of criminal activity. In September, however, the Juvenile Division of the Higher Regional Court sentenced Johann to five months of juvenile detention in Kaiser-Ebersdorf for pilfering and forging identification papers. After serving his sentence, he perished in an Allied air raid.[30]

Two other cases reveal the persistent influence of female social workers in bringing grief to youngsters for minor infractions. The first involved Franz X., who lived with his parents and a sister while his two older brothers were serving in the Wehrmacht. In January 1943, his high-school principal filed a formal complaint to the Juvenile Welfare Board. In sententious language, the educator claimed that by skipping school throughout most of December to play soccer Franz demonstrated a serious "threat to the young." In response, a social worker undertook an extensive investigation, concluding that because the youngster behaved like a "Schlurf" he deserved correctional training. On April 20, Franz was taken briefly into custody. When released he was placed under surveillance by the NSV and the police, who discovered he had taken up with a 17-year-old girl, was absenting himself from the workplace, and hanging out with a small gang. In May 1944, the authorities arrested him, holding him in a police station in the Juchgasse from which he soon escaped. After recapture, Franz was tried and convicted of theft on October 3. Interestingly, the judge paid little attention to the tendentious reports of the welfare workers. In what appears to have been compliance with the new Juvenile Court Law, he imposed a sentence of three weeks in detention. Two months later, however, Franz was hauled before the bench for breaking his labor contract. This time the court was inclined to imprison him as "precocious juvenile criminal," but before passing sentence found that he had been conscripted into the Reich Labor Service.[31]

In the second instance, Stefanie X. had been under the vigilance of the Juvenile Welfare Board since 1936. A home visit shortly before the Anschluß concluded that the father was an alcoholic and the mother inattentive. Given Stefanie's dysfunctional family, the welfare worker worried that her ward might fall prey to "moral danger." Reports filed in 1941, 1942, and 1943 indicated that Stefanie was succeeding as a sewing apprentice, but warned that too much time away from home might result in delinquency or waywardness. On April 9, 1944, she did indeed find herself before a juvenile judge, but not for consciously committing a crime. In February, she had met a young man in a shop, who claimed to be a serviceman home on leave. For two months she provided unstipulated aid and assistance to the soldier, who turned out to be a deserter. Accused of aiding a turncoat, the state prosecutor demanded a stiff prison sentence for her "morally reprehensible deed." The judge ruled, however, that she had acted purely out of affection, sentencing her to four weeks in detention. After completing her sentence, Stefanie returned to her workplace and survived the war. In April 1946, the Juvenile Welfare Board closed the books by reporting she was making a positive contribution to Austria's postwar reconstruction.[32]

Less fortuitous was the fate of three youngsters who in February 1944 knowingly had aided a deserter from an armored division by providing food, clothing, and advice on how to avoid detection. On August 2, the Juvenile Division of the Higher Court sentenced one of the boys to four weeks in detention, a second to five months in jail, and the third to two to four years in jail. The trial transcript reveals that all three had known the deserter before he was called to the colors. However, the oldest, 17-year-old Johann J., had a criminal record. In October 1942, he had been convicted of theft and sentenced to spend nine months to two years in Kaiser-Ebersdorf. After a year, he had been paroled and until his arrest in April 1944 employed as an apprentice purse maker. Given his delinquent past, Johann received the harshest sentence. In imposing a penalty of two years in confinement, Judge Franz Köbl seems to have been of two minds. While ruling that Johann possessed an "injurious predisposition," he refrained from remanding him to criminal court for trial as an adult. Instead, he expressed the hope that incarceration in Kaiser-Ebersdorf would enable him to atone for his misdeeds and through "education" he would become a useful member of the National Community.[33]

Examination of the types of offences committed by Viennese juveniles during the last fifteen months of Nazi rule provides a fairly clear picture of both the impact of the new Juvenile Court Law in the city as well as noticeable changes in society. The documentation is not altogether complete, consisting here and there solely of police reports or formal indictments. Even so, most of the files include extensive investigative evidence and trial transcripts, making it possible to draw certain conclusions. The closing of schools in August 1944, for example, compelled youngsters to work in enterprises essential to the war effort. This led to a significant drop in the miscreant age cohort, which dropped from 17 to barely 16. Overall, there were 128 cases involving 151 individuals. Of these 118 (78 percent) were boys; 33 (22 percent) were girls. The change can also be explained by the large number of teenagers over 16 who had been conscripted into the Reich Labor Service or in the case of the class of 1928 drafted into the armed forces.

Break-Ins and Theft

During the last fifteen months of Hitler's regime, as mentioned above, some 65 percent of juvenile delinquents in Vienna were indicted for break-ins, robbery, or theft. Of these, twenty-seven were tried and convicted after the war by Austrian judges, who as late as July 1947 were handing out relatively harsh sentences. While it is difficult to understand why postwar tribunals imposed stiff penalties for property crimes committed under Nazi rule, the surviving records suggest that the confusion, chaos, and violence toward the end of the conflict hampered Vienna's hard-pressed judiciary in trying the accused. Further, the reports of court-appointed social workers tended to be confined to one or two pages, whereas the records of those brought to justice during the early days of the Second Republic, as we shall see, tended to be more extensive and complete.

1. Break-Ins

Given the large number of hold-ups and robberies, the cases of those convicted of break-ins and theft will be considered first. For the most part, those charged with these offences consisted of one or two boys. The case of 14-year-old

Erwin T. provides a good example. According to the prosecutor's indictment, Erwin had grown up in his parents' home and finished the eighth grade. After the regime shuttered the schools, Erwin was apprenticed to a woodworker but owing to poor health transferred to work in a restaurant. Shortly after Christmas, he had broken into a caretaker's apartment and made off with ration stamps worth RM 800, a winter coat, a hat, a scarf, and a pair of shoes. Thereafter he had gone to ground until apprehended in early March. On March 5, the Juvenile Division of the Higher Regional Court convicted Erwin of theft according to §§ 171, 173, and 174 of the Austrian penal code. In reaching his decision, the judge considered detention too mild, thus sentencing Erwin to two years in confinement. According to surviving documentation, the youngster was released in April immediately after the Soviet liberation of Vienna. Three years later, however, he ran afoul of the law in Innsbruck, where on April 26, 1948, the regional court sentenced him to a year behind bars for theft. Once the magistrates learned that Erwin had been serving time in 1945, they ordered that he complete his previous term, meaning an additional twenty-two months in prison. On September 12, 1949, Erwin appealed the decision from his cell in Stein, claiming mistakenly that his conviction had been based on Nazi wartime ordinances. Because he had been sentenced under Austrian law, he appears to have remained under lock and key.[34]

Another case involved 17-year-old Adolf D. and 16-year-old Johann D. Both boys had grown up in broken or dysfunctional families. As early as 1940, Adolf had been taken from his parents and confined briefly to a children's home. Thereafter, he was placed under supervision until apprenticed first to a lathe operator and next to a shoemaker. In late 1943, he was arrested for stealing a pair of shoes and sentenced to three weeks in detention. While waiting to be conscripted into the Reich Labor Service, he lived with his stepmother in a bombed-out apartment. Johann D. also grew up the son of divorced working-class parents. He did not do well in school and was frequently cited for truancy. Although assigned to work in a textile plant, he suffered from a chronic illness that hampered his performance.

Late at night on December 18, 1944, the boys hammered their way into a tobacco shop, where they stole stocks of tobacco, cigarettes, and other goods worth RM 800. After being taken into custody, they were tried and convicted on January 23, 1945. Because the judge determined they were intellectually and morally mature, he sentenced them to one to four years of "indefinite imprisonment" according to §§ 171–4 of the Austrian penal code and § 36 of the Juvenile Court Law. He concluded by expressing the hope such pedagogical punishment would enable the delinquents to become useful members of the National Community.³⁵

A similar case involved a 16-year-old tailor apprentice, Johann S., and his 15-year-old accomplice, Maximilian S. Following the early death of his mother, Johann had grown up in the care of various family members. He had performed satisfactorily in school, but once his father was called up, social workers reported, he left home and began spending too much time with a girlfriend or watching movies. In 1943, Johann was confined briefly in the Juchgasse jail as punishment for unauthorized excursions to Lake Constance. Upon release, he met Maximilian who had served time in Eggenburg reformatory, apparently for petty theft. Early in the evening of January 7, 1944, the two boys clambered over a wall, breaking into the "Pirate Rowing Club." Here they gulped down bottles of wine, tore open packing crates, and collected piles of clothing, a rifle, phonograph records, and other items worth RM 500. As they sought to make their escape, they were stopped by a woman, whom they threatened with a bayonet. Shortly thereafter they were captured by an off-duty soldier who wrestled them to the ground.

Four months later, the Higher Regional Court sentenced Maximilian and Johann to one to three years of penal servitude in a juvenile correctional facility. According to §§ 171, 173, and 174 of the Austrian penal code as well as § 2 of the Reich Juvenile Court Law, the judges ruled that the failure of previous pedagogical sanctions necessitated severe punishment in order that the delinquents recognize the errors of their ways and atone for their crimes.³⁶

During the last winter of war, a handful of teenage gangs, similar to those roaming the streets of Cologne and bombed-out cities of the "Altreich," carried out a series of break-ins and burglaries in Vienna. At least two were apprehended by the police. The indictment of eight 17-year-old juveniles led by Erich B., a manual worker, casts light on the social background of the members as well as the nature of their crimes. Erich was the son of divorced parents, a member of a family characterized by social workers as "asocial," even before the father had been called up. Three sisters, for example, had served time for absenteeism including one incarcerated in Uckermark. Erich had run afoul of the law in 1938 for deviance (*Verwahrlosung*) and confined to a reformatory in Mödling. Released in August 1942, he became an upholster apprentice, fell into bad company, and the following summer spent a month in detention for bicycle theft. One of Erich's accomplices, Franz L., came from a stable family, but his father was also serving in the Wehrmacht. Following the Anschluß, Franz was picked up several times for petty theft, served two-week detentions, and in 1943 was sentenced to four weeks in jail for bicycle theft. A third accomplice, Franz F., had also spent time in Mödling for indolence, impudence, and unruly behavior.

According to the bill of indictment, Erich and Franz had broken into weekend homes near Schönbrunn as well as numerous tobacco shops between March and May 1944. They were joined by Franz F. and other youngsters, who made off with thousands of cigarettes, numerous tobacco products, and additional items including cash, clothing, shoes, fountain pens, radios, and even rabbits. During the summer months, other gang members sold the purloined cigarettes to foreign workers on the black market. Once taken into custody, State Prosecutor Dr. Heinz Mannl insisted that the Higher Regional Court condemn Erich as precocious juvenile criminal, national parasite, and habitual law breaker, Franz L. as a national parasite, and Franz F. as a dangerous felon. The remaining gang members were charged with grand larceny according to §§ 171, 173, 174, and 176 of the Austrian penal code. Interestingly, the Reich Juvenile Court Law was not invoked. Because no trial transcript has survived, the fate of the juvenile defendants is unknown.[37]

Another teenage gang was led by a 17-year-old welder apprentice, Franz R., and his younger brother, Hubert. Between October 1944 and February 1945, aided by five accomplices, they broke into garden houses, filching clocks, foodstuffs, cameras, and a radio. Undetected by the police, Franz's gang also stole bicycles, one of which they sold to a Russian soldier after liberation. On February 11, 1947, the Juvenile Court sentenced Franz to one year of severe imprisonment to be followed by three years of probation; his brother was sentenced to six months. Two years later, the director of a workhouse in Göllersdorf reported that owing to a failed escape Franz would remain behind bars until April 1950.[38]

The only other group that might be considered a gang, albeit a small one, consisted of five 17-year-old apprentices charged with plundering bombed-out homes in February 1945. Their loot consisted of barber clippers and shears, cameras, film, clocks, table knives, and a variety of kitchen utensils. Looking back, the boys appear to have acted spontaneously, but on May 3, 1946, the postwar juvenile court sentenced the ringleader to six months of severe imprisonment, and the others to terms of four months each. Interestingly, a request to expunge their record twelve years later was met with refusal.[39]

The punishment of individuals convicted of break-ins, primarily of tobacco shops, was not pursued consistently either by Nazi judges or by those of the Second Republic. Eighteen-year-old Josef M., for example, was sentenced on March 21, 1945 to two years in jail, not least for resisting arrest with a pistol.[40] In contrast, 16-year pupil, Herbert F., was sentenced to four weeks of detention for breaking into a cobbler's shop.⁴¹ After the war, on July 7, 1947, a carpenter's apprentice was found guilty of breaking into a Gasthaus on New Year's Eve 1944, where he stole meat, wine, apples, as well as a silver ring, an amber bracelet, and a silk shawl. He was also charged with filching a record player and a leather brief case. On July 7, 1947, the juvenile court acquitted him of several charges, sentencing him to four months of severe detention to be followed by three years of probation.⁴²

2. Hold-Ups and Robberies

The significant increase in juvenile hold-ups and robberies, largely by individuals, during the last months of the war reflects both the breakdown of Viennese society and the desperate plight of many teenage perpetrators. In a number of cases, the magistrates expressed sympathy for the convicted by imposing relatively mild sanctions; in others they handed down harsh sentences. Several examples of the mild sentences are discussed. On January 25, 1945, the judges sentenced 17-year-old Karl S. to eight days in detention for stealing a bicycle from a Hitler Youth lodge.⁴³ Some days later, Walter L. threw himself at the mercy of the court, admitting he had pinched a woolen coat and pair of knickerbockers from a cloakroom in order to protect himself from the freezing cold. He too received a mild sentence, although the exact period of detention does not appear in the documentation.⁴⁴ Similarly, 15-year-old Rudolf K. was sentenced in mid-January 1945 to four weeks in detention for snatching a purse from a woman containing RM 688 in cash.⁴⁵ In an even more remarkable case, Franz., a 17-year-old office trainee, was brought before the bench on January 29, 1945 for stealing two suitcases containing a sweater, two sports shirts, and two bottles of liquor. The court found Franz guilty as charged, but took into account his deprived upbringing and destitute status to invoke § 36 of the Reich Juvenile Court Law, thus imposing a sentence of only three weeks of suspended detention.⁴⁶

In sharp contrast, 18-year-old Otto P. and his 14-year-old brother were sentenced in mid-February 1945 to six months in a juvenile penitentiary for purse-snatching. Court documents reveal that the boys served their time and were released in July 1945.⁴⁷ In mid-March, an 18-year-old domestic was imprisoned for an unspecified period in Stadlau for stealing cigarettes, though in July she also walked free.⁴⁸

Another interesting case was that of 17-year-old Rupert R., whose fate fell between two proverbial stools. On March 28, 1945, only two weeks before the collapse of Nazi rule, the Higher Regional Court found him guilty of stealing two packages of underwear, various items of clothing, and shoes worth RM 167 shortly before Christmas 1944. According to § 6 of the Reich Juvenile Court Law, the judge imposed a sentence of nine months to four years of "indefinite imprisonment," expressing the hope that his behavior would enable him to rejoin the crumbling National Community. In 1946, the judiciary reconsidered the verdict and ordered a second trial, which took place on August 9, 1947. This time the court overruled the Nazi sentence but ordered that Rupert be confined to two months in strict detention. A telegram sent the following year indicated that he had been taken into custody in St. Pölten for an unspecified crime.[49]

The uneven sanctions imposed by juvenile judges in the waning days of Nazi rule for property crimes appear to have diverged in a number of instances from the generally harsh sentences meted out by magistrates of the Second Republic immediately after the war. It is likely, as suggested above, that except in egregious cases, the Nazi judiciary imposed brief detentions as a means of returning delinquents to the wartime workplace as soon as possible.

3. Absenteeism, Indiscipline, and Breach of Contract

In mid-1943, as mentioned above, the Viennese state prosecutor reported a sharp rise in absenteeism from the workplace. At first glance, his alarm appears to have been more prophetic than statistically sound, because only 5.2 percent of those found guilty of violating Nazi ordinances had been convicted of transgressing the War Economy Decree of 1939.[50] On the other hand, over 700 youngsters—mostly "Schlurfs"—were being confined for weekends or longer for "breach of contract" or loitering according to *Jugendarrest*.[51] Further, the number of arrests of foreign workers rose exponentially between February 1943 and March 1944.[52] How many of these were juveniles is unknown. What the 1945 court records indicate is that between August 1944 and the end of the war some 42 Viennese youngsters (29 percent of all delinquents) were formally arrested or convicted for turning up late for work, leaving the workplace, or long-term absenteeism. Of these, twenty-three were boys, and nineteen were girls. Their average age was 16.5. Unsurprisingly, exactly half of those brought to book had stayed away from work for three to four weeks during the 1944 Yuletide season. Some had serious reasons for walking off the jobs; for others, they were more frivolous.

Scrutiny of court records reveal that Viennese justices devoted more assiduous consideration to cases of juveniles accused of "breach of contract" than might be expected. The jurists while weighing the evidence generally took into account the age, personality, and health of the offenders, as well the impact of sanctions on the war effort. Procedurally, employers would file complaints ranging from malingering to insubordination, to walking off the job or, most frequently, to long-term absenteeism. After assessing the charges, officials of the Reich Trustee of Labor would remand the accused to the Higher Regional Court for trial. Given the variety of offences, sentences meted out included a mixture of warnings, fines, brief detentions, as well as confinement in correctional facilities, jail, or disciplinary work camps.[53]

Although difficult to generalize, the available evidence suggests that those juveniles sentenced to jail or a correctional facility for "breach of contract" had previously ran afoul of the law or simply fabricated excuses. The trial transcript of 14-year-old Leopold P. provides a good case in point. Compelled to work for a local firm, Leopold had walked off the shop floor in early November 1943. When apprehended shortly before Christmas, he claimed to have been suffering from a chronic illness. A court-appointed physician reported, however, that the boy was perfectly healthy. And because he had briefly been detained for absenteeism earlier in the year, the court sentenced Leopold to three months in confinement[54] A similar fate befell another youngster, also sentenced to three months behind bars for failing to correct his behavior after two weeks of detention for absenteeism.[55] Even more severe was a seven-month jail term imposed upon 18-year-old Leopold V. for multiple absences since 1940.[56] On the other hand, in February 1944, 14-year-old Wilhelm F. was let off with a warning because of his age.[57]

As the war drew to a close, the justices appear to have taken a closer look at the health and living conditions of youngsters accused of "breach of contract." This may be attributed to growing hardships and shortages as well as the impact of Allied bombing. It is true, for example, that the food distribution system had succeeded in avoiding the sort of "starvation crisis" that engulfed Vienna in the First World War. Nevertheless, a postwar study revealed that 70 percent of adolescent apprentices had emerged from the 1939–1945 conflict severely malnourished, underweight, and prone to illness; for working girls and domestics, the figures were 38 percent.[58] The records of those juveniles tried for "breach of contract" in the last year and a half of the war suggest that the justices weighed the evidence more carefully than might be expected. This was no easy matter as they had to take into consideration the severity of the charge, the age, character, and health of the defendant as well as the impact of sanctions on the war effort. Procedurally, employers would file complaints ranging from insubordination, to indolence, to walking off the job, or most commonly to long-term absenteeism. As previously mentioned, officials of the local Trustee of Labor would process the allegations and present them to the judiciary. In a number of cases, however, prosecutors either downplayed the charges or judges declined to bring the accused to trial.[59]

In a fair number of instances, the magistrates took into consideration medical evidence. On May 2, 1944, for example, 18-year-old Ernst K. claimed that a severe heart condition precluded him from hard labor. Rather than pass sentence, the court ordered a thorough medical examination.[60] In another case tried in 1944, a 15-year-old plumber apprentice argued that a skin infection prevented him from working in a filthy, squalid enterprise. After some months, on January 16, 1945, the Institute for Legal and Criminal Medicine of the University of Vienna reported that the accused did indeed suffer from impetigo, but should be compelled to return to the shop floor.[61]

As mentioned above, the number of cases of adolescent "breach of contract" rose sharply in late 1944, most notably during the Yuletide season. Further, the health and well-being of the accused figured prominently in the deliberations of the judicial magistrates. In December 1944, the Labor Office ordered 16-year-old Josefine F. to resume her job at the Garven machine, pump, and scales factory, which she had left heavily pregnant on August 1. The management responded that the plant's drilling machinery was too cumbersome and dangerous for a young mother to operate, requesting that she be allowed to work at home. The Labor Office replied by filing charges of breach of contract. On March 3, 1945, the District Court expressed sympathy for Josefine, but nevertheless sentenced her to four weeks in detention.[62] In contrast the judges took pity on another 16-year-old girl who had left the workplace in early November without shoes to wear in the cold winter weather. After securing another pair from her sister, she was allowed to resume working without paying a penalty. This also appears to have been the case with another young woman, who had been hospitalized since May 1944.[63] In yet another case, the court seemed ambivalent in assessing the character of the defendant. During the summer, 16-year-old Franz S. had absented himself on and off from a factory in Simmering until dismissed by his employer at the end of September. Assigned to work at another plant in October, he walked off the job after only three days. When tried by the District Court on January 1945, Franz claimed to have been unwell while admitting he had no desire to work. This appeared to be a flimsy excuse, but the court ruled that four weeks in detention should bring him to his senses.[64] The judges imposed the same penalty on another 16-year-old, a plumber's apprentice, who offered no excuse for staying on and off the job for thirty-five days in 1944.[65]

Scrutiny of those youngsters tried for "breach of contract" or absenteeism during Christmastime 1944 reveals a panoply of motives, excuses, and penalties. In two cases, the court acquitted two 16-year-old defendants. In the first instance, Judge Franz Langer ruled on February 2, 1945, that Leopold P. was neither physically nor mentally fit to dig entrenchments. In the second, Langer conceded that Ludwig P. had good reason to stay away from the Franz Reuner firm to which he had been assigned, simply because he lacked the strength to offload pig irons weighing 50 kilograms each. On April 3, however, Judge Staininger overruled this verdict, sentencing Ludwig to four unspecified detentions. As Vienna fell to Soviet troops within ten days, it is unclear whether Ludwig was forced back to work or locked up in a reformatory.[66]

In other cases, the judges imposed relatively light sentences by considering mitigating circumstances such as sickness or serious familial problems. On March 23, 1945, for example, the court found 18-year-old Rudolfine B. guilty of absenteeism but, recognizing the necessity of caring for a gravely ill sister, ordered her detained for merely a week. In two additional cases, the court dismissed all charges owing to a mother's illness.[67] On the other hand, the justices were not always persuaded. A 16-year-old Wehrmacht assistant, Anna S., had spent three weeks away from her post between Christmas and Epiphany, claiming to have cared for her ailing mother. Shortly before war's end, Anna was sentenced to three weeks in strict confinement.[68]

In several cases, the judges relied on the reports of social workers in reaching decisions, although less frequently than in the past. Because of Vienna's chronic housing shortage, 18-year-old Gertrude P. had never lived in a proper home. Her parents were so impoverished that she had spent her childhood dwelling between two sets of grandparents. She did poorly in elementary school and was sent down after one year in high school. As an apprentice, she paid little attention to her work, leaving her job for the entire Christmas season from Advent through Epiphany. On January 31, 1945, she was sentenced to three weeks in detention and upon completion was to be entrusted to the Guardianship Authority.[69] Seventeen-year-old Luwig J. had also taken the month off for Christmas. According to extensive investigation by social workers, Ludwig had suffered from serious childhood illnesses as well as a heart condition. He was nervous, short-tempered, and experienced difficulty sleeping. During his absence, he had spent his time loitering and attending movies. On January 12, 1945, the court sentenced him to two weeks in detention, recommending that thereafter he be assigned to foster parents for proper education.[70] In yet another case of Yuletide absenteeism, NSV social workers filed an extensive report on 16-year-old Josef

Z., a boy who had left school with learning disabilities. At age 14, he had worked briefly in an auto paint shop, but been dismissed for frequent absences. He then became a manual laborer in a metalware firm, though continued to be considered weak and untenable. On January 31, 1945, the District Court sentenced Josef to three weeks in detention. Sadly, the experience had little impact. In late 1953, the judicial authorities refused to efface his record owing to five additional convictions.[71]

The records of other juveniles accused of absenteeism during the Christmas season are less complete but suggest a common pattern. Nearly all of the delinquents had grown up in straitened circumstances, not infrequently in single-room dwellings. By late 1944, their fathers had been serving for years in the Wehrmacht, had gone missing, or had been killed in action. Seventeen-year-old Anastasia M., for example, was one of eight siblings. Born with a learning disability, she had dropped out of school with a fifth-grade education. She was then compelled to work eight months as a housekeeper, after which she spent one and a half years toiling in an engineering firm. That she chose to spend Christmas with her family and a mother who had been reduced to begging seems hardly incomprehensible. But because the NSV claimed her absence cost the mythical National Community 200 man-hours, the District Court sentenced her in late February to four weeks in detention.[72] In a similar case, 17-year-old Wilhelmine L. was compelled to scrub bedpans in an SS hospital after completing three weeks of detention.[73]

The fate of other minors charged with work stoppages or absenteeism is incomplete. At least eight were never brought to trial, of whom two were conscripted by the Reich Labor Service, two others by the *Volkssturm*, and a third killed in an air raid. In one case, 15-year-old Aloisa B. was placed briefly under arrest, but following a brief hospital stay was allowed to return to work.[74] As for the others, their fate is simply unknown. Looking back, the 1944 Juvenile Court Law constituted a logical way to stem juvenile absenteeism during the last fifteen months of Hitler's war. By imposing brief detentions on teenagers who had left the workplace, the regime sought both to reintegrate them as quickly as possible into the war effort and to set an example for others to stay on the job. That virtually all of the convicted delinquents came from impoverished or disadvantaged backgrounds reveals something about the persistence of class divisions in Hitler's National Community. It also says something about gender, as every one of the girls forced to work as scullery maids or domestics for prosperous or well-to-do Viennese families expressed bitter resentment to the authorities. One 16-year-old was taken into custody from a factory floor was reported to have resisted with clenched fists.[75] To what extent the Juvenile Court Law achieved its dual objectives in Vienna thus remains an open question.

4. Assault and Sexual Immorality

While nearly all Viennese adolescents convicted of absenteeism had not committed serious crimes—as even the Nazis conceded—the same cannot be said of those indicted for aggravated assault or sexual immorality. On January 4, 1945, two 17-year-old apprentices, Rudolf F. and Karl B., had seized and gagged a 12-year-old school boy, and stole his wristwatch and a ring. Convicted by the District Court on March 20, they were sentenced to six and seven months in confinement respectively. Here the judges must have taken the new Juvenile Court Law into consideration, as § 192 of the Austrian penal code for violent theft called for ten to twenty years in prison.[76] In another case, two other boys were indicted for assault in October 1944. However, a postwar tribunal sentenced them to three months of strict detention, as they had unwittingly become involved in a brawl over bedcovers while exposed to the elements during the construction of Hitler's Southeast Wall near Zurndorf.[77]

Only a handful of individual minors are known to have been tried for sexual immorality, although others may have been incarcerated by the police or dispatched to concentration camps. In October 1943, Erich B., an 18-year-old carpenter apprentice, was arrested for numerous homosexual encounters, theft, and forgery. Given the gravity of the charges, social workers prepared an extensive pretrial investigative report. Born the illegitimate child of an alcoholic mother, his putative father had committed suicide in 1933. The mother married six years later, but paid little attention to her offspring. Erich completed two years of secondary education, and then dropped out to become a tailor's apprentice. Nervous and abnormally active, he rarely turned up for work. After serving a brief sentence for absenteeism in 1943, he joined two other juveniles at the Roman Sauna, where he serviced at least fifty adult homosexuals, charging RM 5–10 per person. At the time of his arrest, Erich was also found to have stolen suitcases and ration coupons.

Held in custody for a year, Erich was tried, found guilty, and on December 8, 1944, sentenced to ten years in a juvenile penitentiary. As stipulated by § 5 of the Reich Juvenile Court Law, the judges ruled that such a severe sentence was required not only by the needs of the National Community, but also as an acknowledgment of guilt, penance, and awareness of the magnitude of the crimes committed. Further, the defendant's "injurious predisposition" indicated that educative rehabilitation would serve no useful purpose.[78] In contrast, Erich's accomplice, Otto V., received a lighter sentence of one to three years of "indefinite imprisonment," most likely because he was convicted solely of offences "contrary to nature."[79]

Not all moral offences involved homosexual conduct. During the summer of 1944, 16-year-old Rosa S. fell in love with a Polish prisoner of war in Prellenkirchen, east of Vienna. By February 8, 1945, her pregnancy was so advanced that she was indicted for violating the ordinance that required "protecting the German people." There is no record that her case ever came to trial.[80] In another instance, a 16-year-old lathe apprentice was scheduled to be tried on May 4, 1945, for "crimes contrary to nature." Although liable for trial in the Second Republic, there is no evidence that such a legal proceeding ever took place.[81] In another bizarre case, a 16-year-old girl was indicted on February 26, 1945, for incest with her father. The documentation is exiguous but reveals that she received an amnesty shortly after the war. Finally, for some odd reason, a 42-year-old adult was tried by the Juvenile Division of the Higher Regional Court on charges of debauchery. On January 24, 1945, 17-year-old Friedrich P. was found guilty of having exposed himself to a 10-year-old school girl in the Prater and sentenced to six months in jail, followed by three years of probation. Although § 128 of the Austrian penal code called for punishment of one to five years in prison, the judge imposed a lesser penalty by taking into account the plight of Friedrich's innocent family. Three years later, Friedrich petitioned the court to efface his record in order to take a job in the postal service. The magistrates obliged, reporting that Friedrich had fulfilled his debt to society.[82]

5. Petty Thefts, Misbehaviors, and Adolescent Shenanigans

Aside from the small number of major break-ins and robberies discussed above, the upsurge of petty thefts and absenteeism in the last months of the war no doubt reflected the sense of foreboding, disillusionment, and desperation engulfing Viennese society. Nowadays, nearly all of these juvenile offences would be considered minor misdemeanors; others deserving no more than a warning or slap on the wrist. A few examples should suffice. In late 1944, a 17-year-old sales apprentice was sentenced to one week in detention for selling two wild ducks on the black market.[83] In a similar case, a 16-year-old was charged with pinching three geese and a liter of wine.[84] In yet another instance, two younger boys were punished with brief detentions for stealing a rucksack of potatoes.[85] Two other 15-year-olds, one an electrical apprentice, the other a day laborer, were indicted for crawling through a hole in a barbed wire fence surrounding a private garden in Gross Enzendorf, after which they made off with substantial quantities of fruit. Within weeks they were mustered into Hitler's *Volkssturm*, so that the trial was delayed for a year. When brought before the bench, the magistrates of the Second Republic ruled that the youngsters had clearly committed larceny under §§ 171 and 174 of the Austrian penal code, but that their motives had been frivolous rather than malicious. With that in mind, the court sentenced them to two brief detentions.[86] In two additional cases, Nazi judges considered the charges absurd. On February 19, 1945, they found 16-year-old Friedrich T. not guilty of nicking rabbits.[87] Seven weeks later, they issued a warning to a 15-year-old mechanic apprentice for stealing six Christmas trees.[88]

In many ways the adolescent misbehaviors and shenanigans deliberated by the Viennese judiciary during the last weeks of the war are difficult to categorize. They ranged from teenage high jinks to vandalism, to acts of defiance that may or may not have constituted resistance to the regime. In the first instance, 19-year Karl S., joined by three younger boys and a girl, went on a spree in late 1944 of releasing phials of tear gas in a number of cinemas and other public places. Although charged with "indecent assault," Karl was sentenced on January 20, 1945, to a relatively mild punishment of two weeks in severe detention. Oddly, a court document filed on March 6, 1946, indicates that Karl never served time and would not be compelled to do so.[89]

The few surviving records of juvenile arrests for misbehavior or waywardness in the last months of Nazi rule portray spontaneous outbursts of anger and rage similar to those expressed by large numbers of ordinary people in working-class districts of Vienna.[90] On February 8, 1945, for example, a 16-year-old baker's apprentice punched a street car conductor in the face in an overcrowded tram.[91] Three weeks later, two 15-year-olds opened fire with a Steyr pistol in a cable manufacturing plant. Although arrested by the criminal police, they were freed from all charges the following summer.[92] Even more remarkably, in early March, 16-year-old Walter R. brazenly stole a service revolver from a noncommissioned officer in Petronell, a capital offence. For this act of defiance, however, the boy was never brought to trial, as he was killed by an exploding grenade.[93] Other instances that involved teenagers caught with firearms coupled with numerous arrests for petty theft and looting during the last weeks of Nazi rule can be attributed to the rapid deterioration of material conditions and sense of dread in Vienna, particularly in the wake of Allied air raids. Whether they represented the work of teenage hooligans, acts of political resistance, or simply adolescent shenanigans remained a question for the judges of the Second Republic to sort out.

Conclusions

What impact did the 1943 Reich Juvenile Court Law have in Vienna? At least two conclusions may be drawn. First, the new law appears to have had some success in stemming juvenile delinquency during the last fifteen months of the war, or more precisely until mid-February 1945. While it is true that the number of property offences declined slightly, that of hold-ups and thefts rose notably. Further, except for three diminutive cliques, most of the crimes involved petty pilfering and appear to have been committed by individuals or by two or three boys. Unlike other cities of the Greater German Reich such as Cologne, Düsseldorf, and other regions of the Ruhr, no violent teenage gangs ever roamed the streets of Vienna. Indeed, the number of felonious bands appear to have declined during the last year of the war. On the other hand, it is unlikely that large numbers of youngsters refrained from joining in the wave of lawlessness and theft that accompanied the siege and fall of Vienna.[94]

Second, the sentences handed out tended initially to be severe, although generally not as punitive or intermittently capricious as before. Unless convicted of a previous misdemeanor or felony, the court usually imposed a penalty of two to four months strict of confinement, most notably for absence from the workplace. Toward the end of the war, sentences for "breaches of contract" were frequently reduced to two to four weeks in detention. It is true that the justices sometimes imposed lengthy jail terms, generally upon recommendation of the NSV or Juvenile Welfare Board, but the evidence suggests they paid less attention to the advice of social workers than in the past. They also tended to take age into account and in several cases expressed sympathy for youngsters too weak to engage in heavy labor. Moreover, in convicting two youngsters of violent theft, the court imposed a sentence of six to seven months in jail instead of lengthy prison sentences stipulated by Austrian law. None of this is to imply that the 1944 Juvenile Court Law constituted a change in judicial attitudes. Rather, it represented a flawed but pragmatic attempt to control and mobilize wayward and delinquent youngsters for the hard-pressed German war effort. It is within that context that the legislation must be judged and assessed.[95]

6

Postwar and Beyond

On March 30, 1945, Soviet forces drove into the "Ostmark" from Hungary and within a few days reached the outskirts of Vienna. Attacking from the south and west, they overcame stiff resistance from two SS divisions to secure the city by April 13. Ten days earlier, Dr. Karl Renner, the prominent Social Democratic politician and chancellor between 1918 and 1920, emerged from his home in Gloggnitz to contact the Soviet commander. On April 20, Hitler's birthday, an agreement was hammered out to form a provisional government, which took office on April 27. Three days later, the new regime published a proclamation, composed largely by Renner, reestablishing a democratic Austrian republic and declaring the Anschluß null and void. In eloquent language the proclamation listed a bill of particulars, repudiating Nazi usurpations, the wholesale theft of Austrian monetary, proprietorial, and cultural assets, and the dissolution of the federal provinces. The document condemned the Nazi regime for initiating a war of conquest and annihilation that took the lives of millions, including hundreds of thousands of Austrians. It endorsed the Moscow Declaration of 1943 that Austria had been the "first victim of Hitlerite aggression" but also accepted responsibility for the country's participation in the German war effort. Significantly, often overlooked in the literature, Renner's proclamation abrogated the Nuremberg racial laws as well as all laws and ordinances contrary to the fundamental principles of the 1920 constitution.[1]

Throughout early summer, the provisional government annulled no fewer than 250 German laws, ordinances, and decrees that had been imposed in Austria between 1938 and 1945.[2] These included the Law for the Prevention of Diseased Offspring, the Law Against the Formation of New Parties, the Subversion Law, and various supplementary amendments to the Nuremberg Laws. Most important for our study was the repeal of ordinances for the Protection of Juvenile Criminals and the Protection of Youth as well as the Decree Against National Parasites (*Volksschädlinge*). On June 12, Renner's government abrogated the Reich Juvenile Court Law of December 6, 1943, and restored the Juvenile Court Act of 1928, legislation that would remain in force until 1960.[3]

Three weeks later, the new regime formally reinstated the Austrian judicial system as it had existed on March 13, 1938, although it also negated legislation passed by Dollfuss in 1934 altering certain judicial procedures. Further, the provisional government stipulated that judicial law clerks whose careers had been interrupted by racial persecution or military service were to be readmitted to the bar. Various changes introduced after 1938 were also rescinded. Overall, the law published on July 9, 1945, meant the restoration of traditional court procedures such as trial by jury, the appointment of prosecutors and judges, the rights of defendants, and so forth. Most significantly for our study, it officially restored the Austrian penal code, although, as we have seen, it had remained in place throughout the entire Nazi era.[4]

Exactly how and when the Viennese Juvenile Court was reorganized during the early days of the Second Republic is not altogether clear, for example, in the dismissal and retention of judicial personnel. According to surviving records in the municipal archives, the justices decided to dismiss all charges of "breach of contract" but to prosecute youngsters indicted for felonious property crimes. We have already discussed seven of these cases in the previous chapter, primarily because they extended into the postwar period. From today's perspective, it seems inexplicable that magistrates of a liberated country would prosecute youngsters for felonies committed during the last days of the Third Reich. Whether this was a conscious decision or not is unclear. But in doing so, the judges could argue that Austria had been an occupied state in which the existing penal code had remained intact. And there can be little doubt that most sought to retain their positions on the bench, particularly those who had not belonged to the "illegal" NSDAP prior to 1938 and were thus immune from dismissal.[5] Whatever the case, no one can gainsay a continuity of the juvenile justice system in Vienna that extended from the Dollfuss-Schuschnigg dictatorship into the early days of the Second Republic. On the other hand, courtroom procedures had changed significantly. The juvenile bench now consisted of a presiding judge, an associate, two jurors, a prosecutor, a defense attorney, and the defendant accompanied by his parents. All but three of the trials based on Nazi indictments were conducted in 1946.

The first took place on November 3, 1945. It involved the case of two 15-year-old boys indicted in September 1944 for stealing fruit in Gross Enzendorf. As we have already seen, the court convicted them of grand larceny but considered their motives trivial. With that in mind, the boys were sentenced to spend no more than two brief detentions.[6]

The second proceeding was an appeal filed by three 16-year-old inmates on December 20, 1945. In early January of that year, the Higher Regional Court had sentenced them to one to four years of "indefinite imprisonment" for stealing over 6,000 cigars and cigarettes as well as RM 300 in cash. While the judges of the Second Republic may have been inclined to be lenient, they confirmed the sentences primarily because the ringleader of the group had been indicted for a number of other robberies.[7]

Finally, on December 31, the court upheld the conviction of a 17-year-old manual laborer, who in late 1944 and early 1945 had fenced wine and foodstuffs on the black market and stolen over 5,000 cigarettes. The judges sentenced him to three months of strict detention, meaning close confinement, and the payment of court costs to be followed by three years of supervised probation.[8]

When the reconstituted Juvenile Court reconvened after the first of the year in the Gray House, the justices had to adjudicate no fewer than forty-three offences committed in the waning days of the Nazi regime, including seven cases discussed in the previous chapter. Among these were a number of youngsters who had been freed from confinement following the liberation of Vienna in early April but soon thereafter resumed their delinquent behavior.

In early January 1946, the judges dismissed a case on unusual grounds. In late 1945, two 15-year-old boys had cut down and stolen six Christmas trees from a municipal allotment. After examining the evidence, the court ruled that as the allotment had belonged to a Reich German, the youngsters could not be punished under Austrian law for seizing "German assets."[9]

By March, more serious cases were coming before the bench. On the second day of that month, two jobless defendants faced magistrates in the Gray House on charges of theft. In January 1945, Josef R. had stolen hundreds of cigarettes, tobacco, ration coupons, a silver ring, and other items from field post packages. He then entrusted them to Johann W. who attempted to fence them on the black market. In reaching judgment, the court found Josef guilty of larceny, and Johann culpable as his accomplice. Both were sentenced to eight months of strict detention to be followed by three years on probation. The court concluded that both boys would most likely follow a life of crime, but hoped that such a mild sentence might correct their behavior.[10] More severe was the punishment imposed on 16-year-old office trainee, Heinz W. In December 1944, he had purloined a skeleton key from his employer to filch 9 kilograms of sugar, two pairs of women's hose, four handkerchiefs, and two pairs of sandals. The justices seemed bemused that the stolen goods were of little worth, but did not hesitate to sentence him to six months in strict detention.[11] Another

16-year-old, Adalbert K., was convicted of stealing a camera during an air raid. He was sentenced to only three months in detention to be followed by three years on parole. Had Adalbert been tried under Nazi rule, the penalty would most certainly have been more severe. Even so, he was unable to have his record expunged in order to gain employment until 1955.[12]

In late March two 17-year-old apprentices were brought to book for sexual abuse on a cold winter's night the previous year. After spending the day digging trenches as forced laborers near Zurndorf, the two youngsters had attempted masturbating six other boys. Testimony revealed that a row had erupted after one of the victims put up resistance. In passing judgment, the court took into consideration both the defendants' age and the desperate wartime situation. Nevertheless, they sentenced the youngsters to three months in strict detention and the payment of court costs. Two decades later, the record was effaced.[13]

One of the most unusual cases to come before the juvenile justices in early 1946 was that of 16-year-old Hubert S. Like most other adolescent delinquents, Hubert had grown up in straitened circumstances. Born in 1930 to a divorced couple, he was given up for adoption, although never accepted by foster parents. Instead, he spent his childhood in various orphanages, eventually winding up in an apprentices' hostel. Social workers and psychiatrists reported that he had completed four classes of secondary school, was highly intelligent, though also lazy and easily influenced by others. On New Year's Eve 1945, he had assaulted a young woman on the Mariahilfegürtel, snatching her purse that contained valuable ration coupons, RM 300 in cash, and a gold watch. Captured and locked up immediately thereafter, he walked out of a reformatory during the liberation of Vienna.

In early July, Hubert acquired a Hitler Youth blouse, cleverly modifying it to resemble an American uniform. He then approached British occupation authorities, contending that he was a sergeant who had seen combat in Italy and the Western Front. They, in turn, stamped a forged English language certificate that he passed off as a military ID to clueless Viennese officials, a document that enabled him to find lodging and move freely through Lower Austria. However, on July 13, he was apprehended masquerading as the mayor of Eichgraben. When brought to trial on March 9, 1946, the judges expressed sympathy for Hubert's unhappy childhood. Reading between the lines, they seem to have admired his audacity. Even so, they convicted him of theft and forgery according to §§ 190, 197, and 199 of the penal code, imposing a sentence of one-year strict confinement.[14]

In late May, two 16-year-old journeymen trainees, a 15-year-old girl, and a 14-year-old youngster stood accused of multiple thefts between January and March 1945. Operating as a team, they had stolen clothing, including shirts, skirts, trousers, and a fur coat. They had also made off with bottles of champagne, loaves of bread, toilet items, considerable quantities of fruit, tobacco, and even a military pistol. Their success, in retrospect, can be attributed to both shortages of essentials and the breakdown of law and order during the last days of the Nazi regime. Even so, the judges found the perpetrators guilty of grand larceny, sentencing the two oldest to four and six months respectively in strict confinement. The court placed the girl on three years of probation, while releasing the 14-year-old, although not without filing a report that he had been found partially culpable.[15]

Much more severe was the punishment imposed on 16-year-old roofer, Alexander L. Like most delinquents, Alexander had grown up in poverty, not least after his father died in 1938 leaving him under the care of a negligent sickly mother. In March 1945, he and another boy, Franz B., broke into a deserted home during an air raid, stealing a silver watch, several pairs of socks, shoes, playing cards, and a can of sardines. In April, he had pilfered numerous shops and homes in the chaos following the Russian conquest of Vienna. Thereafter he continued his calling as a petty thief until apprehended for stealing vegetables in early September. From today's perspective, Alexander's minor offences would warrant no more than a few weeks in jail, but on May 14, 1946, the Higher Regional Court convicted him of grand larceny. The justices sentenced Alexander to one year of strict detention, primarily for looting during an air raid but also on grounds that he was an indolent layabout. In 1949, after completing his sentence, Alexander, now an adult, was apprehended for breaking into an American jeep. He was subsequently sentenced to six months of heavy labor, but did not walk free until 1951.[16]

To a certain degree, Alexander's case may have been paradigmatic. The evidence suggests that Viennese judges tended to hand down harsh sentences to delinquents who had committed offences both under the Nazi regime and during the early days of the Second Republic. As discussed in the previous chapter, the court sentenced Franz R. in 1947 to one-year strict detention followed by three years on probation. Another case involved Johann R. Born in 1929, he was charged with stealing suitcases of clothing that included suits, dress shirts, ties, underwear, and shoes throughout 1944 and early 1945. After the war, he was arrested for pinching cash, foodstuffs, and two bicycles. On April 26, 1946, the court convicted him of grand larceny according to §§ 171, 173, and 176 of the penal code, sentencing him to one and one and a half years of strict detention. Surviving records indicate that he later spent three months at hard labor and was not released from custody until 1950.[17]

Several other cases seem to prove the point. On June 15, 1946, 18-year-old Ernst M. and 17-year-old Karl K. were found guilty of multiple robberies and thefts in 1944 that continued into early 1946. The stolen items consisted of bicycles, fruits, and various edibles. However, Ernst was also convicted of armed robbery. The judges proceeded to sentence Karl to six months of strict confinement but Ernst to five years behind bars.[18]

Another case involved a single individual, 18-year-old Josef K., an interior decorator trainee. Also the product of a broken home, Josef had been disciplined as a schoolroom bully and troublemaker. In August 1942, he had been briefly jailed in the Juchgasse police station, although it was not until February 1945 that he began his career as a juvenile lawbreaker. In that month, he and several other youngsters stole two suitcases containing a fur coat and food ration coupons from a traveler. In April, he exchanged a pilfered record player with a Soviet soldier for schnapps. In October, he made off with various items from an American post exchange and the following month, foodstuffs from Konsum and other grocery stores. On August 29, 1946, the Viennese Juvenile Court convicted Josef of grand larceny, sentencing him to one to three years strict detention. Had he been found guilty by a Nazi court, it is likely he would have been condemned as a "precocious juvenile criminal." Instead, while the judges of the Second Republic did take into account his antisocial behavior and criminal record, they nevertheless expressed the hope that close confinement would enable him to see the errors of his ways.[19]

At least three other youngsters, between the ages of 15 and 16, were severely punished for petty thefts committed between March 1945 and mid-1946. On March 23, 1945, the boys had been placed in protective custody for stealing 10 kilograms of margarine using force. Released on April 6, they were arrested the following summer for break-ins that yielded them three jars of powdered milk, several loaves of bread, sugar, and an unspecified number of containers of canned fish. On September 26, 1946, the judges took into consideration the delinquents' negligent upbringing and limited education but convicted them of aggravated robbery according to §§ 190, 192, and 194 of the Austrian penal code, primarily for committing crimes under the cover of darkness. Sardonically noting that the previous regime would have condemned them as "national parasites," the justices sentenced each of the youngsters to serve one year of strict detention.[20]

Generally speaking, the Viennese Juvenile Court imposed relatively mild sanctions on juveniles brought to book for offences committed only under Nazi rule. An exception was a case involving 16-year-old Kurt S. and Anton W., both of whom had broken into an allotment home during an air raid shortly before midnight on March 30, 1945. Their loot consisted of two suitcases of clothing, foodstuffs, an alarm clock, three watches, and a radio, which they hauled away in a wheelbarrow. Because both boys had served time in police custody in 1943 and committed burglary during an air raid, the judges sentenced Kurt to one year of strict detention on April 6, 1946, and Anton to nine months. A subsequent document reveals that Anton was released from Kaiser-Ebersdorf on July 30, 1947, but exactly a month later was arrested for breaking and entering.[21] A similar though different case was that of 17-year-old Rupert R., discussed in the previous chapter. On March 28, 1945, only two weeks before the collapse of Nazi rule, he had been sentenced for clothing theft to nine months to four years of "indefinite imprisonment." The following year, the Austrian judiciary reconsidered the verdict and asked for a second trial, which overruled the Nazi sentence but ordered that Rupert be confined to two months in strict detention.[22]

Here it should be reiterated that those sanctions imposed by postwar courts on juveniles for offences committed solely during the waning days of the Anschluß era were handed out according to prewar Austrian law. This may explain, as suggested above, why severe penalties for larceny were frequently reduced or ameliorated by mitigating powers restored to the courts. A good example is that of three 15-year-old apprentices who late at night on January 9, 1945, broke into a Viennese skating rink, making off with a radio, an air-raid mask, linen napkins, a pair of women's shoes, silken underwear, an umbrella, and a kitchen clock. All three had reached puberty in "fatherless" families; one, the son of divorced parents; the other two, children of soldiers missing in action. In passing judgment, the court found the boys guilty of larceny, but took negligence and age into account before sentencing them to four months of strict detention. Their record was not effaced, however, until 1972.[23] A similar case was that of 17-year-old commercial student, Rupert S. On January 26, 1945, he had broken into the private home of Georg Gijurasits and stolen an expensive radio set. Brought to trial on June 13, 1946, he was sentenced to four months of strict detention to be followed by three years on parole.[24]

Without detailing each and every case of the remaining teenagers convicted of theft at the end of the war, roughly half a dozen received sentences of four to six months behind bars, two were ordered to spend two days in custody, and another placed on probation. About half a dozen were not prosecuted or had charges dropped for lack of evidence. Among these were several young women tried for petty theft. A 16-year-old seamstress, for example, was indicted for stealing potatoes, clothing, shoes, and a winter coat from an air-raid shelter on January 20, 1945. Careful investigation by welfare workers revealed that Elsa came from an impoverished family, had done poorly in school, and was sexually involved with a coworker at the time of the offence. On October 10, 1946, the juvenile court found her guilty of larceny, formally sentenced her three months in strict detention, but allowed her to walk free on parole.[25]

One of the most interesting—and revealing—cases to come before a postwar juvenile tribunal was that of 16-year-old commercial student, Franz H. Between February 28 and March 2, 1945, he had seized two cut-out switches from Viennese trams for which he was indicted after the war on charges of grand larceny. On June 14, 1946, Franz filed a formal petition denying the court's judicial authority, arguing that his deeds were deliberate acts of sabotage. As a "Mischling of the Second Degree," he contended, his family had suffered under Hitler's tyranny, impelling him to contribute, albeit in a small way, to Austria's liberation. The justices of the Second Republic were not convinced. Ignoring evidence that fourteen members of Franz's family had perished in the Holocaust, their deliberations revealed the persistence of paternalistic and anti-Semitic attitudes stretching back to the Habsburg monarchy. The magistrates debated whether the youngster had committed a punishable crime. Two weeks later, behind closed doors, they found him guilty of violating §§ 171 and 172 of the penal code, although they did not pass sentence. Franz immediately appealed the verdict that on July 27 was rejected by the Higher Regional Court. Three months later, thanks largely to the efforts of Franz's attorney, Dr. Oskar Franz Trnka, the Juvenile Court ruled that all charges be dropped according to an amnesty issued by the Austrian government.[26]

In reviewing these cases and combining them with those of other delinquents tried by postwar magistrates for property crimes committed under the Nazis, several conclusions may be drawn. First, all defendants appear to have been given a fair trial. The courts followed proper rules of evidence and the justices devoted several weeks in reaching a decision. Second, although two defendants were acquitted on a technicality, all were clearly guilty of some form of larceny as defined by §§ 171–6 of the Austrian penal code. But aside from those convicted of automobile theft, nearly all had filched or stolen relatively inexpensive items in short supply at the end of the war. These usually consisted of staples, foodstuffs, tobacco, clothing, footwear, and even Christmas trees. By the standards of the twenty-first century, the offences would be considered misdemeanors, rather than serious crimes. Nearly all delinquents came from impoverished or "fatherless" families, as had been generally true long before the Anschluß. While some were likely destined to lead a life of crime, others may have settled down and found useful work in the Second Republic. Here it may be noted that none tried as juveniles was sentenced to spend time in prison. Whatever the thinking of Austrian jurists, close confinement in a juvenile detention facility offered some hope of educative rehabilitation.

Postwar Offences, 1945–1946

Because the Viennese Juvenile Court did not resume deliberations until November, 1945, over three-quarters of those youngsters tried the following year were prosecuted for offences committed during the last six months of the Nazi regime. The number of juveniles charged or tried for transgressions in the immediate postwar period was thus much smaller, even though official statistics reveal that overall felonies and misdemeanors soared in 1946. (See Figures 1.2 and 1.3.) Only eleven trial transcripts, including those discussed in the previous chapter, were located for this study, but arrest lists and other data provide information on twenty-two other individuals. A case tried in February 1946 suggests that large numbers of youngsters looted and plundered homes and shops in the weeks following the Soviet occupation of Vienna. Among those brought before the bench were a 17-year-old commercial apprentice, a 16-year-old waiter trainee, and a 17-year-old day laborer. Two of the boys had been convicted for stealing butter, margarine, sugar, and sausage in February 1945. Once freed from custody in April, one of them, Fritz H., made off with various household items from a firm in the 14th District, claiming before the court that the Red Army had considered the loot as German assets. However, in October he and two other boys broke into private homes, stealing phonograph records, a golden bracelet, and other valuables. On February 18, 1946, the Juvenile Court sentenced Franz to five months in strict detention, and his accomplice, Kurt J., to three months. In passing judgment, the justices wrote that a relatively mild punishment had been imposed owing to the youngsters' negligent upbringing.[27]

Much more lenient were the sentences imposed on two teenage brothers, Heinrich and Alfred R., convicted for stealing a rucksack of potatoes in October 1945. They were ordered to spend three days in strict confinement for what the judges clearly considered a minor misdemeanor.[28] Another case that did not come to trial concerned that of a 15-year-old Pietro, who had stolen an accordion from a Russian soldier billeted in a private home. When arrested in June 1945, the boy responded that without income he had nothing to eat and had exchanged both the accordion and a purloined bicycle for food. After five months in protective custody, the penitentiary physician requested that the starving boy be released to a home in order to recover his health. In another case, a juvenile robber brazenly told the court that he had every right to fence stolen goods in order to support his family. According to one authority, scrounging, looting, and black marketeering swept through Vienna to stave off hunger in the months following the war. Many youngsters even acquired discarded pistols and firearms to procure the basic necessities of life.[29]

This is not to imply that the dramatic upsurge of black marketeering, robberies, thefts and other felonies that confronted both the Austrian government and four occupying powers immediately after the war were committed largely by juveniles. On March 25, 1946, for example, the state prosecutor indicted a gang of individuals ranging in age from 18 to 50 for a wide range of offences. These included armed robberies, break-ins, and large-scale thefts of clothing, cameras, radios, typewriters, and particularly foodstuffs. That said, the most culpable were three 18-year-old males and a 20-year-old woman. In April 1945, these four had made off enormous quantities of personal belongings from abandoned dwellings or shops. In June, the ringleader, 18-year-old Franz B., was captured in what came close to an exchange of gunfire. On October 22, Franz escaped from protective custody and found refuge with his 20-year-old girlfriend, Marie R. Together with five other gang members they undertook a series of audacious nocturnal robberies from cafes, cinemas, and even an American post exchange, thereafter selling their booty at the Naschmarkt. As mentioned above, Franz's gang was indicted on multiple counts of grand larceny, although no trial transcript has survived for this study. Because all were tried as adults, it is likely that they were sentenced to lengthy prison terms.[30]

Trial transcripts of two juvenile gangs brought to bench in the immediate postwar period have survived, however. The first tried in March 1946 consisted of five boys and a girl in their late teens. Throughout October and November 1945, they had carried out a series of daring robberies, including one from an American post exchange that netted them twelve pairs of skiing boots, seven pairs of running shoes, and two boxes of liquor. On October 29, the young hooligans broke into a coffee house, making off with 2 kilograms of lard, bottles of wine and cognac, as well as two dozen phonograph records. Other burglaries from residential homes in Aspern as well as various shops and grocery stores elsewhere in Vienna added up to a wide variety of clothes, tobacco products, and personal belongings worth thousands of schillings. In passing judgment on March 30, 1946, the justices noted that the stolen goods were in great demand on the black market. With that in mind they refused to consider mitigating circumstances such as age, negligent upbringing, and admission of guilt, contending that the defendants' contempt for the law warranted severe punishment. The ringleader was thus sentenced to one-year strict detention, his girlfriend to nine months to a year, a third to nine months, and the rest to three years on probationary parole.[31]

On October 30, 1947, eleven members of a teenage gang were ushered into the chambers of the Viennese Juvenile Court. Five of the youngsters were 17 and 18 years old, while the others ages 15 and 16. Three were charged with offences committed just before the collapse of the Nazi regime, and the rest for robberies undertaken both during the initial Soviet conquest and well into 1947. The leader of the group, Walter K., had been born in 1929 into an impoverished family. His mother had succumbed to a lung infection in 1941, leaving him in the hands of a negligent father who was subsequently drafted into the Wehrmacht. Social workers reported that Walter did poorly in school, dropping out after the fourth grade, spending years in Spiegelgrund children's clinic, and briefly becoming a butcher apprentice. The social workers characterized him as "wayward and undisciplined." Walter's principal associate, Kurt K., born in 1930, was the son of divorced parents, who had been reared in institutions, and served jail time in the Juchgasse police station. The other defendants came from similar dysfunctional families, although one had worked in a fire department, another in the Reich Labor Service. According to court records, each and every one was "fatherless" during the war.

Technically speaking, the accused had not initially operated as a gang. In January 1945, Karl and three other boys had broken into a residential home, but stolen only four chickens, a turkey, and a rabbit. However, two other boys made off with clothing, shoes, sheets, and bed covers. After the war, under circumstances not altogether clear, the gang began to coalesce. In February 1946, they came up with a scheme to rob trucks laden with much needed foodstuffs on Schwechat Bridge. As the vehicles parked or backed up after dark, the boys leapt into the cargo vans tossing out sacks of flour, cans of condensed milk, slabs of bacon as well as cartons of sugar, cigarettes, butter, and even croissants. Amazingly, they pulled off these robberies on three separate occasions. Several months later, gang members began frequenting train stations and marshaling yards to fill rucksacks with stolen coal. They also made off with firewood and lumber from a warehouse in the 3rd District. In addition, several individuals stole bicycles and fruit, in one case with a pistol.

In passing judgment, the Juvenile Court imposed relatively mild sentences. Walter was sentenced to eight months of strict detention, Otto Z., born in 1931, to six months, Kurt to five months, and the others to three months. In each and every case, the justices took into account mitigating circumstances, particularly negligent home life owing to poverty or the absence of a father in wartime. In addition, contradictory or insufficient evidence led to acquittal on certain charges, for example, that Walter had stolen rabbits and goats.[32]

Conclusions

In reviewing the cases of juveniles tried for offences committed in 1945, both before and after the collapse of Nazi rule, a distinct pattern can be discerned. Whereas work stoppages and absenteeism shot up during the last months of the war, property crimes remained high, constituting two-thirds of the offences. At the same time, there was a difference. Throughout the Anschluß era, most robberies and thefts had been of bicycles, radios, phonograph records, jewelry, personal belongings, valuables, and cash. There were also instances of minors stealing fruits, vegetables, and rabbits from allotment gardens. In late 1944 and early 1945, the delinquents targeted tobacco shops, stealing substantial quantities of cigarettes, cigars, and ration coupons, which, as we have seen, had become the coin of the realm. Immediately following the Russian capture of Vienna, individuals and small gangs plundered abandoned stores, dwellings, and even warehouses, focusing on valuables and other items readily exchangeable on the black market or even in public in the Naschmarkt. With the development of food shortages during the summer, minors such as 15-year-old Pietro found themselves driven by hunger to theft in order to have enough to eat. By autumn, the situation was becoming so desperate that small gangs had taken to robbing American post exchanges for powdered milk, canned goods, and other edibles. And with winter approaching, a number were driven to steal coal, lumber, and firewood. Once apprehended, those convicted of larceny by the Juvenile Court were required under § 178 of the Austrian penal code to be punished by severe detention for six months to one year, though in extreme cases to five years.[33] Generally speaking, the justices appeared to have adhered to the letter of the law, though frequently taking into consideration mitigating circumstances. To what extent this pattern persisted until the overall crime rate declined in 1949 remains beyond the purview of this study.

Final Thoughts

In reviewing the record of juvenile delinquency in Vienna during the entire Anschluß era, several questions come to mind. To what extent, for example, did Nazi rule constitute a rupture in the Austrian juvenile justice system? As in Vichy France, there were dramatic caesurae but also strong continuities, not least because the Austrian penal code remained in place. Its juvenile clauses, moreover, were rooted in a process of state involvement in the families of delinquent or problem children that developed in the late nineteenth century and persisted into the Second Republic. Even in Red Vienna, elites took a "top-down" approach to juvenile justice. Under Nazi rule, the Danubian metropolis differed from other cities in the "Altreich," not only because the Austrian criminal code remained in place, but also because it persisted largely intact long after the collapse of the Third Reich. In both postwar France and Austria, the persistence of existing legal systems indisputably stabilized society but also reinforced the myths of French resistance and that of Austria as "Hitler's first victim." Indeed it would not be until the Waldheim affair of the 1980s that the Second Republic would come to terms with its Nazi past. Based on our imperfect database, the following conclusions can be drawn.

In the eighteen months prior to the outbreak of the Second World War, the Austrian juvenile judicial system was "aligned" rather than "coordinated" with that in the "Altreich." Indeed, over two-thirds of justices appointed by the Juvenile Division of the Higher Regional Court had not belonged to the NSDAP prior to the Anschluß. Despite certain procedural changes, the judges convicted youngsters charged with property crimes such as break-ins, thefts, and shoplifting under Austrian law. For the most part, they sentenced the delinquents to two to four months in Kaiser-Ebersdorf. Those found guilty of stealing expensive items such as cameras or jewelry, however, were condemned to serve six months at hard labor. Much more severe were sanctions imposed on youngsters convicted of moral offences, particularly homosexuality, as had been customary in

Catholic Austria. Minors under 16 usually received relatively lenient treatment, but older boys and girls endured some form of imprisonment. Overall, juvenile legal proceedings in the eighteen months following the Anschluß did not differ significantly from those of the authoritarian Dollfuss-Schuschnigg regime or in the case of "crimes contrary to nature" from those stretching back to the First Republic and even the monarchy.

In the years following the Hitler's invasion of Poland, Nazi decrees and ordinances indisputably had a major impact on the Austrian juvenile justice system, most notably in sentences meted out by the Higher Regional Court. In this respect, Austrian juvenile law was Nazified or "coordinated" with that in the Third Reich. Even so, just under half of fifty-four known youngsters convicted for larceny received relatively lenient sanctions that ranged from a few weeks to one year of imprisonment. The average punishment was seven to eight weeks in a reformatory. However, several others were condemned to spend three years in a correctional facility for extenuated circumstances and another to seven years for aggravated assault. In none of these cases did the judges rely on wartime ordinances. Rather, they meted out stiff sentences according to § 180 of the Austrian penal code, a paragraph that mandated harsh punishment for felonies committed under the cover of darkness long before the Anschluß. Unsurprisingly, sanctions imposed on delinquents condemned by the Higher Regional Court under Nazi decrees as "national parasites," "precocious juvenile criminals," or "moral degenerates" were more draconian. Between 1940 and 1944, the sentences ranged from four to seven years in prison. In invoking Hitler's decrees, the judges appear to have taken into consideration recommendations of social workers as well as records of previous convictions for robberies committed during blackouts. In one case, a 16-year-old apprentice was sentenced in 1943 to serve six years in prison for multiple felonies and "dishonoring the race." He survived the end of the war in a punishment battalion, but upon registration with the police was forced to complete his term and not released until 1948. Equally harsh, as might be expected, were the punishments imposed on juveniles by Hitler's Special Courts for property crimes, in most cases nocturnal robberies. Of fourteen known Austrian culprits, over half were sentenced to six to seven years in prison and two to death.

By far, the most severe sanctions imposed on juveniles for criminal offences between 1938 and 1945 were for political acts of defiance. As we have seen no fewer than 293 minors were picked up by the Gestapo, of whom roughly 40 percent belonged to the Communist Youth and 13 percent to Catholic conservative or monarchist movements. The remaining half acted for a variety of reasons, though many appear to have been motivated by a sense of particularism or Austrian patriotism. We do not know the fate of most of these adolescent militants, primarily because the available data are based on Gestapo arrest lists, not trial records. Further, those taken into custody for "Jewish-related offences" were usually punished by extralegal means. Two dozen youngsters convicted by the Higher Regional Court for insulting the party and its uniform, radio crimes, subversion, or undermining the war effort were usually condemned to spend six to seven years behind bars. At least seven adolescents prosecuted by the People's Court for high treason were sentenced to death, although the figure may have been higher. This is because defendants under 18 were frequently held in protective custody until coming of age. The most egregious case was that of Friedrich Lachnitt, condemned to death as a minor but not executed until his nineteenth birthday.

The most significant change in the Austrian juvenile justice system to occur under Nazi rule was the introduction of the Reich Juvenile Court Act on January 1, 1944. Whether it constituted a rupture in Austrian jurisprudence is debatable because it was repealed in May 1945 by the Second Austrian Republic. Interestingly, the legislation paralleled a similar measure passed in Vichy France in July 1942. Both laws sought to categorize minors as a distinctive group and to permit judges to decide whether convicted delinquents could be educated or punished as criminals. Both measures were punitive, but both sought to reform petty offenders before they reached adulthood. The objectives, however, were quite different. In the French case, there was an obsessive concern with the country's declining population. Underlying juvenile laws passed in 1912, 1942, and in 1945 was an assumption that minimum corrective punishment of maladjusted or deviant adolescents would produce responsible adults who would procreate healthy offspring. In the German case, the goal was to reduce lengthy sentences for petty misdemeanors in order to mobilize wayward or delinquent youngsters for the Nazi war effort.

During the last fifteen months of Nazi rule, as we have seen, 65 percent of Viennese juvenile delinquents were indicted for break-ins, robbery, and theft. Of those convicted by the Juvenile Division of the Higher Regional Court before the collapse of Hitler's regime, only five were condemned to spend terms of one to four years behind bars, usually for multiple thefts or in one case aggravated assault. Ten others received sentences ranging from three to eight months in a reformatory, while an additional ten to several weeks in a correctional facility. These relatively mild sanctions stand in sharp contrast to the harsh sentences handed down for similar crimes between January 1, 1940 and December 31,

1943. Thereafter, court records reveal that although one youngster was indicted as a "national parasite" neither he nor any other delinquent was convicted of "dishonoring the race."

Between January 1, 1944 and late March 1945, Hitler's judges handed out relatively lenient sentences to twenty-seven boys and girls brought before the bench and convicted for work stoppages or absenteeism, particularly during the last months of the war. Of these, four were sentenced to two weeks in detention, eight to three weeks, and five to a month. The rest were either issued a warning, ordered to return to work, or to perform what would today would be called community service under the supervision of the Guardianship Authority. Only three boys were condemned to spend three to four months in a correctional facility, primarily owing to previous convictions. Because working conditions were often dangerous or difficult, the judges tended to express sympathy for ill or weak boys and girls, although in several instances they ignored medical evidence and ordered defendants to return to the workplace.

While relatively mild, the sanctions imposed by the Juvenile Division of the Higher Regional Court during the last fifteen months of the war for property crimes and absenteeism were anything but altruistic. The available evidence indicates that the Reich Juvenile Court Law stemmed waywardness and delinquency in Vienna, but that convicted miscreants bitterly resented being compelled to work upon leaving school and for that reason showed little sense of remorse for committing petty crimes. Further, many came from such impoverished backgrounds that they felt driven to steal or stay off the job out of sheer desperation.

As for other juvenile crimes, Viennese judges did not hesitate to hand out draconian penalties. The records of those convicted of sexual immorality, for example, are scarce. Nevertheless, the exiguous evidence reveals that in 1944 the Special Court sentenced a servant girl to three years in prison at hard labor for sleeping with a French prisoner of war, another to one year and three months, and two lowly working girls to two years behind bars. That same year, the Higher Regional Court condemned two homosexual boys to lengthy prison terms for crimes "contrary to nature." Nor should it be forgotten that on April 17, 1944, the People's Court condemned two minors to prison terms of five to eight years respectively as members of the "Always Faithful Austria" resistance movement.

During the immediate postwar period, the reconstituted Juvenile Court prosecuted several dozen adolescents for felonious offences committed under the Nazi regime. Of these, the judges dropped charges or acquitted four of the youthful defendants, sentenced fourteen to terms of three to eight months in a juvenile penitentiary, and ordered nine others to be confined in prison for one to four years. Outwardly, the sanctions imposed did not differ much from those meted out by Nazi judges under the Reich Juvenile Court Act, although in many cases the postwar justices took mitigating circumstances into account to reduce sentences. As for those condemned to spend time in prison, nearly all had been convicted of previous transgressions or continued their criminal activities after 1945.

Throughout the entire period of Nazi rule in Vienna, the overwhelming majority of youngsters charged or convicted as delinquents came from working-class backgrounds. The few middle-class or bourgeois exceptions belonged to legitimist or Catholic conservative resistance groups. Most youthful miscreants had left school at age 14, were employed as apprentices, and spent their free time hanging out at street corners, congregating in coffee houses, or spending summer evenings in the Prater. Prior to late 1943, a majority of those convicted of break-ins and theft had been paid sufficiently to make ends meet and enjoyed a sense of freedom after work. But as elsewhere in large cities of Hitler's Reich, they sought to become part of a perceived consumer society through shoplifting, robbery, and theft. Others such as the Schlurfs had opposed the regimentation of the Dollfuss-Schuschnigg regime and after 1938 the mandatory demands of the Hitler Youth. Sarah Fishman in her impressive study of juvenile justice in Vichy France has contended that deprivation, particularly food shortages, as well as frozen wages, inflation, and black marketeering were largely responsible for the juvenile crime wave in wartime Paris. This was generally not the case in Vienna. It is true that poorer teenagers stole rabbits and other edibles from municipal allotments throughout the war, but until late 1944 most delinquents continued to make off with jewelry, bicycles, cash, and other valuables to fence on the black market. Thereafter, the deteriorating material conditions of everyday life in addition to the onerous demands of the German war economy drove teenagers to steal tobacco and food stuffs.

Another difference was the large number of Viennese adolescents prosecuted for moral offences, most notably homosexuality. The exact figures are unavailable, although those adolescents over 16 convicted of crimes "contrary to nature" usually received harsh sentences according to §§ 120 and 130 of the Austrian penal code. As for girls, those charged with illicit intercourse with foreigners were ordered to spend time in a correctional facility, based not on Austrian law but rather on Nazi racial ordinances. In Vichy France and Cologne, by way of contrast, jurists and psychologists devoted considerable attention to the study of "perverse" youngsters, concluding that female delinquents were more likely to become sexual promiscuous than teenage boys. For that reason they were usually confined to state-run institutions.

Overall, few violent crimes were committed by juvenile delinquents in Vichy France or in the major cities of Hitler's Reich during the Second World War. In Vienna, three-quarters of the offences were property crimes, most of which could be categorized as misdemeanors, though many were often tried as felonies. Nearly all of the delinquents came from impoverished or dysfunctional families, many of whom had been under the supervision of the Guardianship Authority since early childhood. And even those who had had a relatively normal upbringing as children lost their fathers to military service as adolescents. Exactly as Nazi authorities feared, offences committed by wayward or youthful delinquents were the offspring of "fatherless" families.

In three respects, juvenile offences in Nazi Vienna appear to have differed from those committed in other cities of Hitler's Greater German Reich. First, nearly 300 teenagers were arrested or prosecuted for acts of political defiance. This is not to deny the heroic opposition of youngsters in other cities such as the White Rose Society in Munich or Hamburg. However, in Vienna, those apprehended by the authorities seem to have been motivated not only by resentment of Nazi tyranny but also by a sense of patriotic resistance to a foreign regime. Second, Vienna did not experience gang violence as did Cologne and other cities of the industrial Ruhr as well as Hanover and Leipzig. This may have been attributed to the dearth of Allied air raids before September 1944, but the gangs of Vienna, most notably the Schlurfs, simply wanted to be left alone. Third, the percentage of offences in Vienna were fewer and far between than those committed in other major towns of the Greater German Reich. For better or worse, in other words, our study suggests that between 1938 and 1945 the Nazi regime succeeded in controlling juvenile crime more effectively in Vienna than in other large cities of Hitler's realm. That said, the validity of this conclusion requires investigation in additional Austrian and German archives.

Notes

Introduction

1 Monika Steinböck, *Die Geschichte der Wiener Jugendwohlfahrt*, http://www.monika-steinboeck, 6.
2 Ibid., 2.
3 http://de.wikipedia.org/wki/Heimerziehung in Österreich; Sigrid Umele, "Zur Geschichte der Kindheit in Österreich. Von den frühen Anfängen des Mittelalters bis zur Gegenwart" (MA thesis, Klagenfurt, 2011), 64–7. For more details see the introductory essays in Ernst Berger (ed.), *Verfolgte Kindheit: Kinder und Jugendliche als Opfer der NS-Sozialverwaltung* (Vienna, 2007), particularly that by Clarissa Rudolf and Gertrud Benetka, "Kontinuität oder Bruch? Zur Geschichte der Intelligenzmessung in Wiener Fürsorgesystem vor und in der NS Zeit," 15–88.
4 Edith Sheffer, *Asperger's Children: The Origins of Autism in Nazi Vienna* (New York, 2018), 32–8.
5 Helmut Gruber, *Red Vienna: Experiment in Working-Class Culture 1919–1934* (New York, 1991), 68, 74–7 ff., Umele, "Zur Geschichte der Kindheit in Österreich," 79 ff.
6 Ibid.
7 Sheffer, *Asperger's Children*, 31.
8 http://de.wikipedia.org/wki/Heimerziehung in Österreich, 2–4. For more favorable assessments of Red Vienna see Anson Rabinbach, *The Crisis of Austrian Socialism: From Red Vienna to Civil War, 1927–1934* (Chicago, 1983) and Eve Blau, *The Architecture of Red Vienna, 1919–1934* (Boston, 1998), especially 88–133, 174.
9 Quoted in Phillip J. Henry, "Democracy's Children: Psychoanalysis, the Great War, and the Cultural Subject of the *Zwischenkriegszeit*," *Contemporary Austrian Studies*, XXVIII (2010), 254.
10 http://de.wikipedia.org/wki/Heimerziehung in Österreich, 2–4.
11 Evan Burr Bukey, *Hitler's Austria: Popular Sentiment in the Nazi Era, 1938–1945* (Chapel Hill, 2000), 73; Michael H. Kater, *Hitler Youth* (Cambridge, MA, 2004), 1.
12 http://de.wikipedia.org/wki/Heimerziehung in Österreich, 4.
13 Jörg Wolff, *Jugendliche vor Gericht im Dritten Reich: Nationalsozialistische Strafrechtpolitik und Justizalltag* (Munich, 1993); Robert George Waite, "Juvenile Delinquency in Nazi Germany, 1933–1945" (Diss., State University of New York at Binghamton, 1980); Detlev Peukert, *Inside Nazi Germany: Conformity, Opposition,*

and Racism in Everyday Life (New Haven, 1987), 145–74; Kurt Schilde (ed.), *Jugendorganisation und Jugendopposition in Berlin Kreuzberg 1933–1945: Eine Dokumentation* (Berlin, 1983); Christian Gerbel, Alexander Mejstrik, and Richard Sieder, "Die 'Schlurfs': Verweigerung und Opposition von Wiener Arbeiterjugendlichen im Dritten Reich," in Emmerich Tálos, Ernst Hanisch, Wolfgang Neugebauer, and Reinhard Sieder (eds.), *NS-Herrschaft in Österreich: Ein Handbuch* (Vienna, 2001), 523–48. See also Petra Göte, *Jugendstrafvollzug im Dritten Reich: diskutiert und realisiert- erlebt und erinnert* (Bad Heilbrunn, 2003). For additional titles and thoughtful analyses see the introduction by Arno Klönne in A. Klönne (ed.), *Jugendkriminalität und Jugendoppostion im NS Staat: Ein sozialgeschichtliches Dokument* (Münster, 1981), I–XVI and Kater, *Hitler Youth*, 299–301. For an excellent summary essay see Wayne Geerling, "Protecting the National Community from Juvenile Delinquency: Nazification of Juvenile Criminal Law in the Third Reich," http://artsonline.monasch.au/eras/publications/eras/edition-2 geerling.pha.

14 Kater, *Hitler Youth*, 112–68. Less subtly and less convincingly H. W. Koch characterizes the three groups of adolescent dissidents as politically oppositional, liberal individualistic, or criminally antisocial. H. W. Koch, *In the Name of the Volk: Political Justice in Hitler's Germany* (New York, 1989), 166.

15 Ernst Fraenkl, *The Dual State: A Contribution to the Theory of Dictatorship* (New York, 1941).

16 Alan F. Steinweis and Robert D. Rachlin, "The Law in Nazi Germany and the Holocaust," in Alan F. Steinweis and Robert D. Rachlin (eds.), *The Law in Nazi Germany: Ideology, Opportunity, and the Perversion of Justice* (New York, 2013), 1–2 ff.

17 For an introduction see the essays in Steinweis and Rachlin, *The Law in Nazi Germany*, particularly Robert D. Rachlin, "Roland Freisler and the Volksgericht: The Court as an Instrument of Terror," 63–87; and Douglas G. Morris, "Discrimination, Degradation, Defiance: Jewish Lawyers under Nazism," 105–35. For more comprehensive studies see Lothar Gruchmann, *Justiz im Dritten Reich 1933–1940: Anpassung und Unterwerfung in der Ära Gürtner* (Munich, 2001), particularly the excellent historiographical introduction, 1–5; Thomas Roth, *"Verbrechungsbekämpfung" und soziale Ausgrenzung in nationalsozialistische Köln: Kriminalpolizei, Strafjustiz und Verbrechungsbekämpfung zwischen Machtübernahme und Kriegsende* (Cologne, 2010); Koch, *In the Name of the Volk*; Ingo Müller, *Hitler's Justice: The Courts of the Third Reich* (Cambridge, MA, 1991), 3–192; Michael Stolleis, *The Law under the Swastika: Studies on Legal History in Nazi Germany* (Chicago, 1998). Also see the pioneering study by Bruno Blau, "Die Kriminalität in Deutschland während des zweiten Weltkrieges." *Zeitschrift für die gesamte Strafrechtswissenschaft* (Berlin, 1952), 31–81.

18 Steinweis and Rachlin, "The Law in Nazi Germany and the Holocaust," 4.
19 Rachlin, "Roland Freisler," 64.

1 Anschluß and Consolidation, 1938–1939

1 For a comprehensive account see Norbert Klatt, *Zum Verhältnis des österreichischen und deutschen Strafrechts in der Zeit des Nationalsozialismus* (Göttingen, 2009), particularly 65–100. See also Ursula Schwarz, "Politische Gerichte in der NS Zeit," in Friedrich Forsthüber, Ursula Schwarz, Johannes Mahl-Anzeiger, and Matthias Keuschnigg (eds.), *Die Geschichte des Grauen Hauses und der österreichischen Strafgerichtsbarkeit* (Vienna, 2012), 94–109. On the massive purge of Jewish and partial-Jewish judges, prosecutors, attorneys, and notaries see Gruchmann, *Justiz im Dritten Reich*, 175–203.
2 Michael Lojowsky, "Hochverrat," in Wolfgang Form, Wolfgang Neugebauer, and Theo Schiller (eds.), *NS-Justiz und politische Verfolgung in Österreich 1938–1945: Analysen zu den Verfahren vor dem Volksgerichtshof und dem Oberlandesgerichtes Wien* (Munich, 2006), 15–52 ff.
3 Specifically Point 19, but also Point 5 stipulating that noncitizens, that is, Jews, be subject to German law as "guests," and Point 19 demanding the death sentence for "habitual criminals." Gruchmann, *Justiz im Dritten Reich*, 747 ff.
4 For details see Gruchmann, *Justiz im Dritten Reich*, 806–13 and Klatt, *Zum Verhältnis des österreichischen und deutschen Strafrechts*, 30–40 ff.
5 Emmerich Tálos, *Das Austrofaschistische Herrrschaftssytem: Österreich 1933–1938* (Vienna, 2013), 47–49, 269–313.
6 Indefinite imprisonment or detention is a sentence imposed by judicial officials on potentially habitual criminals, particularly adolescents or young adults, to protect the community. In many ways it constitutes a half-way house between punishment and rehabilitation. Those subjected to indefinite imprisonment usually receive a maximum sentence according to the law, but made eligible for early release on the basis of good conduct or the recommendation of prison authorities that rehabilitation can be undertaken outside jail. The imposition of indefinite imprisonment had been widely practiced in the German lands during the early modern period, but eliminated in the nineteenth century. Ironically, various forms of indefinite imprisonment or detention had become an integral part of penal codes in Australia and twenty-three states in the United States by 1900. An 1887 New York statute stipulated, for example, that the length of incarceration should be determined by the managers or wardens of reformatories. That indefinite imprisonment was written into Austrian law during the First Republic no doubt reflected a belief in the judgment of fair-minded prison authorities dedicated to rehabilitation. Paragraph

12 of the Juvenile Court Law of 1928 even stipulated that adolescents sentenced to short-term imprisonment might be remanded to educational institutions or court-appointed guardians. Under the Dollfuss-Schuschnigg dictatorship, however, jurists increasingly imposed sentences of indefinite imprisonment as a form of "preventive punishment" to keep convicted malefactors under lock and key. Cf. August Schoetensack, *Unbestimmte Verurteilung* (Leipzig, 1909) 8–14 ff; Geerling, "Protecting the National Community," 16–17; Klatt, *Zum Verhältnis des österreichischen und deutschen Strafrechts*, 184, 196.
7   Stolleis, *The Law under the Swastika*, ix.
8   Müller, *Hitler's Justice*, 79.
9   Roland Grassberger and Helga Nowotny, "Introduction," *The Austrian Penal Act 1852 and 1945 as Amended to 1965* (South Hackensack, NJ, 1966), 1–6; T. C. W. Blanning, *Joseph II* (London, 1994), 81–2, 102, 119.
10 Grassberger and Nowotny, *Austrian Penal Act*, 6–9.
11 Robin Okey, *The Habsburg Monarchy from Enlightenment to Eclipse* (New York, 2001), 66.
12 In accordance of Paragraph 91 of the General Civil Code that stipulated: "The husband is head of the family. In this capacity he retains exclusive legal right to oversee and direct household affairs."
13 Bundesministerium für Justiz, *75 Jahre Wiener Jugendgerichtshilfe* (Vienna, 1987).
14 Frank D. Healy, "Legislation Concerning Juvenile Delinquency in Vienna, Austria," *Journal of Criminal Law and Criminology*, 35, 3 (1944), 152; Ilse Lukas, "Prevention of Juvenile Delinquency and Crime in Austria," *Journal of Criminal Law and Criminology*, 29, 5 (1939), 689–93 ff.
15 Juvenile justice in nineteenth-century France developed into a system based on conflicting views of adolescent crime and social anxieties. For a brilliant description and analysis see Sarah Fishman, *The Battle for Children: World War II and Juvenile Justice in Twentieth Century France* (Cambridge, MA, 2002), 12–34 ff. For Austria Robert Wegs, "Youth Delinquency and 'Crime': The Perception and the Reality," *Journal of Social History*, 32, 3 (Spring, 1999), 603–21.
16 Wegs, "Youth Delinquency," 603–21; Lukas, "Prevention of Juvenile Delinquency and Crime in Austria," 689.
17 Maureen Healy, *Vienna and the Fall of the Habsburg Empire: Total War and Everyday Life in World War I* (Cambridge, 2004), 104–5, 250–5.
18 Ibid.
19 For details see F. L. Carsten, *The First Austrian Republic 1918–1938: A Study Based on British and Austrian Documents* (Cambridge, 1986), 36–43. See also Healy, *Vienna and the Fall of the Habsburg Empire*, 255.
20 For an excellent account of impoverished living conditions leading to incest and other juvenile sexual offences in interwar Vienna see Britta McEwen, *Sexual*

Knowledge: Feeling, Fact, and Social Reform in Vienna, 1900–1934 (New York, 2012), especially 43, 46, 63, 159.
21 W. Gleisbach, "Twenty-Five Years of Criminology in Austria," *Journal of Criminal Law and Criminology*, 24, I (1933), 176–78 ff.
22 Fishman, *Battle for Children*, 14, 26–27.
23 As quoted in Lukas, "Prevention of Juvenile Delinquency and Crime in Austria," 703.
24 Ibid., 705–6; Herbert Exenberger, "Gefängnis statt Erziehung: Jugendgefängnis Kaiser-Ebersdorf 1940-1945" (Vienna, n.d.), 1–13.
25 Ibid.
26 Quoted in Sheffer, *Asperger's Children*, 193.
27 See Figures 1.1–1.4.
28 *Statistisches Jahrbuch für Österreich 1938* (Vienna, 1938), 245. The figures published here are often at variance with those appearing in the *Statistisches Jahrbuch der Stadt Wien*, most likely because of overlapping jurisdictions. Even so, the national percentages approximate those in the Danubian city.
29 See Figures 1.1–1.4.
30 Wiener Stadt- und Landesarchiv (Viennese Municipal and Provincial Archives) (Hereafter WSLA), A 3, Vr. 818/37.
31 See tables XVI–XIX in Waite, "Juvenile Delinquency in Nazi Germany, 1933–1945."
32 See Figure 1.1.
33 Lukas, "Prevention of Juvenile Delinquency and Crime in Austria," 700–1.
34 Among the many excellent accounts of the immediate impact of the Anschluß the standard works remain Gerhard Botz, *Die Eingliederung Österreichs in das Deutsche Reich: Planung und Verwirklichung des politisch-administrativen Anschluss (1938–1940)* (Vienna, 1976) and Radomir Luza, *Austro-German Relations in the Anschluss Era* (Princeton, 1975).
35 For a comprehensive account see Klatt, *Zum Verhältnis des österreichischen und deutschen Strafrechts*, 22–76 ff.
36 *Bundesgesetzblatt für die Republik Österreich*, December 16, 1949, 57, 272: "Kundmachung der Bundesregierung vom 10. November 1949 über die Wiederlautbarung des Jugendgerichtsgesetzes," Artikel I, 112.
37 For details see Gruchmann, *Justiz im Dritten Reich*, 432–53.
38 Waite, "Juvenile Delinquency in Nazi Germany, 1933–1945," 22–43.
39 Cf. Müller, *Hitler's Justice*, 151–5; *Bundesgesetzblatt für die Republik Österreich*, "Kundmachung der Bundesregierung vom 10. November 1949 über die Wiederlautbarung des Jugendgerichtsgesetzes," Artikel I, 112. Also Klatt, *Zum Verhältnis des österreichischen und deutschen Strafrechts*, 114–22.
40 Wolfgang Neugebauer, *The Austrian Resistance 1938–1945* (Vienna, 2014), 42.
41 Dr. Michaela Laichmann, WSLA, to the author, April 30, 2013.
42 WSLA, A 3, Jugendgerichtshof, Strafakten, Vr. 228/39–497/39.

43 Most notably Christian Gerbel, "Lebenswelten von Wiener Arbeiterjugendlichen unter der NS-Herrschaft: Administrative Karriereren und 'Schlurf' Gangs." (Diss., University of Vienna, 1993).
44 These figures do not correspond exactly to the official statistics of all cases tried in 1939. See Figure 1.4.
45 WSLA, A 3, Vr. 226/39.
46 WSLA, A 3, Vr. 327/39.
47 WSLA, A 3, Vr. 458/39.
48 WSLA, A 3, Vr. 447/39.
49 WSLA, A 3, Vr. 442/39; Vr. 443/39; Vr. 455/39; Vr. 456/39; Vr. 476/39.
50 WSLA, A 3, Vr. 476/39.
51 As mitigating circumstances the court also took into consideration that the stolen goods had been returned. WSLA, A 3, Vr. 457/39; Vr. 473/39. On January 16, 1940, the juvenile court expressed similar leniency in placing eight youngsters on probation for crimes of vandalism, petty theft, and break-ins committed the year before in St. Pölten. For details see WSLA, A 3, Vr. 434/39. Had P., his accomplices, and the St. Pölten gang been apprehended after October 9, 1939 they would have been more severely punished according to an ordinance against "dangerous juvenile criminals" passed in that month.
52 WSLA, A 3, Vr. 451/39; Vr. 130/38.
53 There is a vast literature on such prominent figures as Sigmund Freud, Otto Weininger, Arthur Schnitzler, Gustav Klimt, Egon Schiele, Hugo von Hofmannsthal, Arnold Schoenberg, Richard Gerstl, Oskar Kokoschka, and Alma Schindler Mahler. For an introduction see Carl Schorske, *Fin-de-Siècle Vienna: Politics and Culture* (New York, 1980).
54 Ernst Hanisch, *Männlichkeiten: Eine andere Geschichte des 20. Jahrhunderts* (Vienna, 2005), 189–212 ff.
55 Ibid., 212–13 ff.
56 Albert Müller and Christian Fleck, "'Unzucht wider der Naturf'. Gerichtliche Verfolginge der 'Unzucht mit Personen gleichen Geschlechts' in Österreich von den 1930er zu den 1950er Jahren," *Österreichische Zeitschrift für Geschichtswissenschaften*, IX (1998), 3, 400–3 ff. 422.
57 *Statistiches Jahrbuch der Stadt Wien 1939–1942* (Vienna, 1946), 417.
58 Dokumentationsarchiv des österreichischen Widerstandes (Documentation Archives of the Austrian Resistance) (Hereafter DöW), Tagesrapporte Gestapo (Daily Reports of the Viennese Gestapo) (Hereafter TR), January 1–December 31, 1939.
59 WSLA, A 3, 88 Vr. 450/39.
60 WSLA, A 3, 83 Vr. 463/39.
61 WSLA, A 3, Vr. 461/39; Vr. 487/39.
62 WSLA, A 3, 85 Vr. 475/39.
63 WSLA, A 3, 81 Vr. 432/39.

64 WSLA, A 3, 85 Vr. 464/39.
65 *Reichsgesetzblatt*, I., April 6, 1923, 249.
66 WSLA, A 3, 83 Vr. 449/39.
67 WSLA, A 3, 83 Vr. 448/49; 83 Vr. 449/39; 88 Vr. 486/39; 81 Vr. 462/39.
68 WSLA, A 3, 84 Vr. 433/39; 85 Vr. 484/39; 81 Vr. 438/39; 8 Vr. 446/39.
69 For a full discussion of dissident, noncompliant, and oppositional juvenile behavior in the Third Reich, see Kater, *Hitler Youth*, 112–66 and Peukert, *Inside Nazi Germany*, 145–74.
70 Neugebauer, *Austrian Resistance*, 32–4.
71 Ibid.
72 TR, September 2, 1938 to April 1, 1945.
73 Ibid.
74 DöW, 52133: Liste der Novembertoten 1938.
75 For a brief summary see Radomir Luza, *The Resistance in Austria, 1938-1945* (Minneapolis, 1984), 13–18.
76 Cf. Ibid., 103; *Widerstand und Verfolgung in Wien* (Resistance and Persecution in Vienna) (Hereafter WVW), 2, 283.
77 TR, October 5 and October 6–7, 1938; WVW, 2, 282.
78 Luza, *Resistance*, 102–5.
79 TR, October 22, 1938.
80 TR, February 21–22, 1939; WVW, 2, 280–1.
81 TR, April 22–24, 1939.
82 TR, June 27, 1939; WVW, 2, 275–6. M. was sentenced to four years in prison although those underage in 1939 were usually sentenced to two years in jail.
83 TR, July 1–3, 1939.
84 TR, March 11–14, 1939.
85 TR, October 8–10, 1938; October 18–19, 1938.
86 For details see Bukey, *Hitler's Austria*, 102–4.
87 Neugebauer, *Austrian Resistance*, 124–6.
88 TR, November 26–28, 1938.
89 TR, September 21–23, 1938.
90 TR, March 17, 1939.
91 TR, October 12, 1938; October 28, 1938; August 10, 1939.
92 Cf. Knopp, *Kriminalität und Gefährdung der Jugend: Lagebericht bis zum Stande vom 1 Januar 1941* (Berlin, 1941), 58–83 ff; Waite, "Juvenile Delinquency in Nazi Germany, 1933–1945," 62–70 ff.
93 Ulrike Jureit, *Erziehen-Strafen- Vernichten:Jugendkriminalität, und Jugendstrafrecht im Nationalsozialismus* (Münster, 1995), 61–3. That Grynszpan was in the custody of French authorities at the time is not without significance.
94 *Reichseseztblatt*, 1939, I, 2000 (Berlin, 1939).

2 Nazification: The Impact of Wartime Ordinances on the Austrian Juvenile Penal Code, 1940–1944

1 For the best, most thoroughly researched, and comprehensive account of familial problems and juvenile crime in wartime Britain, particularly during the early years of the conflict see Geoffrey G. Field, *Blood, Sweat, and Toil: Remaking the British Working Class, 1939–1945* (Oxford, 2011), 183–216. See also the contemporary study by M. E. Bathurst, "Juvenile Delinquency in Britain during the War," *Journal of Criminal Law and Criminology*, 34, 5 (1944), 291–302.
2 Fishman, *The Battle for Children*, 82 ff.
3 Wolff, *Jugendliche vor Gericht*, 1–24, 81; Geerling, "Protecting the National Community," 10–12.
4 DöW, BMJ-NA (Personnel files).
5 On this issue see the extensive discussion in Klatt, *Zum Verhältnis des österreichischen und deutschen Strafrechts*, 170–97 ff.
6 Gerbel, "Lebenswelten," 1–46.
7 Ibid., 1–46, 265–91. On France see Fishman, *Battle for Children*, 88.
8 In her impressive study of autism in Nazi Vienna, Edith Sheffer suggests that the Third Reich should be considered as a "diagnosis regime," a paradigm that coincides with my own conclusions. Sheffer, *Asperger's Children*, 11–23 ff.
9 Reichsgesetzblatt (*Reich Law Gazette*) (Hereafter RGBl), Jg. 1939, I, 2000
10 For a full explanation and analysis of the Ordinance for the Protection of Dangerous Juvenile Criminals see Waite, "Juvenile Delinquency in Nazi Germany, 1933–1945," 101–18 ff. See also Gerbel, "Lebenswelten," 47–8 and Geerling, "Protecting the National Community," 11–14.
11 Cf. Gerbel, "Lebenswelten," 47; Brigitte Bailer, Wolfgang Maderthaner, and Kurt Scholz, *"Die Vollstreckung verlief ohne Besonderheiten": Hinrichtungen in Wien, 1938 bis 1945* (Vienna, 2013), 62–3; DöW, doc. 3367; WSLA, A 1, Strafakten (Hereafter Str.) 6843, 6891, 5609, 7964, 8094.
12 Nikolaus Wachsmann, *Hitler's Prisons: Legal Terror in Nazi Germany* (New Haven, 2004), 194–6; Geerling, "Protecting the National Community," 13–14; Gruchmann, *Justiz im Dritten Reich*, 901–10.
13 Wolff, *Jugendliche vor Gericht*, 51–54; Geerling, "Protecting the National Community," 15; Anton Tantner, *"Schlurfs" Annäherung an einen subkulturellen Stil Wiener Arbeiterjugendlicher* (Vienna, 2007), 41–6.
14 Österreichisches Staatsarchiv (ÖStA) Archiv der Republik (AdR), Allgemeines Verwaltungsarchiv (AVA), Box 4991: Der Vorstand des Landesgerichtl. Gefängenhausses I an den Generalstaatsanwalt, September 13, 1940.
15 Wolff, *Jugendliche vor Gericht*, 63–7, 104–9, ff.; Geerling, "Protecting the National Community," 15–16; Waite, "Juvenile Delinquency in Nazi Germany,

1933–1945," 108–18. For a statistical data and a brief summary of the impact of Hitler's wartime ordinances in incorporated Austria see Wolfgang Form, " 'Das Strafrecht ist also in erhöhtem Maße ein Kampfrecht ... '. Die Anwendung der Todesstrafe in Österreich während der NS-Zeit," in Claudia Kuretsides-Haider, Heimao Halbrainer, and Elisabeth Ebner (eds.) *Mit dem Tode bestraft: Historische und rechtspolitische Aspekte zur Todesstrafe in Österreich im 20. Jahrhundert und der Kampf um ihre weltweite Abschaffung* (Graz, 2008), 59–84. On the impact of Jugendarrest in Vienna see Tantner, *"Schlurfs,"* 43–4.

16 See Figures 1.1–1.4
17 Cf. Waite, "Juvenile Delinquency in Nazi Germany, 1933–1945," 74–90 ff.; Fishman, *Battle for Children*, 82–104 ff.
18 The activities of the Edelweiß Pirates has been the subject of considerable historical debate, not least because thirteen members, including three teenagers, were hanged by the SS on October 25, 1944. While it is true that the youngsters opposed the Nazi regime and even aided Allied prisoners, they also attacked Polish and Soviet forced laborers and other displaced persons (DPs) after the war. In April 1946, British authorities even tried, convicted, and sentenced one member to death, though shortly thereafter commuting the sentence. The present consensus holds that the Edelwieß Pirates were made up of social outcasts who combined dissident, oppositional, and criminal elements. Oddly, Roth's exhaustive study of crime and criminality in Nazi Cologne devotes only a few pages to the Edelwieß Pirates, aside from describing a shoot-out with the police toward the end of the war. See Roth, *"Verbrechungsbekämpfung,"* 551–2. For extensive analysis and discussion of dissident youth groups, including the famous Hamburg Swings and other gangs in Hitler's Germany see Kater, *Hitler Youth*, 134–66. Also see Peukert, *Inside Nazi Germany*, 145–74. For a relatively complete list of dissident groups see Blau, *"Die Kriminalität,"* 61.
19 Fishman, *Battle for Children*, 67–9.
20 The first arrest of juveniles identified as "Schlurfs" appears to have taken place on March 14, 1941. Tantner, *"Schlurfs,"* 45.
21 Neugebauer, *Austrian Resistance*, 240–1. See also, Tantner, *"Schlurfs,"* 45.
22 On the Schlurfs see Gerbel's comprehensive work, "Lebenswelten"; Gerbel et al., "Die 'Schlurfs,' " 523–48; Tantner, *"Schlurfs"*; Alexander Mejstrik, "Urban Youth, National Socialist Education and Specialized Fun: The Making of the Vienna Schlurfs, 1941–44," in Axel Schildt and Detlef Siegfried (eds.), *European Cities, Youth and the Public Sphere in the Twentieth Century* (Hampshire, 2005), 57–79; Kater, *Hitler Youth*, 134; Bukey, *Hitler's Austria*, 195–6.
23 See Wolff, *Jugendliche vor Gericht*, 305.
24 DöW, G: Vr. 496/43. Interestingly, the percentage of arrests and convictions of adolescents for unnatural sexual behavior in Vienna appears to approximate that of

other cities of Greater Germany. See Robert G. Waite, "Teenage Sexuality in Nazi Germany," *Journal of Sexuality*, XIII (January 3, 1998), 438.
25 Fishman, *Battle for Children*, 101–4.
26 Gerbel, "Lebenswelten," 289–91. For information on similar adolescent motivation and behavior in major cities of the "Altreich" see Blau, *"Die Kriminalität,"* 61.
27 Wolfgang Form and Oliver Uthe (eds.), *NS-Justiz in Österreich: Lage-und Reiseberichte 1938–1945* (Vienna, 2004), 135.
28 DöW, BJM: Vg. Vr. 2050/45 Hv 808/46, October 17, 1946.
29 DöW, G: Vr. 266/40.
30 DöW, G: Vr. 1024/40.
31 DöW, G: Vr. 667/41.
32 DöW, G: Vr. 496; Vr. 197.
33 Gerbel, "Lebenswelten," 201–2.
34 DöW, G: Vr. 692/42. In 1952 and 1964, the Higher Regional Court expunged the records of two of the convicted, both of whom had been underage in 1942.
35 Identified under the pseudonym "Ludwig" by Gerbel in "Lebenswelten," 315–16.
36 For more extensive information and analysis see Gerbel, "Lebenswelten," 315–33.
37 DöW, G: Vr. 389/43.
38 For details see Gerbel, "Lebenswelten," 334–53.
39 Gerbel, "Lebenswelten," 378–400.
40 Kater, *Hitler Youth*, 134.
41 TR, Gestapo, October 2–5, 1942.
42 Gerbel et al., "Die 'Schlurfs,'" 543–46. See also Neugebauer, *Austrian Resistance*, 239–41. In his classic study *Hitler Youth*, Michael Kater examines and analyzes the many forms of juvenile dissent in Hitler's Reich, concluding that youthful dissidents were diverse in social background, behavior, goals, and political views. Ironically, the group most comparable to the working-class Schlurfs may have been the wealthy Hamburg Swing Kids who also simply wanted to be left alone. See Kater, *Hitler Youth*, 113–66, particularly 143–8.
43 Roth, *"Verbrechungsbekämpfung,"* 498 ff.; Fishman, *Battle for Children*, 116–19 ff., 169.
44 DöW, G: Vr. 401/40.
45 DöW, G: Vr. 159/41.
46 DöW, G: Vr. 370/41.
47 DöW, G: Vr. 518/41.
48 DöW, G: Vr. 568/43.
49 DöW, G: Vr. 671/42.
50 DöW, G: Vr. 973/42; Vr. 1784/42; Vr. 2274.
51 DöW, G: Vr. 843.
52 DöW, G: Vr. 1260/40.

53 DöW, G: Vr. 1191/40.
54 DöW, G: Vr. 943/40.
55 DöW, G: Vr. 777/41.
56 DöW. G: Vr. 496/43.
57 DöW, G: Vr. 1076/42. Klementine could have been more severely punished, as the Viennese branch of the Nazi Welfare Office had recommended imprisonment in a juvenile concentration camp, presumably Uckermark. Nevertheless, her time under lock and key was surely difficult. Hirtenberg had been established in 1929 as a correctional facility for delinquent girls, but after the Anschluß, it was transformed into a women's detention center that was set up to manufacture infantry cartridges. To what extent Viennese girls such as Klementine were forced to labor as munitions workers is unclear. In 1944, Hirtenberg became a subcamp of Mauthausen, primarily for women. See Herbert Exenberger, "Vergessene Opfer des NS Regimes," in www. doew. at Heinz Arnberger and Claudia Kuretsides-Haider (eds.), *Gedenken und Mahnen in Niederösterreich: Erinnerungszeichnis zu Widerstand: Exil und Befreiung* (Vienna, 2011), 149–59.
58 Gerbel, "Lebenswelten," 190–4.
59 Fishman, *Battle for Children*, 214.
60 DöW, G: Vr. 2008/42; Vr. 175/42; Vr. 1176/42.
61 DöW, G: Vr. 1162/42.
62 DöW, G: Vr. 2304/42.
63 Roth, "*Verbrechungsbekämpfung*," 24, 77 ff.
64 DöW, G: Vr. 264/43.
65 DöW, G: Vr. 265/43.
66 DöW, G: Vr. 272/43.
67 DöW, G: Vr. 267/43.
68 DöW, G: Vr. 332/43; Vr. 1995/43.
69 Neugebauer, *Austrian Resistance*, 238.
70 The Wage Structure Ordinance of June 25, 1938, stipulated that individuals convicted of disturbing the "industrial peace" were to be jailed and fined. RGBl, I, June 28, 1938, 691. On the impact on juveniles see Gerbel, "Lebenswelten," 112–28, *passim*.
71 *Statistisches Jahrbuch der Stadt Wien, 1943–1945* (Vienna, 1948), 294–5.
72 DöW, G: Vr. 1074/41.
73 DöW, G: Vr. 217/41; Vr. 1242/42; Vr. 8/42.
74 DöW, G: Vr. 595/42; Vr. 1045/42; Vr. 798/40; Vr. 1373/42; Vr. 135/42; Vr. 1375/42; 1373/42; Vr. 266/43; 268/43; Vr. 957/43; Vr. 498/43; WSLA, A 3, Vr. 268/43. M: Vr. 2219/43; Vr. 2347/43.
75 Form and Uthe, *NS-Justiz in Österreich*, 302.

76 Gerbel, "Lebenswelten," 112–30. How many Viennese or Austrian juveniles were dispatched to Hitler's "juvenile protection camps" (*Jugendschtzlager*) is unknown, but see Regina Fritz, "Die 'Jugendschtzlager' Uckermark und Moringen im System nationalsozialistischer Jugendfürsorge," in Berger, *Verfolgte Kindheit*, 305–26.
77 *St.Jb Wien 1939–1942*, 416–20; *1943–1945*, 290.
78 Cf. Waite, "Juvenile Delinquency in Nazi Germany, 1933–1945," 121–6 ff.; Roth, "*Verbrechungsbekämpfung*," 163 ff.; Kater, *Hitler Youth*, 138; Fishman, *Battle for Children*, 50.
79 DöW, G: Vr. 809/41.
80 DöW, G: Vr. E: Vr. 386/41; Vr. 1784/42.
81 Cf. Figure 1.4; Waite, "Teenage Sexuality," 458–62; Hanisch, *Männlichkeiten*, 270–1; Albert Müller and Christian Fleck, "Unzucht wider die Natur," *Österreichische Zeitschrift für Geschichtswissenschaften*, VIII (1998), 402.
82 Form and Uthe, *NS-Justiz in Österreich*, 310.
83 DöW, G: Vr. 1072/40; St. 2187/42.
84 DöW, G: Vr. 278/40.
85 DöW, G: Vr. 1245/40; Vr. 340/43.
86 DöW, G: 88 Vr. 697/41.
87 DöW, M: Vr. 95/44.
88 DöW, M: Vr. 2061.
89 DöW, G: 84 Vr. 74/42.
90 *St.Jb Wien 1939–1942*, 416–20; *1943–1945*, 290.
91 DöW, G: 88 Vr. 275/43.
92 Neugebauer, *Resistance in Austria*, 226–7.
93 DöW, G: 85 Vr. 1875/42.
94 Wolff, *Jugendliche vor Gericht*, 305–20, particularly the chart on 312.
95 Cf. Waite, "Juvenile Delinquency in Nazi Germany, 1933–1945," 78–88 and Figure 1.4.
96 For a brief overview see Waite, "Juvenile Delinquency in Nazi Germany, 1933–1945," 126–9. For background and detailed analysis see Klatt, *Zum Verhältnis des österreichischen und deutschen Strafrechts*, 288–323 ff.; and Wolff, *Jugendliche vor Gericht*, 118–73.

3 Juveniles Tried by Hitler's Special Courts, 1940–1945

1 Quoted in Müller, *Hitler's Justice*, 154.
2 Ibid., 154–9; Klatt, *Zum Verhältnis des österreichischen und deutschen Strafrechts*, 126–32 ff.
3 Maria Szecsi and Karl Stadler, *Die NS-Justiz in Österreich und ihre Opfer* (Vienna, 1962); Neugebauer, *Austrian Resistance*, 46–8; Wolfgang Form, "'Das Strafrecht ist also in erhöhtem Maße ein Kampfrecht...,'" 64.

4   Roth, "*Verbrechungsbekämpfung*," 233 ff.
5   DöW, Bundesministerium für Justiz (BMJ): Frauenberger.
6   DöW, BMJ: Wotawa.
7   DöW, BMJ: Watzek.
8   DöW, BMJ: Hesch.
9   DöW, BMJ: Zednik.
10 DöW, BMJ: Urbanek.
11 WSLA, Sondergericht (Hereafter SG) A 1, Str. 8197; DöW, BMJ: Lahajnar.
12 WSLA, SG, A 1, Str. 5087.
13 In the United States, individuals convicted of postal theft or mail fraud are usually fined $250,000 and sentenced to five years in a federal penitentiary. According to Statue § 1708, extreme cases can be imprisoned for twenty to thirty years. See https:/www. law@cornell mail-theft-or-related-offences.
14 WSLA, SG, A 1, Str. 8367.
15 WSLA, SG. A 1, Str. 8223.
16 WSLA, SG. A 1, Str. 6061.
17 WSLA, SG, A 1, Str. 5210.
18 WSLA, SG, A 1, Str. 8240.
19 WSLA, SG, A 1, Str. 6893.
20 WSLA, SG, A 1, Str. 6891.
21 WSLA, SG, A 1, Str. 7152.
22 WSLA, SG, A 1, Str. 6479. See also the case of a 17-year-old salesgirl, Anna K., who on June 18, 1941, was sentenced to three months in jail for forging butter ration coupons. Her adult accomplice Josefine H., born in 1905, was condemned to two and a half years in prison. WSLA, SG, A 1, Str. 5919.
23 WSLA, SG, A 1, Str. 5616.
24 WSLA, SG, A 1, Str. 7964; 6516.
25 Müller, *Hitler's Justice*, 157.
26 This generalization does not apply to younger Communists, nearly all of whom were condemned by the Higher Regional Court or the dreaded People's Court. See Neugebauer, *Austrian Resistance*, 79–123.
27 Luza, *Resistance,* 54, and Neugebauer, *Austrian Resistance*, 154–5. For the indictment see WSLA, A 1, 6524.
28 WSLA, SG, A 1, Str. 8293.
29 WSLA, SG, A 1, Str. 8239.
30 WSLA, SG, A 1, Str. 5199.
31 WSLA, SG, A 1, Str. 5232.
32 For analysis and discussion of sentences handed out to adults for anti-regime statements, radio crimes, and other subversive activities see Neugebauer, *Austrian Resistance*, 226–39, *passim*.
33 WSLA, SG, A 1, Str. 5583.

34 WSLA, SG, A 1, Str. 5613.
35 WSLA, SG, A 1, Str. 5523. During the summer, Friedrich had spent a week in detention for his rude behavior.
36 WSLA, SG, A 1, Str. 8027.
37 WSLA, SG. A 1, Str. 5526; 5203; 8393; 8410; 8552.
38 WSLA, A 3; Landesgericht für Strafsachen, Cg.
39 Bukey, *Hitler's Austria*, 159–60. For a gripping fictional account see Rolf Hochhuth, *Eine Liebe in Deutschland* (Reinbeck, 1978).
40 Specifically § 4 of the Ordinance for the Protection of the Military Strength of the German People prohibiting intimate relations with prisoners of war. RGBl, I, November 25, 1939, 2319.
41 WSLA, SG, A 1, Str. 6460. Much more draconian was the penalty imposed on Theresia F., a 19-year-old indentured farm girl. Already the mother of an illegitimate son, she was sentenced on November 15, 1941, to five years of hard labor in prison for engaging in disgusting sexual acts in a stable with no fewer than twenty French prisoners of war, who had provided her with cigarettes and perfume. The judges refused to consider extenuating circumstances, because her degenerate behavior constituted a gross violation of female German honor. Whether Theresia served her full sentence is unknown. In 1949, her record was expunged. WSLA, SG, A 1, Str. 8457.
42 WSLA, SG, A 1, Str. 7510.
43 WSLA, SG, A 1, Str. 7401.
44 WSLA, SG, A 1, Str. 7768. The thick file of this case contains police reports, bills of indictment, extensive psychiatric reports, and even photographs of the defendants. It does not include a record of the legal proceedings of the Special Court. Nor does it reveal the sanctions imposed on Franz K. other than a notation that he was too immature to be condemned as a "precocious juvenile criminal."
45 WSLA, A 1, Str. 5249.
46 WSLA, A 1, Str. 6697.
47 WSLA, A 1, Str. 8332.
48 WSLA, SG, A 1, Str. 5609.
49 WSLA, SG, A 1, Str. 5549.
50 WSLA, SG, A 1, Str. 8094.

4 Juvenile Political Crimes, 1940–1944

1 Schwarz, *Grauen Hauses*, 94–101.
2 Luza, *Resistance*, 99–113; Neugebauer, *Austrian Resistance*, 79–82.
3 TR, September 30 to October 1, 1939; WVW, 2, 248, 282–4.

4 TR, November 25–27, 1939, November 30 to December 1, 1939, December 16–18, 1939, December 26–27, 1939.
5 TR, February 24–26, 1940, July 2–3, 1940.
6 Luza, *Resistance*, 109; Neugebauer, *Austrian Resistance*, 82.
7 Luza, *Resistance*, 43–8.
8 TR, February 7–8, February 14–15, 1940; WVW, 3, 90–2; Luza, *Resistance*, 46; Neugebauer, *Austrian Resistance*, 154–5; WSLA, A 1, 6524; http://doew.at/erinnern/biographien.erzählte-geschichte/widerstand/1938 1945/camillo-heger-widerspruchliche-ueber-bord. On November 2, 1948, the Higher Regional Court ruled the sentences of all sixteen defendants null and void. WSLA, A 1, 6564/47.
9 TR, May 25–27, 1940; Neugebauer, *Austrian Resistance*, 152–3; WVW, 3, 92–4.
10 Luza, *Resistance*, 46; Neugebauer, *Austrian Resistance*, 134; WVW, 3, 113–15.
11 Luza, *Resistance*, 49.
12 The literature on Scholz, Kastelic, Lederer, and their respective "Austrian Freedom Movements" is extensive, although both Luza and Neugebauer provide thorough, comprehensive accounts. Luza, *Resistance*, 49–61; Neugebauer, *Austrian Resistance*, 145–56 ff., 284–5.
13 Neugebauer, *Austrian Resistance*, 147.
14 TR, August 29–30, 1940, September 1–2, 1940, October 12–13, 1949; WVW, 3, 97, 101.
15 TR, September 19–20, 1941; DöW, 51618; Luza, *Resistance*, 46; Neugebauer, *Austrian Resistance*, 20–1; Kater, *Hitler Youth*, 119–20; *Wiener Zeitung*, http://www.jura.at/ausstellunglandgraf/jura_ausstellung_landgraf_00.html, 2016.
16 Luza, *Resistance*, 46; Neugebauer, *Austrian Resistance*, 20–1; DöW, 51618.
17 DöW, 20000/L37.
18 http://www.jura.at/ausstellunglandgraf/jura_landgraf_00.html; Winfried Garscha to the author, July 1, 2016.
19 TR, July 20–21, 1942, March 5–8, 1943. See also WVW, 3, 117–18 on the arrest of a 16-year-old pupil, Paul Koutny, the youngest member of a Catholic League devoted to Christian and German principles.
20 Luza, *Resistance*, 115–17.
21 TR, April 21–22, 1941; WVW, 2, 284–5.
22 Luza, *Resistance*, 117. Although the Higher Regional Court handed out nine death sentences for high treason, it sentenced 1,188 individuals to prison terms averaging 24–120 months behind bars and 47 others (2.5 percent) to lengthier terms. It also acquitted 210 individuals for lack of evidence. According to Lojowsky's findings, the judges took into account mitigating circumstances such as age or perceived threats to the National Community. Subversive remarks or activities made by individuals in private or in small groups tended to be less severely punished. Lojowsky, "Hochverrat," 214–40, especially 223.

23 TR, July 7–8, 1941; WVW, 2, 148.
24 TR, July 14–15, 1941; WVW, 2, 367.
25 This summary follows Luza, *Resistance*, 127–33 and Neugebauer, *Austrian Resistance*, 103–4. For further information and biographical details see Willi Weinert, *"Mich könnt ihr löschen, aber nicht das Feuer": Biografien der im Wiener Landesgericht hingerichten Widerstandskämpferinnen: Ein Führer durch die Gruppe 40 am Wiener Zentralfriedhof und zu Opfergräben auf Wiens Friedhöfen* (3rd edition) (Vienna, 2011), 17–50, 100–2, 130–1, 151, 186. On Sassmann, see Lojowsky, "Hochverrat," 224–5 and WVW, 2, 266–8.
26 Luza, *Resistance*, 147.
27 TR, October 7–8, 1941; WVW, 2, 85
28 TR, October 11–12 to December 3–4, 1941.
29 Lothar Gruchmann, "Die Reichstagbeschluβ vom 26 April 1942 und seine Bedeutung für die Maβregelung der Deutschen Richter durch Hitler," *Vierteljahrhefte für Zeitgeschichte* (2003), 509–20. On the impact on the Austrian judiciary see Albrecht Kirschner, "Wehrkraftzersetzung," in Form and Uthe, *NS-Justiz in Österreich*, 502–4.
30 TR, May 19–20, 1942; WVW, 2, 291–4; Willi Weinert, *"Mich könnt ihr löschen, aber nicht das Feuer" Biografen der in Wiener Landesgericht hingerichten Wiederstandskämperinnen. Ein Führer durch die Gruppe 40 am Wiener Zenralfriedhof und zu Opfergräbern auf Wiens Friedhöfen* (Vienna, 2011), 175.
31 https://de.wikipedia.org/wiki/ Anna Gräf; WVW, 2, 268–70; DöW, Nr. 197/93, Urteilschrift der Hauptverhandlung vom October 12, 1943; Walter Schuster, *Deutsch National Nationalsozialistisch Entnazifiziert: Franz Langoth: Eine NS Laufbahn* (Linz, 1999), 149–51; Weinert, *"Mich könnt ihr löschen, aber nicht das Feuer,"* 118–19, 184, 241–2.
32 Neugebauer, *Austrian Resistance*, 104; WVW, 2, 298; WVND, 2, 233–4.
33 TR, August 25–27, 1942, May 1–4, 1944; WVW, 2, 106, 149; DöW, 9233: Urteil des 8. Senates des Oberlandesgerichts Wien, April 21, 1944; *Wiener Zeitung*, "Ich habe als kind gelernt, nicht feig zu sein," October 30, 2012, http://www.augustin.or.at/zeitung/tun-und-lassen/.
34 TR, August 18–19, 1942; WVW, 2, 278.
35 TR, October 6–8, 1942; WVW, 2, 294.
36 TR, May 12–14, 1942, September 9–12, 1942,
37 Neugebauer, *Austrian Resistance*, 155.
38 Ibid., 180.
39 TR, November 7–8, 1940, February 15–17, 1941.
40 TR, June 6–8, 1942.
41 TR, October 27–29, 1942; DöW, Shoah Opfer.

42 Evan Burr Bukey, *Jews and Intermarriage in Nazi Austria* (Cambridge, 2011), 149.
43 TR, March 2–4, 1943; DöW, Shoah Opfer.
44 TR, May 4–6, 1943, January 15–18, 1943, September 21–23, 1943, October 26, 1943.
45 DöW, Shoah Opfer.
46 TR, April 27–28, 1942, October 25–28, 1942; DöW, Shoah Opfer.
47 TR, September 20–22, 1943; WVW, 2, 187,
48 Neugebauer, *Austrian Resistance*, 172–6. On the persecution of the Jehovah's Witnesses throughout Greater Germany see Detlef Garbe, *Between Resistance and Martyrdom: The Jehovah's Witnesses in the Third Reich* (Madison, 2008).
49 WSLA, SG, A 1, Str. 5454.
50 TR, May 11–15, 1940, July 29, 1940, August 21–23, 1940, December 20, 1940 to January 5, 1941.
51 TR, June 9–10, 1941; Bukey, *Hitler's Austria*, 162.
52 TR, July 14–15, 1941.
53 TR, May 12–13, 1941.
54 TR, October 22–23, 1941.
55 TR, March 4–6, 1941, June 2–3, 1941, July 4–6, 1941, July 28–29, 1941, August 8–10 to August 27–28, 1941, October 9–10, 1941.
56 TR, February 1–2, 1942.
57 TR, February 11–12, 1942.
58 TR, June 22–23, 1942.
59 TR, April 22–23, 1942.
60 TR, February 9–10, 1942, July 11–19, 1942, November 3–5, 1942.
61 TR, January 21–22, 1942.
62 TR, January 29 to February 1, 1942.
63 TR, February 1–2, 1942, October 20–22, 1942, April 15–16, 1942, July 29–31, 1942.
64 Kater, *Hitler Youth*, 112–66.
65 Neugebauer, *Austrian Resistance*, 240.
66 TR, April 22–23, 1942, October 2–5, 1942, December 1–3, 1942.
67 TR, Nr. 5, February 1943, May 14–17, 1943.
68 WVW, 3, 525–6.
69 Ernst Hanisch, *Der lange Schatten des Staates: Österreichische Gesellschaftsgeschichte im 20. Jahrhundert: Österreichische Geschichte 1890–1990* (Vienna, 1994), 389; quoted in Neugebauer, *Austrian Resistance*, 389. See also Timothy Kirk, *Nazism and the Working Class in Austria: Industrial Unrest and Political Dissent in the National Community* (Cambridge, 1996), 121.
70 Bukey, *Hitler's Austria*, 186–8.
71 TR, March 20–25, 1943; WVW, 3, 527.
72 Luza, *Resistance*, 38.

73 WVND, 3, 326–30; Weinert, *"Mich könnt ihr löschen, aber nicht das Feuer,"* 118; "Und nie gewesen," *Die Presse,* October 23, 2011; TR, October 27 to November 2, 1944.
74 Luza, *Resistance,* 141.
75 TR, February 2–4, 1943, February 23–25, 1943, February 26 to March 1, 1943, May 1-3 to May 18–20, 1943, June 22–23, 1943, September 21, 1943, September 23, 1943, November 16–23, 1943; WVND, 2, 135.
76 TR, March 5–8, 1943, October 29–31, 1943; WVW, 3, 117–18.
77 TR, March 19–22, 1943.
78 *Statistiches Jahrbuch der Stadt Wien, 1939–1942,* 116, 118, 120; *1943–1945,* 290.
79 Neugebauer, *Austrian Resistance,* 34.
80 This is not to deny the persecution of homosexuals throughout Greater Germany including incorporated Austria. On Austria, see Müller and Fleck, "'Unzucht wider der Natur.'"
81 TR, November 26–28, 1939, December 6–7, 1939, December 20–21, 1939, May 27–28, 1942, October 21–23, 1943.
82 TR, March 7–9, 1941, March 28–30, 1941, July 4–5, 1941, January 26–27, 1942, February 6–7, 1942, March 20–21, 1942, March 25–26, 1942, April 15–16, 1942, June 5–7, 1942, June 26–28, 1942, July 17–19, 1942, July 20–23, 1942,
83 TR, March 28–30, 1941.
84 Form and Uthe, *NS-Justiz in Österreich,* 301–2.
85 Kirk, *Nazism and the Working Class in Austria,* 93–105 (Quotation on 105).
86 TR, October 12–13, 1939.
87 TR, April 9–10, 1940.
88 TR, March 7–9, 1941, June 2–3, 1941, July 4–6, 1941, July 28–29, 1941, July 23, 1941, August 8–10, 1941, August 13–14, 1941, August 27–28, 1941.
89 TR, October 26–28, 1943.

5 Impact of the Juvenile Court Act, 1944–1945

1 Wolff, *Jugendliche vor Gericht,* 353–65 ff.
2 For details see Klatt, *Zum Verhältins des österreichischen und deutschen Strafrechts,* 288–320.
3 Cf. ibid, 310–12 and Wolff, *Jugendliche vor Gericht,* 365–8 ff.
4 Blau, *"Die Kriminalität,"* 65–72.
5 Cf. ibid. and Waite, "Juvenile Delinquency in Nazi Germany, 1933–1945," 118–26.
6 Form and Uthe, *NS-Justiz in Österreich,* 302, 309–10.
7 Waite, "Juvenile Delinquency in Nazi Germany, 1933–1945," 127.
8 RGBl, I, 1943, Nr. 97, November 10, 1943.

9 Heinz Kümmerlein, *Reichsjugendgerichtsgesetz von 6, November 1943 mit den ergänzenden Rechts-und Verwaltungsvorschriften auf dem Gebiet des Jugendstrafrecht, Jugendhilfrechts und des strafrechtlichen Jugendschutzes* (Munich, 1944), 10–11.
10 Ibid., 65–7, as translated by Waite, "Juvenile Delinquency in Nazi Germany, 1933–1945," 127.
11 Kümmerlein, *Reichsjugendgerichtsgesetz*, 83.
12 Ibid., 149.
13 Ibid., 155–6.
14 Ibid., 176–7, as well as an addendum leaving a number of procedural and technical articles of the Austrian penal code in place, 189–203; Waite, "Juvenile Delinquency in Nazi Germany, 1933–1945," 126–9; Wolff, *Jugendliche vor Gericht*, 312–13; RGBl, I, 1943, Nr. 97.
15 ÖStA/AdR/AVA, Box 4991: RdErl. D. RF SSuCadDtPol. V. 3.1.1944–SV A 3 Nr. 860. *Die Behandlung der Kinder und Jugendlichen bei der Polizei*.
16 Ibid., 1–11.
17 Ibid., 11–33 ff.
18 Form and Uthe, *NS-Justiz in Österreich*, 311–15.
19 Ibid., 318–20.
20 Ibid., 289–90, 185.
21 TR, 5–11; 12–18; January 19–25, 1945, followed by the alarmist reports of February 2–8 to February 19–25, 1945, and March 1 to April 23, 1945.
22 TR, April 23, 1944, June 16–22, 1944.
23 TR, March 10–13, 1945.
24 TR, May 12–18, 1944, October 27 to November 2, 1944.
25 TR, January 19–25, 1945.
26 TR, March 1–2, 1944, May 19–25, 1944.
27 TR, May 19–25, 1944.
28 TR, December 8–4, 1944.
29 Gerbel, "Lebenswelten," 154–70.
30 Ibid., 132 47.
31 Ibid., 68–83.
32 Ibid., 232–46.
33 DöW, G: Vr. 618/44.
34 WSLA, A 3, Vr. 170/45.
35 WSLA, A 3, Vr. 14/45–13.
36 DöW, M: Vr. 405/44.
37 DöW, M: Anklageschrift, November 10, 1944.
38 WSLA, A 3, Vr. 117/45.
39 WSLA, A 3, Vr. 279/45
40 WSLA, A 3, Vr. 1/45.

41 WSLA, A 3, Vr. 29/45.
42 WSLA, A 3, Vr. 103/45.
43 WSLA, A 3, Vr. 4/45.
44 WSLA, A 3, Vr. 10/45.
45 WSLA, A 3, Vr. 20/45. Interestingly, long after the war the judiciary refused to efface the record.
46 WSLA, A 3, Vr. 40/45.
47 WSLA, A 3, Vr. 24/45.
48 WSLA, A 3, Vr. 119/45.
49 WSLA, A 3, Vr. 87/45.
50 *Statistisches Jahrbuch der Stadt Wien*, 7 (1943–1945), 295.
51 Tantner, "Schlurfs," 52.
52 Kirk, *Nazism and the Working Class in Austria*, 101.
53 Karoline Gattringer, *Jugend hinter Gittern: Aus den Akten des Wiener Jugendgerichtshofes* 1945–1960 (Vienna, 2016), 8–13.
54 DöW, M: Vr. 2347/43.
55 DöW, M: Vr. 3217/43.
56 DöW, M: Vr. 185/44.
57 DöW, M: Vr. 294/44.
58 Gattringer, *Jugend hinter Gittern*, 12.
59 DöW, M: Vr. 138/44; Vr. 448/44; Vr. 255/45; Vr. 258/44; Vr. 261/45; Vr. 962/44; Vr. 962/44; Vr. 955/44; Vr. 980/44; Vr. 1869/44. WSLA, A 3, Vr. 5/45; Vr. 37/45; Vr. 51/45; Vr. 137/45; Vr. 180/45; Vr. 203/45; Vr. 225/45; Vr. 333/45; Vr. 234/45.
60 DöW, M: Vr. 722/44.
61 DöW, M: Vr. 1550/44.
62 WSLA, A 3, Vr. 178/45.
63 WSLA, A 3, Vr. 99/45; Vr. 98/45.
64 WSLA, A 3, Vr. 8/45.
65 WSLA, A 3, Vr. 127/45.
66 WSLA, A 3, Vr. 66/45; Vr. 179/45.
67 WSLA, A 3, Vr. 207/45; Vr. 19/45; Vr. 149/45.
68 WSLA, A 3, Vr. 64/45.
69 WSLA, A 3, Vr. 63/45.
70 WSLA, A 3, Vr. 21/45.
71 WSLA, A 3, Vr. 36/45.
72 WSLA, A 3, Vr. 124/45.
73 WSLA, A 3, Vr. 134/45.
74 WSLA, A 3, Vr. 98/45.
75 WSLA, A 3, Vr. 73/45.
76 WSLA, A 3, Vr. 55/45.

77 WSLA, A 3, Vr. 70/45.
78 DöW, M: Vr. 95/44.
79 DöW, M: Vr. 1837/43.
80 WSLA, A 3, Vr. 186/45
81 WSLA, A 3, Vr. 181/45.
82 WSLA, A 3, Vr. 3/45.
83 DöW, M: Vr. 408/44.
84 WSLA, A 3, Vr. 35/45.
85 WSLA, A 3, Vr. 263/45.
86 WSLA, A 3, Vr. 118/45.
87 WSLA, A 3, Vr. 7/45.
88 WSLA, A 3, Vr. 143/45.
89 WSLA, A 3, Vr. 15/45.
90 See, for example, Luza, *Austro-German Relations*, 343–6.
91 WSLA, A 3, Vr. 165/45.
92 WSLA, A 3, Vr. 235/45.
93 WSLA, A 3, Vr. 281/45.
94 Bukey, *Hitler's Austria*, 22–4.
95 Wolff, *Jugendliche vor Gericht*, 370–2.

6 Postwar and Beyond

1 Luza, *Austro-German Relations*, 349–52; *Staatsgesetzblatt für die Republik Österreich*, Jg, 1945, St. 1, May 1, 1945, 1–6.
2 *Staatsgesetzblatt für die Republik Österreich*, Jg. 1945, St. 1–14.
3 *Staatsgesetzblatt für die Republik Österreich*, Jg. St. 9, June 23, 1945, 47.
4 For details see *Staatsgesetzblatt für die Republik Österreich,* Jg. St. 13, July 9, 1945, 67–70.
5 For details on the first de-Nazification law see Luza, *Austro-German Relations*, 354, fn.62.
6 WSLA, A 3, Vr. 118/45, Box 8.
7 WSLA, A 3, Vr. 14/45, Box 5.
8 WSLA, A 3, Vr. 286/45, Box 15.
9 WSLA, A 3, Vr. 176/45, Box 14.
10 WSLA, A 3, Vr. 196/4, Box 11.
11 WSLA, A 3, Vr. 182/45, Box 18.
12 WSLA, A 3, Vr. 172/45, Box 10.
13 WSLA, A 3, Vr. 70/45, Box 7.
14 WSLA, A 3, Vr. 28/45, Box 5.

15 WSLA, A 3, Vr. 268/45, Box 15.
16 WSLA, A 3, Vr. 276/45, Box 15.
17 WSLA, A 3, Vr. 270/45, Box 15.
18 WSLA, A 3, Vr. 219/45, Box 11.
19 WSLA, A 3, Vr, 243/45, Box 14.
20 WSLA, A 3, Vr. 278/45. Box 15. In 1953, the record was effaced.
21 WSLA, A 3, Vr. 292/45, Box 16.
22 WSLA, A 3, Vr. 87/45, Box 7.
23 WSLA, A 3, Vr. 103/45.
24 WSLA, A 3, Vr. 198/45.
25 WSLA, A 3, Vr. 81/45, Box 7.
26 DöW, M; WSLA, A 3, Vr. 290/45, Box 16.
27 WSLA, A 3, Vr. 222/45, Box 11.
28 WSLA, A 3, Vr. 261/45, Box 15.
29 Gattringer, *Jugend hinter Gittern*, 12–14.
30 WSLA, A 3, Vr. 4483/45, Box 10.
31 WSAL, A 3, 243/45, Box 14. The record of the ringleader, Martin B., was effaced in 1955.
32 WSLA, A 3, Vr. 249/45, Box 10.
33 Grassberger and Nowotny, *Austrian Penal Act*, 79–80.

Bibliography

Unpublished Documents

Dokumentationsarchiv des österreichischen Widerstandes (DöW), Vienna.
  Bundesjustizministerium (BJM-NA), 1946–1947.
  Docs. 197/93; 496/43;3367; 9233; 20000//L7
  Geheime Staatspolizei Wien (Gestapo) Tagesrapporte (TR), 1939–1945.
  Gerbelakten (G), 1939–1945.
  Mejstrikakten (M), 1943–1946.
  Shoah Opfer.

Österreichisches Staatsarchiv (ÖStA), Archiv der Republik (AdR),
  Allgemeines Verwaltungs Archiv (AVA), Vienna.
  Der Vorstand des Landessgericht Gefägenhausses I an den
    Generalstaatsanwalt, September 13, 1940, Box 4991.
  RdErl. D. RF SSuCadDtPol. V. 3. 1. 1944-SV A Nr860/43. Box 4991.

Wiener Stadt- und Landesarchiv (WSLA)
  Jugendgerichtshof Strafakten, A 3, 1939, 1943, 1945.
  Sondergericht Strafakten, A 1, 1939–1945.

Published Documents

Allgemeines Reichs-und Regierungsblatt für das Kaiserthum Österreich 1852.
The Austrian Penal Act 1852 and 1945 as Amended to 1965. Edited
  by Roland Grassberger and Helga Nowtny. London: Sweet and
  Maxwell, 1966.
Bundesgesetzblatt für die Republik Österreich, Jahrgang 1949. Vienna, 1949.
*Jugendorganisation und Jugendopposition in Berlin Kreuzberg 1933–
  1945: Eine Dokumentation.* Edited by Kurt Schilde. Berlin, 1983.
Reichsgesetzblatt (RGBl), I, 1923, 249; 1938 I, 1938, 691; 1939, I, 2000;
  1943, I, 97.

Staatsgesetzblatt für die Republik Österreich. Jahrgang 1945. Vienna: Staatsegesetzblatt, 1945.

Statistisches Jahrbuch der Stadt Wien, 1937, 1938, 1939–1942, 1943–1945, 1948. Vienna: Magistrat der Stadt Wien, 1937–1948.

Statistisches Jahrbuch für Österreich 1938. Vienna: Statitisches Jahrbuch, 1938.

Widerstand und Verfolgung in Niederösterreich (WVN) *1934–1945: Eine Dokumentation.* 3 vols. Edited by Heinz Arnberger, Christa Mitterruntzer, and Wolfgang Neugebauer. Vienna: Österreichischer Bundesverlag, 1987.

Widerstand und Verfolging in Wien (WVW) *1934–1945: Eine Dokumentation.* 3 vols. Edited by Herbert Steiner, Peter Eppel, and Johannes Holzner. Vienna: Österreichischer Bundesverlag, 1975.

Secondary Volumes, Articles, and Memoirs

Arnberger, Heinz and Claudia Kuretsides-Haider (eds.). *Gedenken und Mahnen in Niederösterreich: Erinnerungzeichnis zu Widerstand: Exil und Befreiung* (Vienna, 2011).

Bailer, Brigitte, Wolfgang Maderthaner, and Kurt Scholz. *"Die Vollstreckung verlief ohne Besonderheiten": Hinrichtungen in Wien, 1938 bis 1945* (Vienna, 2013).

*Bathurst, M. E. "Juvenile Delinquency in Britain during the War," *Journal of Criminal Law and Criminology,* 34, 5 (1943–4).

Berg, Mathew P. and Maia Mesner (eds.). *After Fascism: European Case Studies in Politics, Society, and Identity since 1945* (Vienna, 2009).

Berger, Else (ed.). *Verfolgte Kindheit: Kinder und Jugendliche als Opfer der NS-Sozialverwaltung* (Vienna, 2007).

Blanning, T. C. W. *Joseph II* (London, 1994).

Blau, Bruno. "Die Kriminalität in Deutschland während des zweiten Weltkrieges." *Zeitschrift für die gesamte Strafrechtswissenschaft* (Berlin, 1952).

Botz, Gerhard. *Die Eingliederung Österreichs in das Deutsche Reich: Planung und Verwirklichung des politisch-administrativen Anschluss (1938–1940)* (Vienna, 1976).

Bukey, Evan Burr. *Hitler's Austria: Popular Sentiment in the Nazi Era, 1938–1945* (Chapel Hill, 2000).

Bukey, Evan Burr. *Jews and Intermarriage in Nazi Austria, 1938–1945* (Cambridge, 2011).

Bundesministerium für Justiz. *75 Jahre Wiener Jugendgerichtshilfe* (Vienna, 1987).

Carsten, F. L. *The First Austrian Republic 1918–1938: A Study Based on British and Austrian Documents* (Cambridge, 1986).

Exenberger, Herbert. "Gefängnis statt Erziehung: Jugendgefängnis Kaiser-Ebersdorf 1940–1945" (Vienna, n.d.).
Field, Geoffrey G. *Blood, Sweat, and Toil: Remaking the British Working Class, 1939–1945* (Oxford, 2011).
Fischer-Nebmaier, Wladimir, Mathew P. Berg, and Anastasia Christou (eds.). *Narrating the City: Histories, Space, and the Everyday* (New York and Oxford, 2015).
Fishman, Sarah. *The Battle for Children: World War II, Youth Crime, and Juvenile Justice in Twentieth-Century France* (Cambridge, MA, 2002).
Form, Wolfgang and Oliver Uthe (eds.). *NS-Justiz in Österreich: Lage und Reiseberichte 1938–1945* (Vienna, 2004).
Form, Wolfgang, Wolfgang Neugebauer, and Theo Schiller (eds.). *NS-Justiz und politische Verfolgung in Österreich 1938–1945: Analysen zu den Verfahren vor dem Volksgerichtshof und dem Oberlandesgerichtes Wien* (Munich, 2006).
Forsthuber, Friedrich, Ursula Schwarz, Johannes Mahl-Anzeiger, and Mattius Keuschigg (eds.). *Die Geschichte des Grauen Hauses und der österreichischen Strafgerichtsbarkeit* (Vienna, 2012).
Fraenkl, Ernst. *The Dual State: A Contribution to the Theory of Dictatorship* (New York, 1941).
Garbe, Detlef. *Between Resistance and Martyrdom: The Jehovah's Witnesses in the Third Reich* (Madison, 2008).
Gattinger, Karoline, *Jugend hinter Gittern: Aus den Akten des Wiener Jugengerichtshofes 1945-1960* (Vienna, 2016).
Geerling, Wayne. "Protecting the National Community from Juvenile Delinquency: Nazification of Juvenile Criminal Law in the Third Reich," http://artsonline.monasch.au/eras/edition-2 gerling.pha.
Gerbel, Christian. "Lebenswelten von Wiener Arbeiterjugendlichen unter der NS-Herrschaft: Administrative Karrieren und 'Schlurf' Gangs" (Diss., University of Vienna, 1993).
Gerbel, Christian, Alexander Mejstrik, and Reinhard Sieder. "Die 'Schlurfs': Verweigerung und Opposition von Wiener Arbeiterjugendlichen im Dritten Reich," in Emmerch Tálos, Ernst Hanisch, and Wolfgang Neugebauer (eds.) *NS-Herrschaft in Österreich: Ein Handbuch* (Vienna, 2001).
*Gleisbach, W. "Twenty-Five Years of Criminology in Austria," *Journal of Criminal Law and Criminology*, 24, 1 (1933).
Göte, Petra. *Jugendstrafvollzug im Dritten Reich: diskutiert und realisiert- erlebt und erinnert* (Bad Heilbrunn, 2003).
Gruber, Helmut. *Red Vienna: Experiment in Working-Class Culture 1919-1934* (New York, 1991).
Gruchmann, Lothar. "Die Reichstagbeschluß vom 26 April 1942 und seine Bedeutung für die Maßregelung der Deutschen Richter durch Hitler," *Vierteljahrhefte für Zeitgeschichte*, 51 (October 2003), 501–20.

Gruchmann, Lothar. *Justiz im Dritten Reich 1933–1940: Anpassung und Unterwerfung in der Ära Gürtner* (Munich, 2001).
Hanisch, Ernst. *Der lange Schatten des Staates: Österreichische Gesellschaftsgeschichte im 20. Jahrhundert: Österreichische Geschichte 1890–1990* (Vienna, 1994).
Hanisch, Ernst. *Männlichkeiten: Eine andere Geschichte des 20. Jahrhunderts* (Vienna, 2005).
*Healy, Frank D. "Legislation Concerning Juvenile Delinquency in Vienna, Austria," *Journal of Criminal Law and Criminology*, 29, 5 (1939).
Healy, Maureen. *Vienna and the Fall of the Habsburg Empire: Total War and Everyday Life in World War I* (Cambridge, 2004).
http://doew.at/erinnern/biographien erzählte-geschichte/widerstand/1938 1945/ camillo-heger-widersruchliche-ueberbord. http://de.wikepedia.org/wiki/ Anna Graf.
http://www.monika-steinboeck.at/wp-content/uploads/Die Geschichte -der Wiener-Jugendwohlfahrt1.pdf (v.a. ab S.5).
http://de.wikipedia.org/wiki/ Heimerziehung in Österreich.
Kater, Michael H. *Hitler Youth* (Cambridge, MA, 2004).
Kirk, Timothy. *Nazism and the Working Class in Austria: Industrial Unrest and Political Dissent in the National Community* (Cambridge, 1996).
Klatt, Norbert. *Zum Verhältnis des österreichischen und deutschen Strafrechts in der Zeit des Nationalsozialismus* (Göttingen, 2009).
Klönne, Arno. *Jugendkriminalität und Jugendoppostion im NS Staat: Ein sozialgeschichtliches Dokument* (Münster, 1981).
Koch, H. W. *In the Name of the Volk: Political Justice in Hitler's Germany* (New York, 1989).
Kuretsides-Haider, Claudia, Heimao Halbrainer, and Elisabeth Ebner (eds.). *Mit dem Tode betraft: Historische und rechtspolitische Aspekte zur Todesstrafe in Österreich im 20. Jahrhundert und der* Kampf *um ihre weltweite Abschafung* (Graz, 2008).
*Lukas, Ilse. "Prevention of Juvenile Delinquency and Crime in Austria," *Journal of Criminal Law and Criminology*, 29, 5 (1939).
Luza, Radomir. *Austro-German Relations in the Anschluss Era* (Princeton, 1975).
McEwen, Britta. *Sexual Knowledge: Feeling, Fact, and Social Reform in Vienna 1900–1934* (New York, 2012).
*Müller, Albert and Christian Fleck. "'Unzucht wider der Natur': Gerichtliche Verfolgung der 'Unzucht mit Personen gleichen Geschlechts' in Österrereich von den 1930er zu den 1950er Jahren," *Österreichische Zeitschrift für Geschichtswissenschaften*, IX (1998), 400–22.
Müller, Ingo. *Hitler's Justice: The Courts of the Third Reich* (Cambridge, MA, 1991).
Neugebauer, Wolfgang. *The Austrian Resistance 1938–1945* (Vienna, 2014).
Okey, Robin. *The Habsburg Monarchy from Enlightenment to Eclipse* (New York, 2001).
Peukert, Detlev. *Inside Nazi Germany: Conformity, Opposition, and Racism in Everyday Life* (New Haven, 1987).

Roth, Thomas. *"Verbrechungsbekämpfung" und soziale Ausgrenzung in nationalsozialistische Köln: Kriminalpolizei, Strafjustiz und Verbrechungsbekämpfung zwischen Machtübernahme und Kriegsende* (Cologne, 2010).
Schildt, Axel and Detlef Siegfried (eds.). *European Cities, Youth and the Public Sphere in the Twentieth Century* (Aldershot, 2005).
Schoetensack, August. *Unbestimmte Verurteilung* (Leipzig, 1909).
Schorske, Carl. *Fin-de-Siècle Vienna: Politics and Culture* (New York, 1980).
Schuster, Walter. *Deutsch National Nationlsozialistisch Entnazifiziert: Franz Longoth: eine NS Laufbahn* (Linz, 1999).
Sheffer, Edith. *Asperger's Children: The Origins of Autism in Nazi Vienna* (New York, 2018).
Steinweis, Alan F. and Robert D. Rachlin (eds.). *The Law in Nazi Germany: Ideology, Opportunity, and the Perversion of Justice* (New York, 2013).
Stolleis, Michael. *The Law under the Swastika: Studies in Legal History in Nazi Germany* (Chicago, 1998).
Szecsi, Maria and Karl Stadler. *Die NS-Justiz in Österreich und ihre Opfer* (Vienna, 1962).
Tálos, Emmerich, *Das Austrofaschistische Herrschaftssytem: Österreich 1933–1938* (Vienna, 2013).
Tatner, Anton. *Schlurfs Annährung an einen subkulturen Stil Wiener Arbeiterjugendlicher* (Vienna, 2007).
Umele, Sigrid. "Zur Geschichte der Kindheit in Österreich. Von den frühen Anfängen des Mittelalters bis zur Gegenwart" (MA Thesis, Klagenfurt, 2001).
Wachsmann, Nikolaus. *Hitler's Prisons: Legal Terror in Nazi Germany* (New Haven, 2004).
Waite, Robert George. "Juvenile Delinquency in Nazi Germany, 1933–1945" (Diss., Tate University of New York at Binghamton, 1980).
Waite, Robert George. "Serious Juvenile Crime in Nazi Germany," in Robert F. Wetzell (ed.) *Crime and Criminal Justice in Modern Germany* (New York, 2014), 247–69.
Waite, Robert George. "Teenage Sexuality in Nazi Germany," *Journal of Sexuality*, XIII, (1998), 434–76.
*Wegs, Robert. "Youth Delinquency and 'Crime': The Perception and the Reality," *Journal of Social History*, 32, 3 (1999), 603–22.
Weinert, Willi. *"Mich könnt ihr löschen, aber nicht das Feuer" Biografen der in Wiener Landesgericht hingerichten Wiederstandskämperinnen. Ein Führer durch die Gruppe 40 am WienerZentralfriedhof und zu Opfergräbern auf Wiens Friedhöfen* (Vienna, 2011).
Wiener Zeitung. http:/www.jura.at/ausstellunglandgraf/jura-ausstellung 00.html, 2016.
Wiener Zeitung. "Ich habe als kind gelernt, nicht feig zu sein." http://www.austin.or.at/tun-undlassen/, October 30, 2012.
Wolff, Jörg. *Jugendliche vor Gericht im Dritten Reich: Nationalsozialistischt Strafrechtspolitik und Justizalltag* (Munich, 1993).

Index

abnormal sexual behavior 28, 29
abortion 26, 30, 39
absenteeism/breach of contract
  (Arbeitsvertragsbruch) 64–6, 127,
  135–40, 146
acts of subversion *(Heimtücke)* 75
Adler, Alfred 4
adolescents 2, 12
  crime 13
  deviancy and normality 6
  disenchantment 1
  dissidence in wartime Vienna 20
  flirtation 68
agricultural laborers 95
Aichorn, August 4
all-embracing National Socialist law
  (Verreichlichung) 9
Allied bombing 120, 124, 136
Altreich 39, 56, 70, 132, 157, 172 n.26
"Always Faithful Austria" 113
American air raids on industrial
  centers 123
Anschluß 1, 4, 5, 7, 9, 42
  ministerial bureaucrats 119
anti-Hitler jokes, charged with 111
anti-Nazi demonstration 99
anti-Nazi fly sheets 102
anti-Nazi jokes 87
anti-Nazi leaflets 106
anti-Nazi literature 103
anti-Nazi outbursts 111
anti-social saboteurs 44
Arlow, Otto 100
asocials 43, 64, 75, 87, 109, 132
assaults 49, 127, 148
Augustinian monastery 100
Austria
  jurists, forced retirement 9
  reunification with the German Reich 18
Austrian civil and penal codes 119
Austrian Civil Code of 1811 9
Austrian Communist Newsletter 98

Austrian criminal code 10, 42, 51,
  73, 157
Austrian criminal law 11
Austrian Freedom Movement 100, 101
Austrian Juvenile Penal Code 81
Austrian juveniles 80–6
Austrian legal system 78
Austrian Ministry of Justice 78
Austrian Movement 99
Austrian patriotism 97
Austrian penal code 27, 44, 46, 67
  Articles 101 82
  Articles 120 161
  Articles 125–33 67–70
  Articles 130 161
  Articles 171–4 51, 57, 59, 84
  Articles 178 57
  Articles 180 58
  Articles 190 80
Austrian Refugee's Society 78
Austrian Youth League 33
Austro-Hungarian army 78

Bamberger, Kurt 58, 70
Bettauer, Hugo 28–9
biological-racial diagnoses 77
black marketeering 16, 39, 52, 55, 62, 83
blackouts 39, 41
  break-ins during 51
  exploiters 44, 45, 50
  felonies during 54
  multiple thefts during 51
  robbery and theft committed during 60,
    72, 77, 149, 158,
Blau, Bruno 120
Bogner, Peter 50, 56
Bolshevism 99
bourgeois elites 2
Boy Scouts 100
Brunner, Anton 102
Bühler, Charlotte 4
Budin, Karl 106

capital punishment 11, 12
Catholic conservatives 97, 99
Catholic resistance movements 101, 104
Cernoch, Johann 111
child criminals 12
childhood socialization 3, 6
Christian Corporative dictatorship 48
Christian Corporative Youth Group 99
civil liberties 11–12
Civil War (1934) 106
"cleansing of the soul" 28
Communism 99
Communists
   activists 103, 106, 108
   in Vienna and Lower Austria 105
Communist Youth League (KJV) 37, 5, 35, 98, 99, 103, 106, 108, 116
competitive enterprises 50
corporal punishment, abolishment 12
corrective education 62, 63
crimes "contrary to nature" (homosexuality) 26, 29, 30, 37, 67–70, 91, 97, 161, 168
   see also lesbianism
"criminal biological types" 63, 64, 66
criminal penalties 11
curative education 3

"dangerous habitual criminals" 44
"dangerous juvenile criminals" 44, 45
dangerous youth 13
Danzig 5
Dean, James 48
death penalties 10, 44, 45, 63, 77, 98
death sentences 63, 76, 79, 100, 106, 165 n.3, 177 n.22
Decree against National Parasites (*Volksschädlinge*) 44, 51, 145
Decree Against Violent Criminals 45
Decree for Protection of Dangerous Juvenile Criminals 44, 120, 121
defense of Christianity 99
degree of political intention 115
detentions (*Jugendarrest*) 121
deviance (*Verwahrlosung*) 132
"dishonoring the race" 83
Documentation Archives of the Austrian Resistance 5
Dollfuss-Schuschnigg dictatorship 10, 15, 29, 42, 55, 110, 146, 165 n.6

Dubber, Bruno 32

Ebert, Friedrich 31
Edelwei β Pirates 46, 171, n. 18
endangered youth 13
espionage 111
excessive violence 76
Exner, Franz 45
expeditious trial (*kurzer Prozess*) 20

Federal Institution for the Educational Needy 15
Federal Ministry of Justice 80
felonies 46
   Austrian juveniles 80–6
   foreign juveniles 86–7
   political offences 87–91
   sexual offences 91–2
   in Vienna 50, 54–7
   violence and assault felonies 92–4
female detention facility 62
female homosexuality 70
female social workers 43, 63, 66, 69, 127–9, 155
Fexer, Felix, 101–2
firearms violations 127
Fishman, Sarah 161
Flemish National Socialist 89
foreign juveniles 86–7
Four Year Plan Law 9
Fraenkel, Ernst 6
Frauenberger, Friedrich 78
Freischar Ostmark 113
Freisler, Roland 44, 45, 76
Freud, Anna 4
Freud, Sigmund 4
Frick, Hans 9
Friedrich Theiss's Austrian Movement 87
Führer decree 18

"gangsterism" 76
Geltungsjuden 109
General Civil Code of 1811 9, 11, 12
German Common Law 10, 42
German Labor Front (DAF) 71
German Reich
   reunification of Austria with 18
   teenage moral offences 17
Gestapo 97
   arrest lists 108

reports 125–6
terror and fissures 99
Glöckel, Otto 3
Glück, Friedrich 111
Golden Party Badge 80
Goldsteiner, Anna 113–14
Gräf, Anna, 105–6
Gray House in Vienna 96
Great Depression of 1929 4, 17–18
Guardianship Authority 2, 12, 14, 43, 69, 123, 162
Gürtner, Franz 9, 18

Haan, Otto 100
"habitual criminals" 51, 58, 94
Habsburg Hereditary Lands 11
Habsburg monarchy 113
half-Jew (Mischling) 109
Hanisch, Ernst 29
Hartmann, Otto
"healthy sensitivity" 122
Heger, Camillo 99
Hesch, Otto 78, 79
Hess, Rudolf 9
Higher Regional Court 10, 42, 76, 78, 98, 107, 111, 131
high treason *(Hochverrat)* 10
Himmler, Heinrich 56
Hirtenberg 46
Hitler, Adolf
  angry denunciations 56, 80
  defeat in Stalingrad 53, 113
  Golden Party Badge 80
  National Community 56
  Poland, invasion of 43
  Reunification of Austria with the German Reich 18
Hitler-Stalin Pact 98
Hitler Youth (HJ) 1, 5, 19, 42, 48, 52, 54, 55, 81, 98, 101–2, 113, 119, 122, 148
  Utopian revolt in Pulkau 117
Hofmacher, Herbert 67
homosexuality 16, 17, 26, 29, 30, 37, 67–70, 91, 97, 161, 168

illegal border-crossing 89
illegal possession 26
illegitimate births 2
illicit intercourse 97

indefinite imprisonment 10, 12, 15, 119, 122, 124, 131, 147, 165 n.6
indiscipline 64–6
industrialization 2
Inter Allied Relief Commission 14
internal enemies 44
International Association of Bible Students 110
International Committee of Criminal Police 41

Jägerstätter, Franz 87
Jgalffy, Ludwig 101–2
jazz music 55
Jehovah's Witnesses 97, 130
Jewish-related offenses 97
Jewish-related transgressions 108
Josef P's gang 68
Joseph, Francis (emperor) 11
Joseph II 2, 11
Judaism 99
juvenile concentration camp 122
juvenile correctional facility 63, 81
Juvenile Court 42
Juvenile Court Act, impact of 15, 119–23
  absenteeism, indiscipline, and breach of contract 135–40
  assault and sexual immorality 140–1
  break-ins 130–4
  Court Records 126–30
  Gestapo reports 125–6
  hold-ups and robberies 134–5
  judicial reports 123–4
  petty thefts, misbehaviors, and adolescent shenanigans 141–3
Juvenile Court Decisions, 1940–1944 48–50
  juvenile gangs 50–6
  moral offences and homosexuality 67–70
  noncompliant behavior, indiscipline, work stoppages, absenteeism 64–6
  small rings and individuals 56–64
  subversive behavior 70–1
  violent crimes 66–7
Juvenile Court Law of 1923 42
Juvenile Court Law of 1928 12, 165 n.6
Juvenile Court Law of 1943 119, 125

juvenile crime 5, 6
  during the Second World War 41
Juvenile Criminals Act of October 4, 1939 71
juvenile delinquents 1, 120
juvenile detention *(Jugendarrest)* 45, 46, 89
Juvenile Division of the Higher Regional Court 46, 48, 56
Juvenile gangs 50–6
juvenile jail 123
juvenile judicial system 66
juvenile justice 166 n.15
  after Anschluß, 1938–1939 18–25
  Great Depression, impact of 17–18
  origins and evolution 12–17
  political crimes 32–8
  post-Anschluß deviance, 1938–1939 25–38
  traditional offences 25–32
juvenile larceny 19
Juvenile Legal Support Agency (JSLA) 2, 42–3
juvenile misdemeanors 46
juvenile negligence and delinquency 14
juvenile political crimes 20, 32–8, 97–116
juvenile prostitutes 69
juvenile thieves 60–4
juvenile transgressions 120, 127
juvenile waywardness and delinquency 15
Juvenile Welfare Board 14, 42, 129

Kaiser-Ebersdorf 46, 52, 58, 60, 66, 92, 103, 128
"Karo" gang 54, 158
Kater, Michael 5
Kirk, Timothy 115
Kramer, Stanley 6
Kümmerlein, Heinz 121

"Laaberg" gang 55
Lachnitt, Friedrich 105, 159
Landgraf, Josef 101 103
Langoth, Franz 78, 106
Law Against Insidious Attacks 75
Law Against the Formation of New Parties 9, 145
Lazar, Erwin 2
League of German Girls 5, 19, 42, 48, 54, 55, 98
legitimist fly sheets 103

legitimist movements 97
Leichter, Kathe 4
lesbianism 70
liquidation of the bourgeois family 28
"loathsome personalities" and deeds 93
loitering 13, 16, 45, 49, 51, 57, 135, 138

magistrates of Special Courts *(Sondergerichte)* 77–80
Mann, Abby 6
Mann, Heinrich 106
manual-training workshops 16
Maria Theresia 11
Marius, Silvio 100
masturbation 68, 148
Maximilian I 11
Melzer, Kurt, 110–11
misdemeanors involving food 76
misuse of firearms 26
"morally degenerate youngsters" 3
moral offences 67–70, 161
Morawitz, Leopoldine 103
Moringen 119, 128
Moscow Declaration 145
Müller, Ingo 77
murder, attempt to 66
mutual masturbation 68, 70
  see also lesbianism

Napoleonic model of dividing offences 11
National Community 11, 114, 132, 135
"national parasites" 51, 77, 83, 93, 143, 146
National Socialism 5, 6, 43, 80, 86, 99, 119
National Socialist League of Jurists 79
National Socialist Motor Corps (NSKK) 36
National Socialist Revolution 75
National Socialist Sisterhood 71
National Socialist Student League 110
National Socialist Welfare Association 5
Nazification of the Austrian legal system 1, 10
Nazi ideology 20
Nazi judicial system 108
Nazi movement 78
Nazi-occupied Paris 46, 48, 49
Nazi ordinances 1, 135
Nazi racial ordinances 161
Nazi shop steward *(Betriebsobmann)* 65
Nazi-Soviet conquest 98

negligent education 60
Nirschl, Anton 53
nocturnal robberies 81, 83
noncompliant behavior 64–6
nonconformity 1
nullum crimen sine lege 11
Nuremberg Laws 7, 9

oath of loyalty to Hitler 82
Ordinance for Protection Against Dangerous Juvenile Criminals 40, 44, 85
Ostarbeiter 115

parallel judicial universe 7
Parasite Decree 52, 58, 59, 60, 61, 68, 77, 80, 81, 82
  violations 81–2
parasitic or mischievous behavior 49, 58
Penal Code of 1852 9, 12
penalties 94
penitentiaries 46, 65
People's Court (*Volksgerichtshof*) 76
  sentenced to death 106
personality principle 10, 119
petty offences 76
Pirate Rowing Club 132
plunderers 44
Police Decree for the Protection of Youth 45
police regulations 12
political crimes 20, 32–8, 97–116
political offences 87–91
post-Anschluß law on treason 10
post anti-Nazi graffiti 98
postwar offences 153–6
potentially habitual criminals 165 n.6
"precocious juvenile criminals" 44, 77, 82, 106, 120, 129
  guidelines for sentencing 121–2
premature sexuality 62
preventive punishment 166 n.6
prisoners of war 77
problematic maturity 15
property crimes 56
Property Transfer Agency 28
prostitutes 76
Protection Against Dangerous Juvenile Criminals 40
Protection of Dangerous Criminals 77

Protection of Juvenile Criminals 145
Protection of Youth 145
Protection of Youth Decree 45
punishment battalion 61

Rachlin, Robert 7
racial-biological guidelines 42
racial defilement *(Rassenschande)* 76, 91, 108, 115
radio crimes 75, 108, 111
Radio Ordinance of 1939 89
Red Falcons 4
Red Vienna 3, 4, 163, n. 5
Reich Flag Law 9
Reich Juvenile Code, 1944 71
Reich Juvenile Court Law 20, 121, 146
Reich Labor Service 60, 82, 129, 130
Reich Ministry of Justice 115
Reichstag Fire Decree 75
Reich Trustee of Labor 66
Renner, Karl 145
Reunification of Austria with the German Reich 18
Revolutionary Socialists 97
robberies 27, 142, 150, 153, 154
Roman Catholicism 110
Roman Sauna 69

"Sandleiten" gang 53
Schlurfs 48–56, 135
Schmitt, Carl 19
Sicka, Leopoldine 106
Sikuta, Franz 106
Scholz, Karl Roman 100
Schwarz, Ursula 97
security police (SD) 25
Seidl, Friedrich 111
self-styled Marxists 103
sentenced to death 106
"serious dangerous criminals" 93
sex crimes 46, 77
sexual affairs with prisoners of war 95
sexual experimentation 67
sexual immorality 49, 127, 140–3
  see also homosexuality
sexual liaisons 91
sexual offences 28, 77, 91–2
sexual relationships with Jews and non-Aryans, prohibiting 114
Seyss-Inquart, Artur, 57

Seyss-Inquart, Richard 15, 16
Sheffer, Edith 3
short-term detention centers 119
Simplification Decree 75
smuggling Jews 38
social workers 15
Special Courts in Vienna 87, 95
Special Courts *(Sondergerichte)* 6, 75
   magistrates of 77–80
Staininger, Anton 50
state treason *(Landesverrat)* 10
stealing 60
Steinweis, Alan 7
Stich, Johann Karl 115, 120, 124
Sturma, Leo 124
subversion 111
Subversion Law 70
subversive behavior 70–1, 77
Sumdits, Kathe 107
Swing Kids 56

Tandler, Julius 3, 4
teenage crime 13–14
   pattern of 50
teenage gangs 42, 52
teenage girls
   sexual relationships with foreigners 92
   see also sexual offences
teenage high jinks 55
teenage homosexuality 49
   see also homosexuality
teenage sexuality 91
teenage street urchins 4
teenage transgressions 61
teenage violence 44
theft 26–8, 76
   during blackouts 51, 60, 72, 77, 149, 150, 158
   Juvenile Court Act, impact of 141–3
Theiss group 100
theocratic offences 11
Thierack, Otto 119
Third Reich 1, 6, 43, 78, 79
   teenage sexuality 91
tobacco shops *(Tabaktrafik)* 126, 127, 131, 132, 133, 156
"Tobogan" gang 54–5
traditional offenses 25–32
transgression 70

transgressions 97
Trnka, Franz 152
Tyrol 99

unauthorized border-crossings 26, 31–2
undermining military strength 75
unemployment 4
urban teenagers 17
Urbanek, Hans 79

Vagrancy Act of 1885 13
vandalism 127
Vichy France 26, 66
victory army 102
Vienna
   adolescent crime in 46
   disintegration of Habsburg monarchy 14
   fashion-conscious 48
   Juvenile Division of the Higher Regional Court 59, 64
   juvenile justice 42
   juvenile nonconformist behavior 55
   Special Courts *(Sondergerichte)* 75
   starvation crisis 13
   teenage gangs 53
   transgressions 49
Viennese Gestapo 64, 125
Viennese Juvenile Court 57, 151
Viennese Juvenile Welfare Board 29
Viennese Municipal and Provincial Archives 5
Viennese Special Court 93
violation of the Subversion Law 89
violence and assault felonies 92–4
violent crimes 66–7
von Pirquet, Clemens 3

Wage Structure Ordinance of 1938 65
War Economy Decree of 1939 44, 135
War Economy Ordinance 85
Wartime Ordinances (1939–1940) 43–8
   Nazification and 43–4
Wärtl, Gertrude 111
war-torn Cologne 63
Watzek, Hans 78
Weapons Act of 1938 32
weekend detentions (Jugendarrest) 65
Wehrmacht Law 9

Weimar Republic 31, 42
White Rose Society in Munich 32, 63, 162
Wiener Neustadt 125
working-class Meidling 53
work stoppages 64–6, 127
Wotawa, Alois 78, 80

youngsters
　felonies in Vienna 50

Youth Delinquency 166 n.16
youthful convictions 19
youthful defendants 76
youthful miscreants 16
Youth Welfare Office 122

Zednik, Georg 78, 79, 88
Zurndorf 148

www.ingramcontent.com/pod-product-compliance
Lightning Source LLC
Chambersburg PA
CBHW052044300426
44117CB00012B/1962